THE INCAS
AND THEIR ANCESTORS

MICHAEL E. MOSELEY

THE INCAS
AND THEIR ANCESTORS

THE ARCHAEOLOGY OF PERU

With 225 illustrations

THAMES AND HUDSON

Author's Note

Knowledge about the ancient Andes is increasing rapidly. A great
deal of new information remains unpublished, and I am indebted to
multitudes of colleagues for generously sharing their findings. I also
draw upon my own research which began in the Ancon-Chillon area,
shifted north to the Moche valley, and then moved to the southern
Moquegua drainage. Investigating the national patrimony of Peru
has been a great privilege, and I warmly acknowledge the people,
scholars and officials who have graciously hosted my field studies for
many years.
Rather than deal with all aspects of Peruvian prehistory, I have
attempted to weave together evolutionary themes that highlight the
major Andean developments. I have also sought to bring native
Quechua and Aymara people into the picture. They provide rich
insights into the past accomplishments of their ancestors. This
volume is dedicated to these people as well as to Maya Elena and the
younger generation.

*Frontispiece: A female Staff God representation on painted cotton cloth
found at Karwa.*

© 1992 Thames and Hudson Ltd, London

First published in the United States of America in 1992
by Thames and Hudson Inc., 500 Fifth Avenue,
New York, New York 10110

First paperback edition 1993
Reprinted 1999

Library of Congress Catalog Card Number 91-65309
ISBN 0-500-27723-0

Printed and bound in Slovenia

Contents

CHAPTER ONE

Introduction

The Inca called their sprawling realm Tahuantinsuyu, or 'Land of the Four Quarters', and on the eve of Columbus' Caribbean landfall it probably surpassed Ming China and the Ottoman Empire as the largest nation on earth. Stretching down the mountainous Andean backbone of South America for more than 5,500 km, it was the biggest native state to arise in the western hemisphere, and also the largest empire of antiquity ever to develop south of the equator. By dint of armed conquest the masters of Tahuantinsuyu governed the most rugged mountain chain on the face of the earth, second only to the Himalayas in height and harshness. To the west their sovereignty reached over the dry Atacama desert; to the east it included the flanks of the Amazon rainforest. Inca legions – like their Roman counterparts – marched far beyond the frontiers of civilization to dominate barbarian tribes, and heterogeneous societies. At its height, the imperial capital of Cuzco exercised rule over northern Chile, upland Argentina, Bolivia, Peru, Ecuador, and the south of Colombia. No contemporary Andean nation compares in magnitude or prosperity, and the great wealth of Tahuantinsuyu fostered its downfall.

The conquest of Mexico whetted the Spanish appetite for gold. Yet hopes of securing truly prodigious quantities of precious metal eluded the *conquistadores* until 1532. That year Francisco Pizarro and a small contingent of mercenaries disembarked on the desert coast and ventured into the Andean uplands. At the town of Cajamarca the Inca emperor was enticed to a supposedly peaceful meeting, then kidnapped and ransomed for a room full of gold, and two of silver. After payment of about $50 million by today's bullion standards, the soldiers of fortune garroted the monarch, and marched to Cuzco, the capital and heart of Tahuantinsuyu.

The great metropolis was first sighted by a cavalry vanguard. By all accounts it was unbelievable – it was alien – and it was magnificent. The many distant buildings were clustered so close to the clouds that men and horses of the expeditionary force fought for breath in the oxygen-deficient altitude. Catching and reflecting the sun, towering stone walls shimmered with brilliant hues of gold and silver. Ascending a broad highway into the urban nexus, the party of mounted men was greeted by a brilliantly clad entourage of nobles and attendants, stately but fully foreign in physique and attire. Led across spacious malls with sparkling fountains, and along paved avenues flanked by cut-rock palaces, villas, halls, temples, and shrines, the awe-struck visitors beheld imposing edifices encrusted with precious metals that played dazzling light on all beholders near and far.

Plates 12–14 The city was unbelievable because there was nothing of comparable splendor in the soldiers' Castilian homeland. It was alien because the troops had journeyed from an old, familiar world to a new and unusual one. It was magnificent because Cuzco was the home of the Sun, the god Inti, and gold was his essence. Inti was the sacred patron of the city and its empire. Images of the solar deity and other luminaries of the imperial pantheon resided in an opulent sanctuary, the Coricancha or 'House of the Sun'. A glimpse of this remarkable palace of the gods survives in the thoughtful reflections of Cieza de León, *conquistador* and author of *Chronicle of Peru*. Striding around the temple he found that it measured 'more than four hundred paces in circuit' and was of finely hewn masonry.

> The stone appeared to me to be of a dusky or black color, and most excellent for building purposes. The wall had many openings, and the doorways were very well carved. Round the wall, half way up, there was a band of gold, two *palmos* wide and four *dedos* in thickness. The doorways and doors were covered with plates of the same metal. Within were four houses, not very large, but with walls of the same kind and covered with plates of gold within and without . . .
>
> In one of these houses, which was the richest, there was the figure of the sun, very large and made of gold, very ingeniously worked, and enriched with many precious stones. . . .
>
> They had also a garden, the clods of which were made of pieces of fine gold; and it was artificially sown with golden maize, the stalks, as well as the leaves and cobs, being of that metal. . . . Besides all this, they had more than twenty golden sheep [llamas] with their lambs, and the shepherds with their slings and crooks to watch them, all made of the same metal. There was a great quantity of jars of gold and silver, set with emeralds; vases, pots, and all sorts of utensils, all of fine gold.

Indeed the splendor of the Coricancha and the elegant wealth of Cuzco were so overpowering that the narrator was compelled to conclude, ' . . . it seems to me that I have said enough to show what a grand place it was; so I shall not treat further of the silver work of the *chaquira* [beads], of the plumes of gold and other things, which, if I wrote down, I should not be believed.'

If a *conquistador* felt his eye-witness account of Inca accomplishment would be beyond belief, then it is little wonder that four centuries later archaeologists confront a uniquely difficult task in attempting to reconstruct this bygone achievement, describe its evolution, and make Andean civilization intelligible to Western society.

Many aspects of Andean accomplishment are only intelligible as adaptations to environmental extremes, particularly life at extremely high elevations. The towering Cordillera is, after all, the only cradle of ancient civilizations where tourists must worry about heart seizures in the rarefied air, and visitors regularly experience altitude sickness due to anoxia. If an eminent empire had once flourished atop the Himalayas, then Tahuantinsuyu could be studied in

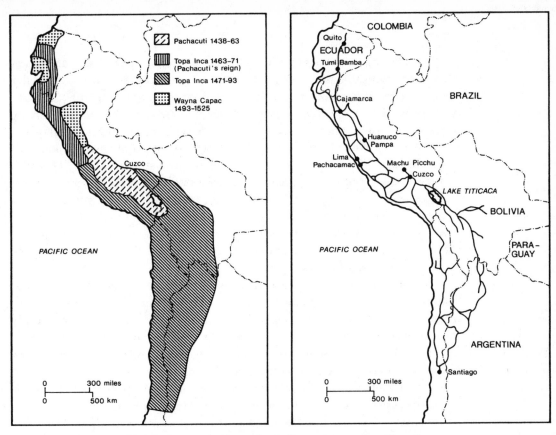

1, 2 *(Left) The growth of the Inca empire. Dates for the Inca rulers are the subject of scholarly debate, and are given here as a general guide only. (Right) The Inca road network.*

comparative perspective and might seem less alien. Yet, this is not the case, and many aspects of Andean civilization are unprecedented, and thus unique.

Because of these factors we must first understand the geography of Tahuantinsuyu and the nature of Inca rule before turning to the prehistoric record to examine how this way of life and government evolved. An understanding of Inca society and statecraft will serve as a guide for interpreting the archaeological data. However, after reviewing the Inca as an interpretative model, I will turn to the earliest inhabitants of the Andes and trace the evolution of native society and statecraft forward in time to its culmination on the eve of Spanish conquest.

The Inca

It is important to note that the term 'Inca' refers only to a small group of kindred, less than 40,000 individuals, who built a great Andean state by force of arms, and who ruled as the realm's governing nobility. The head of this royal family was the head of state, and at the height of the empire his dominion extended over ten million people or more. These individuals were Inca *subjects*, but they were *not* Incas because this was a closed ethnic body.

The Inca empire incorporated multitudes of polities, chiefdoms, and tribes that the Spanish loosely referred to as *señorios* and *parcialidades*. Major mountain chains are notorious refuges for divergent types of plants, animals, and people. The many ethnic groups sheltered in these topographic pockets are often not at peace either among themselves or with the greater political order. The rugged Andean Cordillera housed a myriad large and small populations with distinct ethnic identities and strong separatist tendencies. This rich diversity played both for and against empire-building. Ethnic separatism made conquest relatively easy, but consolidation extremely difficult. Small competing polities were played one against another and conquered piecemeal or coerced into allegiance with Tahuantinsuyu. But to integrate these hostile groups into a national whole under a *Pax Incaica* was the single greatest task confronting Cuzco's rulers.

To govern this multitude Inca organizers amalgamated different peoples and polities into larger administrative units. This still left Tahuantinsuyu with more than 80 political provinces, each administratively distinct if not ethnically heterogeneous. Linguistic variance was formidable and incompatible with centralized administration. An official tongue was therefore imposed – *Runa Simi*, a version of Quechua – as the lingua franca and medium of governmental communication. Communication and contact with the provinces was strengthened by a vast all-weather highway system. Major thoroughfares and trunk lines covered some 30,000 to 40,000 km, and comprised among the best engineered roadways up to the advent of the automobile.

Other integrative policies included relocating entire communities. Called *mitamaqs*, communities from loyal provinces were resettled in new or hostile territories and subversive villages were moved to consolidated regions. At a higher social level, the offspring of conquered rulers were brought to Cuzco to be educated in Inca ways before returning to their homelands to assume the reins of government.

The formidable task of integrating the New World's largest, most diverse empire was disrupted by European contact. Tahuantinsuyu had not submerged ethnic and political opposition, nor matured into a fully monolithic state by the time Wayna Capac, the last Pre-Hispanic emperor died. Insurrections continued during his rule and revolt became rampant upon his demise. When Wayna Capac became the head of state much of Tahuantinsuyu was controlled by the estates of his predecessors. The greatest potential for his own betterment lay with imperial expansion in the north. The monarch therefore took the best of the Inca officer corps and the empire's élite legions, and spent almost all his reign campaigning in Ecuador, where he consolidated a major power base at Tumi Bamba. Near the end of his reign there are suggestions that Wayna Capac was planning to create a second imperial capital at Tumi Bamba, a move not welcomed by the Cuzco nobility. The plan might well have succeeded were it not for the emperor's sudden death in 1526. In many ways the death of Wayna Capac marks the onset of the conquest of Tahuantinsuyu, although almost a decade passed before Pizarro arrived.

The conquest

How could Pizarro's small fighting force of only 260 Spanish mercenaries – 62 horsemen and 198 foot soldiers – topple what in 1532 was potentially the largest nation in the world? This extraordinary event was largely due to the fact that at the time Wayna Capac died so did most of his subjects. Medical historians leave little doubt that Old World infectious diseases, particularly smallpox, worked decisively to Castilian advantage in the conquest of Latin America by swiftly eradicating millions of opponents and occasioning social upheaval in the wake of demographic devastation. The first New World incidence of smallpox was implanted on the Mexican mainland in 1520. It spread further and faster than did the Castilian explorers. Within five years the natives of Panama were largely gone and once across the isthmus there were no barriers to inhibit its southward progress through the Andes and the continent in general, creating the first great New World pandemic. It was the single most severe and far-reaching loss of life that ever occurred in the Americas. Among unvaccinated groups case mortality is about 30 per cent. Because the New World peoples lacked immunity, mortality estimates are as high as two-thirds and more of the population.

The impact on Tahuantinsuyu was devastating. Wayna Capac was suddenly struck down, as was his heir apparent, and many of the governing élite in Tumi Bamba and Cuzco. The tumultuous consequences must have been broadly akin to the upheavals that racked Europe in the aftermath of the Black Death. Demographic collapse ushered in both a power vacuum and a widespread loss of confidence in the established order. Insurrection spread to many quarters of Tahuantinsuyu, and a violent civil war broke out, pitting remnants of the established Cuzco nobility, under one claimant son Huascaran, against the survivors of the Tumi Bamba court led by Atahualpa, one of the dead emperor's many other sons. The war raged on for more than half a decade.

On the eve of the Spanish arrival civil hostilities had only drawn to a partial close. Huascaran had been captured, and Atahualpa was marching south through the mountains in slow and stately procession with much of his court and thousands of troops to take possession of Cuzco. Landing on the desert coast, Pizarro learned of Atahualpa's general itinerary and without opposition moved the small Spanish expeditionary force up the Cordillera and into the highland town of Cajamarca. Atahualpa accepted a treacherous offer to go unarmed and without troops to meet the alien interlopers who kidnapped, ransomed and killed the king. This reignited the Tumi Bamba–Cuzco civil conflict, and aligned Pizarro with the latter faction, who then provided the Spanish with auxiliary troops and welcomed their presumed liberators into the capital. Initiated by disease and concluded with deceit, the conquest of Tahuantinsuyu was largely accomplished without major battles. Violent opposition and fierce battles did ensue. However, Atahualpa's ransom and the sack of Inti's golden city produced such immediate wealth that well-armed *Plate 25* Castilian reinforcements arrived in great numbers, and Pizarro's concerns shifted from conquest to consolidation.

The historical record

Demographic devastation by disease, protracted civil war, and Castilian conquest pose problems for understanding what Tahuantinsuyu may have been like in a pristine state. Record-keeping is essential to all empires, and Inca lords kept a vast body of information – ranging from census and tax data to imperial history – recorded upon *quipu*. Deriving its name from the word 'knot' (*Khipu*), a *quipu* consisted of a length of cord held horizontally and from which numerous other yarns of various colors were vertically suspended. Each of these secondary members, in turn, supported a descending hierarchy of dependent colored strings. Different numerical data were entered by different types of knots, and other information was encoded by cord length, color, and hierarchical position. Unfortunately, in the wake of foreign conquest the entire record keeping system disintegrated as rapidly as the royal court that had supported it.

Neither Pizarro nor those under his command were concerned with recording current events, or the achievements of their native adversaries. Indeed, most of the mercenaries were illiterate, and with few members of the initial expeditionary force leaving memoirs there is woefully little information about the Castilian side of the conquest, and even less from the Inca perspective. One insightful account from a native point of view was written by Felipe Guaman Poma de Ayala, who illustrated his observations with hundreds of charming drawings. Yet he wrote long after the fall of the Inca. Almost all records about Tahuantinsuyu were written well after the conquest and extracted from Indian witnesses who were not unbiased by their circumstances. Arriving with troop reinforcements two decades after the death of Atahualpa, Pedro Cieza de León was one of the first chroniclers sympathetic to the natives. Yet even his detailed account of Tahuantinsuyu must be regarded as an historical reconstruction, and all later writings by other authors are of similar nature. These early accounts about the Inca contain a great deal of fundamental information, but the sources are often contradictory and must be assessed with care. For centuries scholars have taken the early chronicles to be relatively realistic and historically accurate. However, a recent school of analysis sees the accounts as rather idealized expressions of Inca values and norms shaped by how the surviving lords of Cuzco and other native informants wished to have the nature and history of Tahuantinsuyu portrayed to their alien conquerors. No doubt there is a mixture of fact and fiction.

I believe that what colonial sources reported about matters such as native organization and statecraft is substantially more reliable than what is reported about Inca history. Historical information about Tahuantinsuyu suffers from the problem that Andean people conceived of time as cyclical. This was little understood by the Spanish, who framed what the Inca said about history in lineal time. There has been little awareness of this problem and Inca historical lore has traditionally been accepted at face value. This viewpoint has had a pervasive and lasting impact on Western perceptions of Andean civilization,

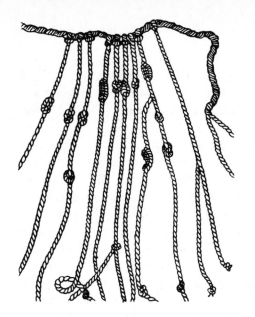

3 *Part of a quipu recording device of cord and string.*
4 *Guamán Poma's sketch of an imperial clerk with a quipu record made of cord and string.*

and on the development of Andean archaeology. For example conquerors often rationalize their acts both to themselves and to their new subjects. For the lords of Cuzco the rationalization process came to include a special creation myth. Inti, the essence of the Sun, was declared the progenitor and spiritual father of the Inca. By this doctrine, the Inca were Inti's chosen 'children of the sun', and the emperor, a demigod, was his executor on earth. From Inti came divine edicts for his children to transform Cuzco into the imperial navel of the universe and to conquer the world as its empire. Dogma held that before Tahuantinsuyu there was only savagery and barbarism, while in the wake of Cuzco's holy wars came civilization and enlightenment. Two remarkably able emperors, Pachacuti and his son Topa Inca, reputedly spread this enlightenment and conquered more than three quarters of Tahuantinsuyu. The historical message was simple: civilization originated at Cuzco and then spread over the Cordillera as a vast horizon of enlightenment within a span of two generations. This is the basis for what may be termed the *origin center →
civilization horizon* concept by which Western society has long interpreted the Andean past.

The oral traditions behind this concept reach back several centuries before the coming of the *conquistadores*, to times when the Cuzco or Huantanay Valley housed a number of small peasant populations who were hostile to one another. These rude conditions purportedly typified the universe in general following its relatively recent creation. Called Viracocha, the Creator had caused the sun to emerge from the waters of Lake Titicaca. He then went to the ancient lakeside metropolis of Tiwanaku, which in a former time had been inhabited by a race of giants. Here he gathered primordial clay and modeled animals and people. On the human models Viracocha painted the different clothes and distinct costumes that would distinguish the many different ethnicities of the

Andes, and each group was instructed in its different language and customs. The creator ordered the people to descend deep into the earth and mountains and then to emerge separately from caves, springs, lakes and hills in different homelands.

In some stories the founder of the Inca royal family, Manco Capac, along with three brothers and four sisters, emerged from Lake Titicaca, while in other versions they emerged from a cave southeast of the Río Huantanay. Gathering a small following, the siblings set off in search of a place with rich soils to settle. A long and adventurous journey sees several of the brothers turned to stone, entombed in mountains, and the like. Eventually, Manco Capac and his sister, Mama Oqlyo (his bride and wife) arrived near the spot where the Río Tullamayo joins the Huantanay. Here the founder plunged a golden staff into the soil to test it. Finding it auspicious, they drove away the local inhabitants and established a settlement at the locality that would become the Coricancha. After founding Cuzco and establishing a family, Manco Capac turned to stone. This ancestral stone was one of the Incas' most sacred objects or *huacas*.

By official accounts Cuzco remained a simple village through the reign of its eighth headman, Viracocha Inca. Late in life, after rule had been passed to his chosen heir, Inca Urcon, a powerful chiefdom from the northwest, the Chanca, amassed to attack Cuzco. The threat was so great that Viracocha and his heir fled the town and took refuge in a distant fort. However, a once troublesome royal son, Yupanqui, some capable generals and various settlers refused to desert their homes. Defenses were hurriedly organized under Yupanqui's command and reinforcements from neighborhood groups secured. When the more numerous Chanca pressed their attack and tried to take Cuzco by storm, they were heroically resisted. In the heat of the great battle, just when it appeared defenses might give way, Yupanqui cried out that the very stones in the fields were turning to armed men to repel the attackers. Cuzco's forces rallied and the Chanca were bloodily repulsed. The thankful commander immediately had the field stones collected and distributed among the city's shrines which they had helped to save.

The victorious Yupanqui, Cuzco's savior, then turned his attention to practical matters and usurped the throne. Although his father was allowed to live out the rest of his life in disgrace, his brother Inca Urcon's name was stricken from the dynastic king lists. I suspect that the usurper – who assumed the imperial title of Pachacuti or 'Earthshaker' – recast far more Inca history than simply striking his brother's name and memory from the royal record. This is because his reign marks a sudden, major change in Inca official history. After having rallied Cuzco's forces behind the banners of defense, Pachacuti Inca Yupanqui unfurled the banners of offense for a long series of aggressive foreign wars. He united the inhabitants of the Huantanay Valley and made local Quechua-speakers honorary Inca citizens, and then turned abroad to the great Titicaca Basin, largest demographic center in the Andean uplands. Credited with subjugating the Lupaqa, Colla, and other kingdoms around Lake

Titicaca, the great defender of Cuzco had amassed a tremendous power base and became concerned with developing institutions of statecraft that would consolidate Inca gains. He therefore returned to Cuzco, relinquishing the imperial legions to his son, Topa Inca. While Topa pursued a victorious career, Pachacuti invented statecraft and institutions such as the national taxation system, the highway and communication system, and the state's extensive warehousing system.

Inti, the Sun God, had appeared to Pachacuti in a vision when he was a young man and provided inspiration for the great deeds that had to be accomplished for humanity's betterment. In appreciation the emperor elevated the cult of the sun to that of Cuzco's patron god and commissioned construction of the marvelous Coricancha. Cuzco had been little more than a humble village until the defeat of the Chanca. Pachacuti tore down the old *Plate 15* settlement and designed a new one befitting Cuzco's status as the navel of the civilized universe. By some accounts streets and buildings were laid out so that the new celestial city looked, in outline, like a vast puma. At his death in 1471 the deeds and accomplishments of Pachacuti were so numerous and far-reaching that he had literally transformed the Inca realm from the Creator, Viracocha's, humble and somewhat unfinished handiwork, to that of Inti's divinely commissioned center of the civilized universe.

Although not the reputed inventor of statecraft that his father was, Topa Inca was by official accounts the Alexander the Great of the continent. From the time of first assuming command of the army to the end of his reign one year after Columbus' discovery of the Caribbean, this gifted tactician expanded the imperial frontiers along more than 4,000 km of the Cordillera, from central Ecuador to central Chile. Subsequently, Wayna Capac's reign was one of consolidation, with relatively modest imperial expansion into the tropical frontiers of Tahuantinsuyu before the chaos of the first smallpox pandemic and the ensuing civil war.

This brief synopsis of Inca historical lore does injustice to its rich but often contradictory detail. It does, however, capture two basic tenets of imperial propaganda: first, that civilization did not exist before the Incas; second, that it was invented at Cuzco and spread from there with remarkable rapidity to the rest of the Cordillera. The first tenet denied any time-depth to Andean development, and it took almost four centuries for Europeans to discover this to be in error. The second tenet limited development of civilization to a single ancient city serving as the fountainhead for invention and diffusion, and it has taken even longer to assess the legitimacy of this notion.

It did not befit the Incas' self image to admit that powerful states had contested Cuzco's rule, or that great civilizations had thrived long before the rise of Tahuantinsuyu. Yet, there were a few great cities in their vast realm that the masters of the Inca realm did not claim. Ultimately each would rise like an archaeological phoenix to challenge the claims of Cuzco. One was the venerable monument of Tiwanaku (Tiahuanaco) on the shores of Lake Titicaca. *Plates 79–83* Renowned for towering stelae in human form, the site figured as a primordial center, built and inhabited long ago by giants whom Viracocha had turned to stone before he created people. Cieza de León visited the site and wrote that the Inca had found it in ruins and regarded it with great reverence.

Plate 6   Pachacamac was another great city that the Inca could not claim. Located near the sea at the mouth of the Río Lurin, south of Lima, it was the home of a widely sought oracle with a powerful cult following. Drawing pilgrims and devotees from all quarters of the Cordillera, Pachacamac was the most revered city in the Andes. Probably something of a thorn in the imperial side, the Inca told Pizarro that the city contained immense riches, whereupon the *conquistador* dispatched his brother and a contingent of troops to sack the sacred center. Although great wealth was not found one officer did provide a short eyewitness account of finding and destroying the idol which was the oracle.

Plate 99   Finally, the Inca admitted to conquering the sprawling metropolis of Chan Chan at the mouth of the Río Moche on the northern coastal desert. This was the capital of Chimor, the second largest New World empire, whose frontiers were recorded by Spanish ethnohistorical sources. Spanning 1,000 km and encompassing two-thirds of the irrigated Andean coastlands, Chimor reached from southern Ecuador to just north of Pachacamac. It was the largest nation to contest Tahuantinsuyu and a protracted struggle was won by the Incas several generations before Pizarro's arrival. The official history of Cuzco made but passing mention of their greatest adversary, but survivors of the old empire made the Spanish aware that it had not been of Inca origin.

The archaeological record

Just as the historical accounts of Tahuantinsuyu are not without prejudice, the archaeological record did not remain unbiased by the Spanish arrival. The conquering forces quickly learned that great stores of precious metal existed in the ground. Much was purely geological in context, but the tombs of past lords and nobles also contained enormous stores of gold and silver. Within a generation of the conquest, looting operations grew so large and financially rewarding that they became legally synonymous with mining. Ancient monuments were divided into claim areas with titles registered in notarial archives. Title holders established chartered corporations to mobilize massive work forces and systematically quarry ruins. As with geological mines, the Castilian king was entitled to a 20 per cent tax on all wealth extracted from the ground. Within a short span the Crown established a royal smelter in the Moche Valley, not because of any local geological wealth but because the royal mausoleums of Chan Chan had been discovered and looting of the nearby Pyramid of the Sun was underway. By rendering the plundered treasures into bullion, overseers of the Crown foundry ensured collection of the royal tax.

From these lucrative beginnings commercial exploitation of antiquities has remained a large-scale business, and the Andean Cordillera is probably the most intensively looted ancient center of civilization in the world. Early in the

1960s several men plowing a field in a northern desert valley discovered the entrance shaft to a deep tomb with rich accompaniments of gold and silver work and fine pottery. The find revealed a cemetery, known as Loma Negra, and within several days 800 looters, called *huaqueros*, reportedly amassed to pillage the newly discovered graveyard. Grave robbing is not limited to *huaqueros* but is now a national pastime tied to the religious calendar and reverently pursued by multitudes on All Saints' Eve. *Semana Santa*, as the annual occasion is known, is considered a particularly auspicious time for discovering ancient tombs and families regularly go to the countryside to picnic atop ancient cemeteries where child and adult alike dig about searching for treasures and trinkets.

One by-product from the four centuries of monument-mining and ruin-quarrying has been the exposure of vast quantities of artifacts. Enormous quantities of fine ceramics, exquisite textiles, wood and lapidary work survived as curios and gradually stocked the shelves of museums and private collections around the world. But apart from the fact that these collections came mostly from graves, there was little information as to where they were found and with what monuments or other materials they were once associated. Therefore as Andean archaeology began to develop as a discipline, analysis and interpretation was largely art-historical. Objects were grouped on the basis of physical similarities and organized into styles, and subsequent excavations concentrated on establishing the spatial distributions of pottery and art styles and on fixing their stratigraphic positions in time.

Although pillaging was the norm, a few individuals pursued a more enlightened attitude, and sought to preserve ancient works by describing, illustrating, collecting, and safeguarding them. In the sixteenth century Cieza de León was a pioneer of this attitude. Near the end of the eighteenth century another was Martínez de Compañón, Bishop of Trujillo in the Moche Valley. He commissioned the mapping of ancient monuments, including Chan Chan and the Huaca del Sol (Pyramid of the Sun), probably the largest mud brick mound ever erected in the continent. Extensive looting had already taken place at the Huaca del Sol, including the diversion of the Río Moche to undercut it, causing two-thirds of the monument to be washed away by the time the Bishop mapped the pyramid.

The Prussian-born naturalist, Alexander von Humboldt, was the first to draw international attention to Andean antiquities and those of Latin America in general. Traveling widely in Spain's colonies, he took notes on ancient monuments, buildings, and works such as the vast highway system of the Cordillera, and in 1814 published *Vues de Cordillères et Monuments des Peuples Indigènes de l'Amérique*. As the first attempt at a systematic overview of the monuments of New World civilizations, von Humboldt's treatise had a lasting impact on later investigators and established recording and commenting upon ruins and monuments as a legitimate field of scholarly endeavor.

Other traveling naturalists made further contributions. After training in Europe as a geologist, Mariano Eduardo de Rivero returned to Peru in 1825 and began systematically gathering information on ancient works. He was joined by the Swiss naturalist, J. J. Diego de Tschudi, and in 1851 they published a two-volume work that was the first treatise to concentrate on the archaeology of the central Andes. But Rivero and Tschudi only described the ruins. The notion that they reflected change and development over millennia was initially put forward by E. G. Squier, who spent over a year traveling, mapping, photographing, and recording prehistoric sites and cities in the central Andes in the 1870s. In the Titicaca Basin he encountered a landscape dotted with *chullpas*, masonry burial towers, which he realized could be grouped into a number of different types which had probably been built at different times. For his time this was an innovative insight, although chronological matters were not a significant theme in his work, *Peru: Incidents of Travel and Exploration in the Land of the Incas*, which was a travel narrative with unusually high standards of archaeological mapping and description. For North American readers it conveyed the important message that the Andes were a legitimate aspect of Americanist, rather than Hispanic, studies. This stimulated scholars such as Adolph Bandelier who spent a decade (1893–1903) exploring monuments of the Cordillera for the American Museum of Natural History.

The ancient city of Tiwanaku (or Tiahuanaco), on the main colonial and modern route from the sea to Bolivia's capital La Paz, had been visited by Squier and many others interested in antiquities. In 1876–7 the distinguished German investigator Alphons Stubel made an extensive and detailed series of measurements and drawings of the sprawling ruins, its many stelae, and artistically rich stonework. Upon returning to Dresden he analyzed these materials with a young museum worker, Max Uhle. Although he had never visited Peru, Uhle had written on New World languages and was actively studying Andean artifacts in his homeland, including large archaeological collections procured from Cuzco. In 1892 the co-workers published their monumental *Die Ruinenstätten von Tiahuanaco*, in which they defined the art style of Tiwanaku, chronologically important because the Inca reported the metropolis to have been in ruins when they first entered the region in the fourteenth century.

Uhle was fired with the desire to excavate at Tiwanaku, which he visited several years later, but could not obtain a permit to excavate. Traveling to Peru, he obtained permission to work at the great oracle center of Pachacamac and there carried out extensive explorations during 1896–7. He supported his research by supplying the University of Pennsylvania with museum quality artifacts. These were most commonly encountered in graves, and in the course of excavating tombs he encountered materials with ties to both Cuzco and Tiwanaku. He recognized that each style was distinct, and related this to the Inca information about the relative ages of the cities. Uhle was also a pioneer in the use of the principles of stratigraphy, for beneath Inca burials he encountered graves with a local pottery style; under these were earlier burials with materials related to the Tiwanaku style, and deeper still were burials with a second local pottery style. Thus, at Pachacamac Uhle had identified solid evidence for time-depth in the Andes, and thereby demonstrated that civilization had developed and flourished long before the Inca.

Supported by the University of California, Uhle went on to excavate at desert cemeteries and sites in the Ica and Nazca Valleys in southern Peru and Moche sites in the north. Over this coastal region he encountered archaeological successions generally similar to those at Pachacamac. Inca remains were the most recent, preceded by local styles which varied from area to area, then by Tiwanaku-like remains, then by other local styles. Earliest of all were coastal villages which Uhle attributed to 'Fisherfolk'. Uhle was rightfully impressed with the widespread occurrence of tombs containing pottery and other artwork broadly similar to the Tiwanaku style. He quite naturally assumed that these remains reflected an early empire which had conquered much of the Cordillera, and he further concluded that the Bolivian metropolis of Tiwanaku had been its capital. The obvious analogy with Cuzco and Tahuantinsuyu lay close at hand. It was only a short step from this conclusion to the hypothesis that Tiwanaku was the source of an earlier horizon of civilization that had spread rapidly across the landscape subduing less developed populations by force of arms. In effect Uhle simply applied Inca propaganda to his interpretation of Tiwanaku.

The grave goods on which Uhle based these pioneering conclusions went to the University of California at Berkeley where they were studied and published by A. L. Kroeber and his students. Appearing in the 1920s and 1930s, these reports supported Uhle's conclusions and established widespread horizons alternating with local traditions of intermediate development as the conceptual framework for interpreting central Andean prehistory. In the 1950s Professor John H. Rowe and his students began to reanalyze the collections, refining the basic notion that the evolution of Andean civilization was marked by periods of unity interspersed with periods of intermediate development. Uhle's work thus gave rise to the prestigious 'Berkeley school' of Andean studies which has shaped the course of Peruvian archaeology more than any other institution.

The founder of another school, the 'Peruvian school', was born in 1890. At this time Peru's native Indian population was viewed with contempt, but one superbly energetic and talented native youth, Julio C. Tello, won a fellowship to Harvard and from there worked his way to the first fully international career in Peruvian archaeology. Well known for directing the national archaeological museum in Lima, this charismatic scientist was also elected to the country's senate. Tello's popularity and international success as a scholar attracted talented young students to archaeology and established it as a respected national discipline.

Tello concentrated on elucidating the early aspects of civilization that had eluded Uhle. He located and excavated the rich seaside necropolis of Paracas, and the enormous coastal mound of Sechín Alto and its associated architectural complexes in the Casma Valley. Yet, Tello's ethnic ancestry drew him to the little-known eastern flanks of the Cordillera. Here his most far-reaching discoveries were at the primordial platform complex of Chavín de Huantar, a *Plates 43,47–49* great masonry monument rich in stelae and artistically carved stonework displaying a vivid iconography dominated by felines, raptorial birds, and serpents. The naturalist E. W. Middendorf had previously visited the ruins and thought them to be early, but it was Tello who demonstrated that Chavín de Huantar was the most elaborate and ornate center of a previously unknown stylistic complex which had been widely disseminated across the central Andes at an early date. He viewed the Chavín complex as a 'mother culture' that nurtured the rise of civilization in Peru, and Chavín de Huantar as its upland center of origin. Nevertheless Chavín iconography was richly charged with jungle beasts, and the roots of Chavín de Huantar, Tello argued, were to be discovered in the Amazonian forests along the eastern flanks of the Cordillera.

Lima, out of which Uhle and Tello operated, was far removed from the realities of highland life and Cuzco. The old city and its mountain hinterlands remained ethnically Indian, albeit with a Castilian overlay. Around the turn of the century Cuzco's Universidad San Antonio Abad became a center for the study of native communities. Here a 'neo-Inca' vogue was encouraged by the Yale University expeditions of Hiram Bingham, one of which rediscovered the lost city of Machu Picchu in 1911. Cuzco's emerging pride in its past led to archaeological exploration of the city's greatest surviving monument, the megalithic citadel of Sacsahuaman, directed by a talented young scholar from the local university, Luis E. Valcarcel. In the succeeding years, Valcarcel came to understand the ruins as reflecting deep-seated native traditions. Spanish conquest and disruption were but threads interwoven with the fabric of ongoing Indian society that persisted throughout the highlands.

Assuming the directorship of the national museum from Tello in 1930, Valcarcel added this vision of unity and continuity to the 'Peruvian school'. For decades he worked actively to promote ethnology, ethnohistory, and archaeology to make the wholeness of the Andean past and present intelligible. This underscored continuing traditions of community organization, reciprocity, labor exchange, and subsistence strategies. They represent the filaments of life that make ancient Andean civilization intelligible in terms of people and not simply potsherds.

The foundations laid by Uhle, Tello and Valcarcel have been built upon by increasing numbers of scholars and students. When Geoffrey Bushnell wrote the 1956 edition of *Peru* for the 'Ancient Peoples and Places' series, the archaeological record was organized in terms of horizons and intermediate periods, as Uhle had first proposed. According to Bushnell, in the cases of Cuzco and of Tiwanaku, pan-Andean integration was achieved by force of arms, but in the case of Chavín de Huantar, a missionizing cult was involved. Since Bushnell's synthesis there has been a tremendous increase in Andean studies and more archaeological, historical, and anthropological research has been carried out during the current generation than during all prior centuries. Thus the brief chapters that follow can only touch upon the dominant evolutionary processes and the large political formations of Andean prehistory.

Owing to this surge of new information our understanding of the development of Andean prehistory is undergoing a profound and exciting revolution, and the results defy easy synthesis. The *origin center* → *civilization horizon* concept does not work the way the Inca portrayed it nor the way Uhle thought it did. Horizons do identify times of widespread interaction and movement of ideas and people. But they are not as Bushnell portrayed them. Chavín de Huantar did not exert Early Horizon influence until relatively late, around 400 BC. The Middle Horizon was influenced by two metropolitan centres, Tiwanaku in the south and Huari in the north. And finally, Chan Chan, the capital of Chimor, evinces almost all the major principles of Andean statecraft that Pachacuti supposedly invented at Cuzco.

When Bushnell wrote, the changes demarcated by horizons were only explained in cultural terms, such as marching armies and conquest, or missionizing movements and conversion. Now other potential sources of change have been revealed by recent advances in the geological, marine, and meteorological sciences. The 'Theory of Plate Tectonics' has shown the Andes to be the New World's most actively growing cordillera, associated with high rates of tectonic, seismic, and volcanic activity that produce natural disasters of regional scope. The 'Theory of Ocean-Atmosphere Interaction' indicates that disasters of pan-Andean scope have been rare but predictably recurrent events. Known as 'El Niño' phenomena, normal marine and meteorological cycles break down and catastrophic rains flood the desert while drought envelops the highlands. It is now obvious that Andean civilization matured within a very dynamic landscape.

In reviewing the archaeological record new interpretations of horizons and intermediate periods are called for. But, as yet, there is nothing to replace the established tradition of chronologically ordering sites, styles, and phases in terms of horizons and periods. If understood simply as epochs of time, devoid of other overtones, then they continue to be useful. The chronological subdivisions I will employ are presented on the following two pages. They begin with a long Lithic Period and a shorter Preceramic Period. Following an Initial Period of pottery use, there are Early, Middle, and Late Horizons, separated by Early and Late Intermediate Periods. The Periods and Horizons are defined by the Berkeley school's 'master sequence' in the Ica Valley. This scheme has its greatest applicability in central Peru where Uhle worked. It is less satisfactory to the north and south, where cross-ties must be projected to more distant regions which are geographically, if not culturally, distinct.

Time Scale	North Coast	Central Coast	South Coast	Periods/Horizons
1500 —	INCA	INCA	INCA	Late Horizon
1250 —	CHIMU	CHANCAY		Late Intermediate
1000 —	SICAN		ICA	Period
750 —				Middle Horizon
500 —		HUARI		
	MOCHE	Pachacamac		Early
250 —		LIMA	NAZCA	Intermediate Period
A.D.				
B.C.	GALLINAZO	Miramar		
	SALINAR	Baños de Boza		Early Horizon
500 —	CUPISNIQUE	Ancon	PARACAS	
1000 —	Caballo Muerto Cerro Sechin	Garagay		Initial Period
2000 —	Huaca Prieta	La Florida		Preceramic Period
		El Paraiso		
4000 —		La Palma		
6000 —				
	PAIJAN			Lithic Period
8000 —		Luz		
10000 —				

5 Chronology for coastal Peru.

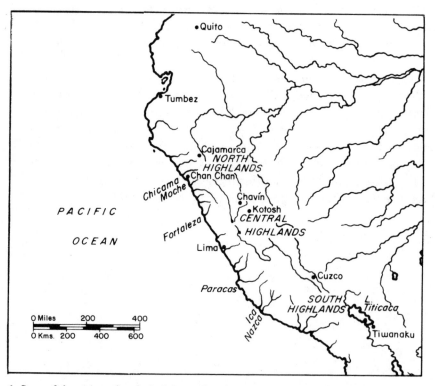

6 Some of the main archaeological sites and modern towns of Peru.

Time Scale	North	Central	South	Periods/Horizons
1500	INCA	INCA	INCA	Late Horizon
1250		Wanka	KILLKE	Late Intermediate Period
1000				
750	Marcahuamachuca	HUARI	Pikillaqta	Middle Horizon
500				Early Intermediate Period
250	RECUAY	HUARPA		
A.D. / B.C.				
500	Kotosh / CHAVIN		Chanapata	Early Horizon
1000	Huacaloma		Marcavalle	Initial Period
2000	Galgada			Preceramic Period
4000				
6000	Lauricocha	Pachamachay		
8000	Guitarrero			Lithic Period
10000				

7 *Chronology for highland Peru.*

Time Scale	Moquegua	Arica	Titicaca-Altiplano	Periods/Horizons
1500	INCA		INCA	Late Horizon
1250	CHIRIBAYA	GENTILAR	AYMARA KINGDOMS	Late Intermediate Period
1000	Tumilaca			Middle Horizon
750	Chen Chen			
500	OMO		TIWANAKU	Early Intermediate Period
250				
A.D. / B.C.	HUARICANI	Faldas el Moro	PUKARA	
500			CHIRIPA	Early Horizon
1000				Initial Period
2000		CHINCHOROS		Preceramic Period
4000				
6000			Asana	
8000	Ring Site		Toquepala	Lithic Period
10000				

8 *Chronology for the Titicaca region.*

Guayas R.

Gulf of Guayaquil

Chira

Piura

Lambayeque

Zaña
Jequetepeque
Chicama
Moche
Viru
Santa
Nepeña
Casma
Huarmay
Pativilca
Supe
Huaura
Chancay
Chillon
Rimac

Lurin
Chilca
Cañete
Chincha

Ica
Nazca

Acari
Yauca

Atica
Ocana
Majes
Sihuas

Moquegua

Azapa

Peru

Brazil

Marañon R.

Huallaga R.

Callejon de Huaylas

Lima

Apurimac R.

Urubamba R.

Cuzco

Lake Titicaca

Lake Popo

Arica
Chile

San Pedro
de
Atacama

Salar
de Atacama

Pacific Ocean

0 100 200 300
Kilometers

N
W   E
S

- - - International Boundaries

D.R.S. 1990

9 *The main rivers of Peru.*

CHAPTER TWO

Land of the Four Quarters

Andean civilization is very different from other great civilizations of antiquity. Tahuantinsuyu arose from human mastery over global extremes in environmental conditions. If thriving civilizations had matured atop the Himalayas while simultaneously accommodating a Sahara desert, a coastal fishery richer than the Bering Sea, and a jungle larger than the Congo, then Tahuantinsuyu might seem less alien. Fundamental contrasts in the Andean Cordillera's habitats confronted humans with radically disparate conditions and dissimilar resources. Simultaneous adaptation to all niches by a single population or society remained an untrodden evolutionary avenue. Instead people pursued more selective proficiency in making a living in one or another environment. The mountain, marine, desert and jungle habitats required distinctive adaptive strategies and promoted different evolutionary pathways, called Arid Montane, Maritime-Oasis, and Tropical Forest lifeways. The Inca were a montane society, but the land of the four quarters incorporated people adapted to other conditions.

The Cordillera

From a geophysical perspective two energy sources, solar and tectonic, molded the South American Cordillera into a land of ecological extremes. The sun powers the ebb and flow of marine and meteorological currents, channeled by the Andes. Tectonic energy compels the westward-moving continental plate to converge on the eastward-moving sea floor of the Nazca Plate at rates of 9 to 15 cm a year. The sea floor slides under the land mass in a narrow oceanic trench and compression buckles the continental margin, folding it into thin, parallel ranges stretching from the Caribbean coast of Colombia to Tierra del Fuego, the world's longest cordillera.

Where the Andes are highest and widest the mountain plan forms a gigantic H, the cross-bar formed by the Nudo de Vilcanota peaks. The western range, the Cordillera Negra, fronts the Atacama desert. The taller eastern range, the Cordillera Blanca, fronts the Amazon and buffers clouds from the Atlantic carrying almost all of the Andes' rainfall. South of the Vilcanota peaks the two ranges diverge to frame the altiplano, an immense landlocked trough of high plains some 800 km in length. Drainage flows south through a string of lake basins. In southern Chile these form salt pans and the sparse grasslands there are called salt puna. As the Andes become higher they become drier, but the puna pasturage is not salty in the northern altiplano, which forms the largest

10 *The four quarters of the Inca realm emanating from Cuzco, the imperial capital.*

expanse of uninterrupted agricultural flatlands in the Andes, around Lake Titicaca, which drains south to Bolivia's Lake Popo.

North of the Vilcanota mountains the uplands splinter into long, narrow ranges paralleling the Cordilleras Negra and Blanca, cross-cut by numerous short ranges which frame high, but fractured, puna grasslands and a string of lower sierra basins, eventually reaching a slim tropical low point in Ecuador. As altitude decreases rainfall increases and the grasslands and sierra basins of northern Peru are relatively lush. About 90 per cent of Andean runoff descends to the Atlantic watershed, while only 10 per cent descends to the Pacific.

The Andes also channel marine currents. Strong daily winds off the ocean are deflected northward by the Cordillera Negra causing the sea to flow northward along the continental margin. Upwelling currents rise from the depths of the tectonic trench propelling extremely cold but nutrient-rich waters to the surface, and supporting a prodigious maritime food chain. The cold currents generate a temperature inversion, inhibiting coastal rainfall and producing the Atacama desert. From central Chile to the mouth of the Río Santa in northern Peru there is little or no continental shelf. The Río Santa breaks through the Cordillera Negra and disgorges abundant runoff into the ocean. North of it the Andes pull back from the shore as a wide continental shelf and coastal plain emerge and expand northward, comprising agricultural lands irrigated by abundant runoff from the lower, wetter Cordillera and large oasis valleys in northern Peru.

Stress

Andean landscapes subject people to stress from a variety of sources. For the majority, who traditionally resided above 3,000 m, the corollaries of high altitude include elevated solar radiation, cold, high winds, rough terrain, limited farm land, poor soils, aridity, erratic rainfall, short growing seasons, diminished nutrition, and hypoxia. Hypoxia is the technical term for low oxygen tension due to elevational decrease in barometric pressure. It stands out as the most pervasive form of constant strain, affecting all physiological functions. Anoxia, or low air availability at the beginning of the oxygen supply chain, causes modified cellular metabolism, higher red blood cell counts, and increased circulation and ventilation associated with large chests and lung capacity. Anoxia also affects highland flora and fauna, and the rise of civilization in these high plains depended upon the domestication of plants and animals capable of contending with the condition. Through the generations native mountain people adjusted physically and economically, and increased their numbers. But biological adjustments to oxygen stress are not necessarily inherited, and with time people born at lower altitudes acclimatize to higher altitudes and vice versa. Yet, the experience of seventeenth-century Spanish colonists at high altitude was reputedly one of low sperm counts, infertility, inability to carry a fetus to full term, and in the event of live birth, neonatal death. Subnormal reproduction may have been a major factor in European preference for settlement along the coast and at low altitudes. Native lowlanders may not have suffered as grievously in the Cordillera, but comparison of ancient skeletal remains from the coast and from the highlands shows that littoral populations appear more closely related to one another than to mountain populations and vice versa. Therefore it is reasonable to suspect that anoxia reinforced economic and cultural separation of Arid Montane, Maritime-Oasis and Tropical Forest adaptations.

Tectonic activity also subjects Andean populations to erratic stress. Earthquakes occur every generation or so, triggering hundreds of mountain avalanches, reshaping the landscape, and killing thousands of people. Major volcanic eruptions are less frequent but they too alter landscapes. In February AD 1600, Huayna Putina in southern Peru exploded with such force that it destroyed the entire mountain and left only a gaping crater. Tens of thousands perished. Thick cinder deposits destroyed large tracts of agricultural land, but further afield the ash enhanced soils. In Ecuador, where volcanoes are numerous, archaeologists are unraveling a long series of violent calamities that scattered survivors far and wide. Finally, tectonic creep causes slow, imperceptible earth movement, straining canal-based irrigation systems sensitive to ground slope change.

In the central Andes rainfall is extremely erratic. Annual precipitation (rainfall) deviates enormously around a statistical average that sees 'normal' rains less often than one year in three. At the extreme end of this variability are 'El Niño events', complete breakdowns of meteorological and marine currents that often last as long as 18 months. These events are of such force and magnitude that they slow the earth's rotational momentum, altering the length of day and causing temporary reordering of the food chain both on land and in the sea. In the north and along the desert coast there is cataclysmic rainfall, while in the southern mountains there is devastating drought. Both trigger large-scale population movements, to interior highlands in the north and to lower, eastern elevations and deserts in the south.

The sediment layers in ice cores drilled from the Quelccaya glacier south of Cuzco provide a record of annual precipitation for the past 1,500 years. This evidence shows that El Niño events were not uncommon, and that some of them may have lasted much longer than 18 months. Archaeological evidence has revealed episodes of exceptional flood destruction on the north coast. The most recent and securely documented of these occurred around AD 1100, but there are also traces of extensive flooding and landscape alteration 500 years earlier, and of still earlier episodes of drastic disturbance within a century or so of 500 BC. Finally, there are ice core signatures of rare, but severe, climatological anomalies spanning decades, such as a great drought between AD 562 and 594. Recurrent natural disasters of this scale must have affected the processes of cultural evolution, requiring rapid adaptation followed by relative stability.

Distribution of resources

Distinct Andean environments provided different kinds and amounts of resources, and the manner in which ecological assets were distributed was particularly critical in influencing the development of Andean cultures. In the vast continental lowlands societies, even though thousands of kilometers apart, all depended upon manioc, kindred basic crops, and corresponding wild resources. The inhabitants of the oasis valleys of the Andean desert likewise shared similar resources.

Whereas continental lowlands stretch ecological zones and separate them horizontally, towering mountains compress and stack these zones one above the other. Andean people can trek as little as 100 km as the crow flies and go from tropical lowland forests to alpine equivalents of boreal tundra in the mountains, crossing counterparts of major continental environmental zones. Contrasts between heterogeneous, stacked mountain resources and homogenous, detached lowland ones resulted in different strategies for collecting and using them. The mountain tactic is referred to as 'verticality' and the lowland one is called 'horizontality', reflecting the directions that goods had to be moved. Horizontal strategies emphasized moving goods over great distances by watercraft, in the east along the Amazon and its tributaries and in the west along the Humboldt Current up and down the coast. The fractured topography of the Cordillera made vertical movement of products more difficult.

The eastern flanks of the Andes, well watered and lush, are referred to as montaña. Montaña and jungle lowlands make up some 58 per cent of Peru. The highlands, including those of Bolivia and Chile, are characterized by scarce to insufficient rainfall. Arid Montane cultural evolution was strongly influenced

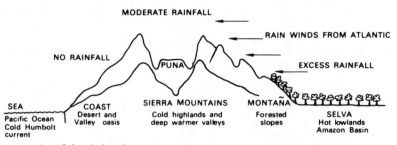

MODERATE RAINFALL

RAIN WINDS FROM ATLANTIC

NO RAINFALL

PUNA

EXCESS RAINFALL

SEA	COAST	SIERRA MOUNTAINS	MONTAÑA	SELVA
Pacific Ocean Cold Humbolt current	Desert and Valley oasis	Cold highlands and deep warmer valleys	Forested slopes	Hot lowlands Amazon Basin

11 Cross-section of the Andes, showing general environmental conditions. Irrigation was vital to agriculture in the dry coastal zone.

by north to south differences in annual rainfall because precipitation governed the distribution, density, and abundance of plant resources and agricultural potential. Peru comprises about 14 per cent puna grasslands, about 11.5 per cent sierra basins, and about 16.5 per cent western desert. In the better watered north the grasslands and basins could support independent populations of hunter-gatherers, but in the south puna and sierra resources grew more impoverished as the Cordillera grew higher, wider, and drier. Lower rainfall caused greater movement between higher and lower Cordillera habitats. In the far south hunters and later herders in the wastelands of Chile trekked up and down from the salt puna, through the dry sierra, to coastal oases. Along the coast decreasing highland rainfall created oasis valleys decreasing in size from north to south.

Farming in the Andes

Andean agriculture depends upon domesticated plants, arable land, and moisture, as well as temperature and sunshine which influence the growing season. At different elevations crops must be sown and harvested at distinct times, and as altitude increases the growing season decreases. In the drier, higher Cordillera, flat land with sufficient rainfall to sustain farming is not common north of the Titicaca altiplano, where the range fractures into predominantly steep and tortuous terrain. Andean agriculture is plagued by the problem that where there is land there is little or no water and vice versa. To mitigate this situation montane and desert populations moved truly prodigious quantities of earth and water to create artificial agrarian niches. One tale about how the Cordillera got its name holds that the *conquistadores* named the Andes for their greatest monument to human endeavor – *andenes*, the abandoned *Plate 2* agricultural terraces found throughout the highlands built by Pre-Hispanic populations to facilitate irrigation. Although the tale may be apocryphal, andenes, canal networks and other abandoned agricultural works cover millions of hectares; the sight no doubt impressed Spanish explorers and it continues to awe contemporary travelers, for abandoned Andean agricultural systems comprise the largest archaeological phenomena of the Western Hemisphere.

Many techniques were used to create farmland. Around the margins of Lake Titicaca soil was mounded up to create 'ridged fields' – long planting ridges

	Annual Mean Temperature °C	Annual Rainfall (dm)	Altitude (m)
Aracacia xanthorrhiza (arracacha)	15-23	7-15	850-956
Arachis hypogaea (peanut)	11-27	3-40	46-1000
Capsicum annuum (chili pepper)	9-27	3-40	2-1000
Capsicum frutescens (chili pepper)	8-27	30-40	385-1000
Chenopodium quinoa (quinoa)	5-27	6-26	28-3878
Cucurbita ficifolia (squash)	11-23	3-17	850-956
Cucurbita maxima (squash)	7-27	3-27	385-1000
Cucurbita moschata (squash)	7-27	3-28	28-1000
Erythroxylon coca (coca)	17-27	7-40	450-1200
Gossypium barbadense (cotton)	9-26	5-40	320-1006
Ipomoea batatas (sweet potato)	9-27	3-42	28-1000
Lagenaria siceraria (gourd)	15-27	7-28	850-956
Manihot esculenta (manioc)	15-29	5-40	46-1006
Nicotiana tabacum (tobacco)	7-27	3-40	57-1000
Oxalis tuberosa (oca)	12-25	5-25	850-1700
Persea americana (avocado)	13-27	3-40	320-1750
Phaseolus lunatus (lima bean)	9-27	3-42	28-1000
Phaseolus vulgaris (common bean)	5-27	3-42	2-3700
Psidium guajava (guava)	15-29	2-42	28-1000
Solanum tuberosum (potato)	4-27	3-26	2-3830
Tropaelum tuberosum (mashwa)	8-25	7-14	850-3700
Ullucus tuberosus (olluco)	11-12	14	3700-3830
Zea mays (maize)	5-29	3-40	2-3350

12 Approximate elevational growing ranges of Andean domesticated plants.

separated by deep furrows that held standing water. Further from the lake people dug great pond–like structures, called *cochas*. After filling with wet season runoff, their sides and bottoms were farmed as their water levels lowered during the dry season. On the coast vast pits were dug down to the water table so that soil moisture could sustain farming in sunken gardens.

Irrigating land from canals fed by streams and springs remains the most prevalent technique for transforming terrain. Along the arid Pacific watershed both on the coast and in the terraced highlands more than 85 per cent of all farming is sustained by canal irrigation, and it is critical in sierra basins as a supplement to seasonal precipitation. Archaeologists agree that social organization is influenced by irrigation and varies with hydrological conditions. More than 60 short, steep rivers descend the arid Andean watershed and cross a length of desert greater than that traversed by the Nile or Tigris rivers. Whereas the Near Eastern rivers seemed to unite the people living along their courses, Andean rivers promoted isolation and segregation. Coastal valleys and sierra basins can be irrigated by multiple canals feeding off a single river, but each canal is capable of operating independently. Therefore, each can form an autonomous economic system capable of supporting an independent group of people.

Andean agrarian adaptations are strongly influenced by an inverse relationship between areas where large numbers of crops will grow and those where large numbers of people can live. There is significantly more farmland at higher altitudes than at lower elevations, but far fewer types of crops will grow at high altitudes. Of the major varieties of Andean cultigens 90 per cent thrive below 1,000 m and fewer than 20 per cent do well above 3,000 m. This elevational inversion of land availability and crop diversity had a profound and lasting structural effect upon agricultural life, creating far-reaching supply and demand problems that lie at the heart of Arid Montane adaptations.

Geography of the Four Quarters

The Inca viewed Cuzco as a sacred city and as the navel of their imperial realm. Boundary lines that quartered Tahuantinsuyu originated in the main plaza of the capital, with one running roughly northwest–southeast, and the other pursuing a perpendicular course. These divisions reflect the fact that for Quechua inhabitants of the high Andes the cosmos was structured by checks and balances between oppositional, though complementary, spheres and forces. This organization was sometimes a dual one and sometimes quadrilateral, and was widespread in the New World. Indeed, the Inca nobility was divided between the royal lineages of *hanan* or upper, and *hurin* or lower Cuzco. Anthropologists call such complementary division moiety organization. Thus, the 'Land of the Four Quarters' was, in part, an expression of how the Inca perceived their universe, with Cuzco midway between lowland desert and jungle, and close to the north–south Cordillera divide.

Collasuyu was the largest and southernmost quarter of Tahuantinsuyu, stretching from the Pacific shores of the Atacama desert, over the mountains to the eastern tropical forest. It was dominated by the high plains of the altiplano, where in the region of Lake Titicaca seasonal rainfall was 50 cm or more, with cool but tolerable temperatures. Here the Aymara-speaking kingdoms were densely settled and became the first target of Inca conquest. The lands along Lake Titicaca formed the bread basket and power base of highland Tahuantinsuyu.

The huge lake holds a wealth of resources and its deep waters trap and release warmth which mitigates frost damage to adjacent fields. Abundant, relatively flat farm land lies mostly within a narrow zone between about 3500 m and the upper alpine limits of plant growth. Altitude, frost, hail, erratic rainfall, a short growing season, and poor soils that must be fallowed frequently allow only the most hardy and specialized of crops. Staples included a variety of tubers, such as oca (*Oxalis tuberosa*), ulluco (*Ullucus tuberosus*), and potatoes (*Solanum*), of which there are more than 60 varieties tended by altiplano folk. Robust chenopods called quiñoa and cañihuas (*Chenopodium quinoa* and *Chenopodium pallidicaula*) were domesticated for grains. Above about 3,900 m vast expanses of dry puna grasslands provided grazing for herds of llama and alpaca, which in *Plate 4* turn provided fertilizer critical to crops when pastured on the stubble of harvested or fallowed fields. This reciprocal arrangement between farming and herding, called 'agropastoralism', transformed the Titicaca altiplano into the most populated region of the Andes, and its rich archaeological heritage includes the ancient cities of Pukara and Tiwanaku at the northern and southern ends of the lake.

South of Titicaca the Atacama desert sweeps over the Cordillera Negra and transforms the uplands into salt puna and salt lakes. There are occasional highland oases but runoff from rainfall is scarce and even the coastal valleys are small. Maritime exploitation, however, dates back 9,000 years along the narrow band of upwelling currents that hug the desert shores and provide the richest fishery and marine biomass of the Western Hemisphere. Mollusks, large fish, sea mammals and marine birds were taken; and small fish such as anchovies were harvested throughout the year with simple nets from small water craft, then dried whole or after being ground into meal, and stored. This maritime adaptation remained basically independent of valley oasis agriculture.

Antisuyu, the eastern quarter of Tahuantinsuyu, stretched into the rugged montaña forests overlooking the Amazon. The boundaries of this province are less clear, but included the rugged sierra and puna uplands forming the eastern rim of the Cuzco Basin. The steep eastern Cordillera dominates the landscape, the sheer mountainsides drained by fast-flowing streams and rivers in deep canyons and valleys providing negligible flat land. Here the highest degree of natural diversity found in the continent is compressed into narrow stratified ecological zones that follow the horizontal, but irregular contours of the mountainsides, creating a vertical series of stacked agricultural zones. From potatoes and quiñoa near mountaintops to manioc and tropical fruits on the jungle floor, each habitat is characterized by particular patterns of rainfall, sunshine, and temperature, and calls for different techniques and times of cultivation. The rugged topography provides relatively little land suitable for farming, but is highly prized because of the many different types of crops that can be grown. Altiplano and sierra villagers regularly descend to the montaña to tend fields of maize, coca, cotton, and other staples.

The extremely broken topography could not accommodate large populations. The Inca empire incorporated much of the montaña but their penetration of the jungle below about 1,500 m was negligible. The lords of Cuzco actively developed their Antisuyu holdings, particularly in the Urubamba Valley where the hillsides were carved into great flights of terraces. A string of monumental settlements were built, including the mountaintop *Plate 3* retreats of Machu Picchu and Wina-Wayna as well as the larger complexes of Pisaq and Ollantaytambo. Antisuyu provided a refuge for the Inca court following Pizarro's capture of Cuzco, and a base for guerrilla warfare.

Cuntisuyu, the small, southwestern quarter of Tahuantinsuyu, stretched from Cuzco to the Pacific coast near the Ica Valley in the north and the Moquegua Valley in the south, including sierra habitats. However, the dominant geographical features of the province were the dry western slopes of the Cordillera and the bleak coastal desert. Normally there is no annual rainfall below elevations of about 1,800 m, leaving the western Andean escarpment and Pacific coastlands barren. Stratified ecological zones occur along the mountain

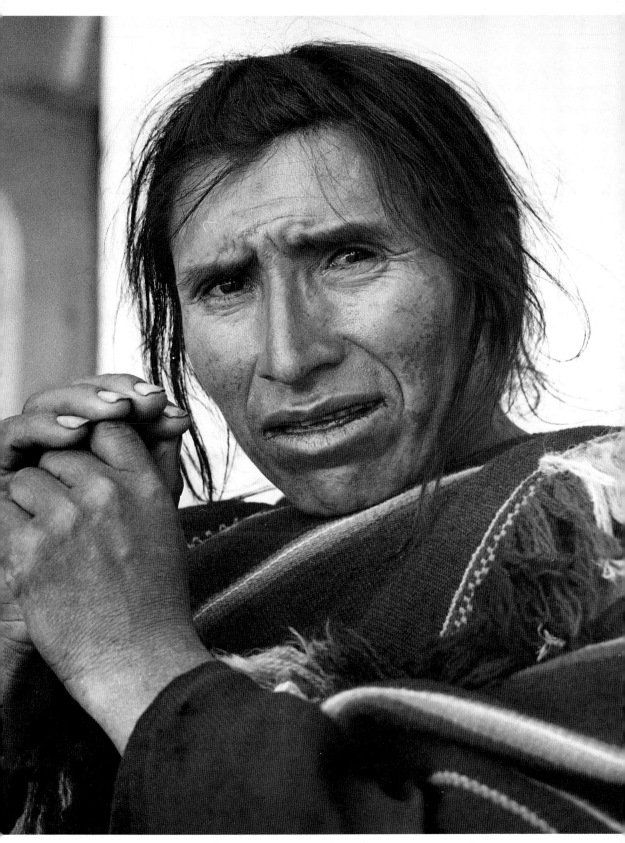

1 Modern highland Indians still pursue many of the traditional adaptations to mountain life that evolved centuries ago, providing insights into the beliefs, languages and customs of their ancient Andean ancestors.

Arid Montane adaptations

2 (left) Terracing is vital to farming the rugged Andes mountains, and steep flights of stone-faced terraces such as these in the Urubamba Valley (center) were an Inca tradition not duplicated by modern farmers.

3 (right) The Inca city of Machu Picchu overlooks the rugged mountains of Antisuyu.

4 (below) Llamas and alpacas, which pasture on the puna, above the elevational limits of agriculture, are essential to survival in the high mountains.

5 (above) *The Río Paramonga (bottom) supplies water to large canals that transformed the barren desert into agricultural oases. Built late in prehistory, the imposing hill-top bastion sanctuary of Fortaleza de Paramonga overlooks the verdant valley.*

6 (below) *View of the coastal city of Pachacamac from the air.*

7 (opposite) *A space shuttle view of the desert coast showing (from top to bottom) the Moche, Viru, Chao, Santa and Nepeña Valleys.*

Maritime-Oasis adaptations

Coast and Tropical Forest adaptations

8 (left) A fisherboy on a balsa raft. Watercraft were fashioned from reeds because the desert yields no wood.

9 (above) Supplying fish and other foodstuffs, jungle rivers were vital to life in the tropical forest. Seasonal flooding enriched adjacent soils for farming, and the waterways provided routes for long-distance trade and commerce.

10 (right) Feathered cloth, such as this coastal tunic, was highly prized and manufactured by skilled specialists.

11 (overleaf) Mountain adaptations united herding and farming, with llamas supplying both fertilizer for crops and a means of transporting produce between far-flung mountain habitats.

slopes, but extreme aridity leaves these habitats impoverished in comparison with those of Antisuyu. The Cuntisuyu desert is crossed by 15 short rivers, which support terrace farming along the sierra headwaters where irrigation supplements seasonal rainfall. At mid-course they flow in deep canyon-like courses offering few farming potentials. Near the ocean they widen out to form V-shaped valleys with greater agricultural potential, but decreasing runoff from southern mountain rainfall leaves populations small.

Here desert dwellers made intensive use of marine assets and another resource complex called *lomas*. During the cool southern winter the coastlands are enveloped by dense sea fogs, which condense on certain slopes and plains to support a remarkable flora for a few short months. These lomas provide feed for cattle, sheep and goats, and during very moist years and El Niño years can support crops. In the past, herds of guanaco – wild camelids related to the llama and alpaca – pastured on the fog plants and were intensively hunted.

Chinchaysuyu, the second largest quarter of Tahuantinsuyu, encompassed Ecuador and more than two-thirds of Peru. Reaching from the Pacific coast to the montaña, it stretched north from Cuzco, past Quito where the Cordillera is low and tropical, and ended on the fringes of present-day Colombia. Chinchaysuyu embraced the fractured sierra and included large expanses of dry grasslands gradually giving way to wet puna splintered into long meandering ridges and mesas separated by deep streams and rivers. At high elevation near their headwaters, sierra drainages tend to be wide and basin-shaped, with steeply sloping sides sometimes called the *quichua* zone. But with decreasing altitude, the rivers cut into deep gorges with little farmland.

By flowing north and then east to feed the Amazon, the sierra drainage pattern tended to draw highlanders into closer contact with the montaña and jungle. In Ecuador Chinchaysuyu loses its purely Andean characteristics as tropical vegetation envelops both the Atlantic and Pacific watershed, and mangrove swamps dot the humid coast.

The desert in the northern quarter is crossed by 40 streams and rivers, *Plate 7* including 10 of the 12 largest that descend the desert watershed. Along the wide flat coastal plain above the Río Santa it was possible to construct canal networks fed by two or more rivers. The largest such system united the Ríos Motupe, Leche, Lambayeque, Zana, and Jequetepeque and formed the so-called Lambayeque canal complex. To the south the Ríos Chicama and Moche were also once linked. The ten valleys of the Ríos Motupe and Viru and those in between comprised almost one-third of all land reclaimed along the desert coast and held about one-third of the coastal population. As the heartland of Chimor, the Incas' greatest rival, this region imparted a duality to Andean geopolitics: northern coastlands and southern uplands.

The largest desert river, Río Santa, disgorges where there is no coastal plain for agriculture. Although streams and rivers to the south are largely isolated from one another by mountains, canal link-ups between adjacent valleys were built across the difficult terrain between the Ríos Supe, Pativilca and Fortaleza and at the mouths of the Ríos Chillon and Rimac. These irrigated oasis valleys of the western desert gave the highest yields per unit in the Inca realm, and it was in this setting that Pizarro founded Lima as 'the City of Kings', after his sack of Tahuantinsuyu.

The area of coastal desert used for agriculture was less than ten per cent of the total and therefore small in comparison with the Titicaca altiplano or the sierra basins. Many more people lived in the mountains than along the littoral. However, the mountain populations were scattered while those on the coast were densely concentrated in oases. Andean civilizations were products of large numbers of people living close together, and the distribution of large architectural monuments broadly mirrors the past distribution of dense populations. The highland cities of Cuzco, Huari, Pukara and Tiwanaku reflect the southern, upland demographic pole, while the large architectural complexes of the coastal valleys of Chinchaysuyu reflect the northern counterpart, including the biggest pyramidal mounds of South America in the valleys of the Ríos Lambayeque, Moche, and Casma.

Making a living

Evolutionary pathways diverged in the arid central Andes because distinct environments offered different types and spatial arrangements of resources. With the domestication of plants and animals people secured carbohydrates by farming, and protein by herding or fishing. Each of these vocations can be pursued individually or in combination depending upon the ecological setting. Because mountain farming and herding are more productive when practiced together, Arid Montane adaptations are characterized by people doing both simultaneously. In contrast, in coastal Maritime-Oasis traditions protein and carbohydrate production are independent adaptations pursued by separate groups. People in each region must adapt to different problems: lowland specialists exchange farm and fish products, whereas highland generalists need not traffic in plants and animals since each family produces its own.

Differences in vertical and horizontal distribution of resources also require different solutions to supply and demand. Along the desert coast securing foreign goods by long-distance seafaring was well established when the Spanish arrived. They report that in the valley of Chincha alone there were 6,000 maritime merchants who regularly sailed to Ecuador to procure exotic goods such as colorful *Spondylus* shells, considered sacred by the Inca. In Ecuador, where the Cordillera is low and forested, the Spanish encountered local exchange specialists called *mindalaes*, who supplied northern chiefs and lords with valued goods such as precious minerals and stones from distant sources. In contrast trade, merchants, and thriving marketplaces – all hallmarks of the great empires of antiquity – are uniquely inconspicuous in the higher, drier reaches of Tahuantinsuyu. This does not reflect a lack of commodity movement, but is characteristic of Arid Montane adaptations in which the resources of different ecological zones are exploited by individual families, communities and ethnic groups.

13 *Grown at low altitudes, coca leaves are chewed with lime kept in small gourd vessels. The lime is removed with a thin spatula and transferred to the mouth as depicted in this Moche ceramic painting.*

Arid Montane adaptations

Mountain life depended upon herding and farming concurrently, and large populations were feasible where mountain farmland lay near puna pasturage. Nevertheless few crop types will grow at such heights, and the large populations of the mountains required prodigious quantities of basic commodities from the lowlands: marine salt, seaweed, fish, fruit, beans, maize, coca, and cotton. In the case of Tahuantinsuyu's numerically dominant upland populations, ethnographic and ethnohistorical sources document a persistent strategy of securing outside goods by maintaining rights to exploit patches of land in distant ecological settings. These holdings were discrete and separate from one another, forming a chain of economic islands, and the strategy of maintaining direct control over such dispersed environmental settings is called 'ecological complementarity' by the ethnohistorian John V. Murra, who first described the adaptive practice. It is also known as 'verticality', because altitude differences produce resource variation over the shortest distance, and because holdings tend to be distributed along elevational or vertical axes.

Altiplano lands surrounding high altitude communities receive sufficient seasonal rainfall to sustain cultivation of hardy tubers and chenopod grains. Variations of frost, hail, and drought however, concede only one good harvest every three or four years. Storage is therefore important and potatoes can be freeze-dried to produce *chuño*, and stored for times of uncertainty. Because the mountain soils are shallow and poorly developed, crops must be rotated frequently, and the whole community decides which lands to fertilize with *Plates 4,11* llama and alpaca dung from their herds. Both men and women work in the fields and share the tasks of farming. The herds provide wool, serve as pack animals, and are slaughtered and their flesh sun-dried to make *charqui* (jerky), also important for storage against uncertain times. When not pastured in fallow fields the herds are tended by youngsters in nearby alpine pastures.

Alternative crops with different planting and harvesting seasons are grown

14 Guamán Poma's illustrations of Inca agriculture: left to right, maize planting, guarding the young shoots from birds and animals, and harvesting.

on irrigated terraces at warmer elevations below 3,000 m. By cultivating different ecological tiers with different growth cycles labor can be distributed over the year. Still lower village holdings must also be worked to procure commodities such as iodine-rich marine products, coca leaves – chewed to relieve high altitude fatigue and rich in calcium and vitamin B – and maize for brewing *chicha* beer. Depending on topography such holdings may be two to ten days' trek away, and may be seasonally or permanently occupied by a few individuals or by a number of families. Yields are transported back to the parent community where bonds of kinship require the pooling and redistribution of commodities.

One reason verticality adaptations focus upon the exploitation of a series of environmental zones is that changes in precipitation or temperature, which often produce poor yields at one altitudinal setting, may result in good harvests in another ecological tier. Working different tiers spreads risks and rewards, working against specialization by promoting diversification. Because people must scatter far and wide to secure yields vital to the parent community as a whole, kin bonds are essential to cohesion. Distant colonists retain full privileges of membership in the home community, and it is the community rather than the household that decides basic matters such as pasture allocations, lands to be fallowed, and lands to be farmed or irrigated. Thus, the strategy of exploiting many scattered land holdings to promote self-sufficiency is nested in a kin-based notion of reciprocity. Reciprocation may be with labor or service, or with commodities ranging from subsistence goods to manufactured goods such as fine textiles.

Vertical complementarity appears in the Alps, Himalayas, and Andes, where people exhibit important similarities in their manner of making a living: tight integration of agricultural and pastoral production, exploitation of multiple ecological zones, reliance on crop variety, frequent rotation and fallowing, use of dung as fertilizer, sequential timing of production tasks in different altitudinal belts, emphasis on long-term storage of plant and animal products, relatively little sexual division of labor, cooperation in task sharing, and a mixture of household and communal control of land. All of these features characterize what is termed a 'Montane Production Strategy', an adaptive response to the constraints of mountain environments including low temperature, short growing seasons, shallow, eroding soils, risks of frost and hail, rugged topography with steep slopes, and marked variation of precipitation over short distances. Because these constraints increase with altitude, it is not surprising that broadly parallel human adaptations have arisen in the world's highest cordilleras.

Verticality varies in form and intensity with elevation, aridity, topography, and other conditions. It can be 'compact', with few foreign holdings because different resource tiers are closely spaced and within easy walking distance; or it can be 'dispersed', where resources are widely spaced over long distances with scattered colonies. The forested eastern flanks of the Cordillera supported more compact forms of verticality than did the arid Pacific watershed. In terms of longitude, the strategy is least pronounced in the north equatorial zone where the mountains are low and tropical. Intensity and elaboration increase to the south and are most pronounced in the Titicaca Basin and the salt puna uplands of Chile. Verticality was pursued by households, communities, and states, and at different levels of organization it assumed different configurations.

In the Titicaca region verticality was pursued by the Lupaqa and other Aymara kingdoms, whose people not only controlled potato- and tuber-producing lands as well as high elevation pasture near their capitals, but also held numerous, often large, colonies on both flanks of the Cordillera. Emphasizing discontinuous land holdings and scattered colonies these ancient mountain states were *extensive* in terms of being far-flung, but not *intensive* in terms of political control because vast tracts of terrain separating colonies were often held by others. From this perspective Tahuantinsuyu was not so much a monolithic state such as ancient Rome as it was an extensive dominion, an imperial net cast over the Cordillera that loosely bound heterogeneous people together by a vast highway system.

The origins of verticality adaptations reach far back in time and vary somewhat in different regions of the Cordillera. Where the altiplano turns to

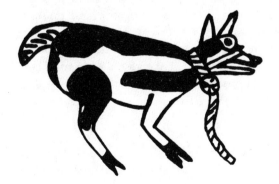

15 Important on the coast as well as in the mountains, llamas were depicted on Moche ceramics.

brine lakes and salt pans, Chilean archaeologists propose that early hunter-gatherers pursued migratory guanaco herds through annual rounds between salt puna and arid sierra if not down to coastal lomas. Here the domestication of llamas and alpacas transformed long distance transhumance into an extreme form of verticality, based on great caravans of camelids moving goods between distant settlements. Alternatively, in the northern wet puna where guanaco did not migrate into sierra basins, plant domestication played a greater role in fostering verticality for two reasons. First, domestication exacerbated natural disparities in the elevational distribution of resources because few crops grew at high altitudes with arable land, whereas many domesticates thrived at lower elevations. Second, successful cultivation required fertilizers as well as the movement of bulk cargo around the landscape, and both factors promoted the integration of herding and farming.

As highland populations grew in size, and low elevation domesticates grew in diversity, the strategy of securing direct control of foreign holdings must have arisen first at the household and community level, long before states developed. The Andean archaeological record is characterized by the recurrent presence of high altitude items and cultural influences in lower ecological settings, and vice versa. The means by which goods and ideas moved are not always clear. Yet, a dramatic increase in the evidence of interchange accompanies the rise of economic reliance upon domesticated plants and animals. By fostering larger populations in high environmental tiers but greater crop diversity in low ones, farming imparted a downward thrust to the economic demands that verticality alleviated.

Verticality promoted long-lasting relationships between major sierra basins and lower adjacent drainages feeding into the Pacific and Amazon. Highland territorial control over the headwaters of drainages and the presence of highlanders in elevations down to 1,000 m was normal. Along the Pacific watershed long-lasting linkages are evident between the Titicaca Basin and the valleys of Moquegua to Azapa; the Ayacucho sierra and the Ica and Nazca Valleys, the Callejon de Huaylas and the valleys from Santa to Casma; and the Cajamarca sierra and the Jequetepeque Valley. As highland agripastoralists grew in numbers, highland demands for lowland resources influenced the broader political prehistory of the Cordillera. Expansion by mountain centers such as Cuzco, Tiwanaku, and Huari throughout the uplands and into the lowlands shows an expectable correlation between verticality and military tactics. The coastal populations were markedly different. Here conquest and consolidation by centers such as Chimor and Moche expanded along the Pacific littoral, with little penetration into the highlands above about 2,000 m. Their aim was to monopolize the single most productive ecological tier in the Andes: the lower Pacific watershed and its near-shore fishery.

Maritime-Oasis adaptations

Maritime-Oasis ways of life rely on economic specialization and commodity exchange, beginning at the fundamental level of protein and carbohydrate production. Peru's distinguished ethnohistorian, Maria Rostworowski de Diez Canseco, has shown that by the eve of the Spanish conquest, fishing and farming had evolved into non-overlapping ethnic specializations. Within the dominion of Chimor, fisherfolk spoke their own language or dialects, married among themselves, and resided in separate communities under their own hierarchy of leaders. Using sunken gardens along the beaches they grew 'totora', or bulrush reeds, for watercraft, cotton for fish-nets and lines, and gourds for net floats. But for agricultural staples they exchanged maritime products for crops from farmers, who did not fish. This fundamental division between coastal fishing and farming reflects the fact that each produces higher yields in the hands of specialists. The near-shore upwelling currents of the Peruvian coastline support the greatest biomass in the Pacific Ocean. Net-harvesting of small fish from small craft with small crews is possible 280 days a year, and the diversity of marine life is such that fishermen can specialize in other products ranging from mollusks to large fish and sea mammals.

Plate 8

In contrast, less than ten per cent of the desert can be farmed because agriculture is dependent upon irrigation. Irrigation of the desert with runoff from the rugged mountains requires large canal systems and large, coordinated labor forces. Yields per hectare are the highest in Tahuantinsuyu, and, given water, farming is possible year round. However, highland runoff tends to be seasonal, which creates an agricultural cycle with nonproductive times occupied by canal cleaning and maintenance of the irrigation systems. Specialized maritime adaptations arose early in the Lithic Period, then persisted as an independent pursuit. Intensive agriculture was only grafted on to the coastal economy about 4,000 years ago. Its late advent, relative to tropical and mountain farming, was in part due to the technological difficulties involved in building large irrigation works. Yet, once in place agriculture too persisted as an independent pursuit. Fishing and farming remained separate ways of life because they involved different risks, tied to different cycles – one lunar, governing tides and fish movements, and the other solar, governing precipitation and plant growth – and involved different beliefs.

Plate 5

Within this fundamental division of marine and terrestrial adaptations there was further economic specialization. Some seafarers focused on exploiting particular marine products, whereas others were merchants who sailed regularly to the Guayaquil Gulf of Ecuador to procure exotic goods. Similarly different farming communities focused on particular crops. Specialization extended to the arts and crafts: metallurgical production in Chimor was in the hands of skilled technicians organized in a guild-like manner and subsidized by the state; the design and layout of canal networks was in the hands of skilled technicians. And task specialization permeated the dynastic courts, where nobles held titles such as steward of the shell trumpet, drink master, and master of feathered cloth makers. Some social groups, such as deer hunters and cooks, were also named for their particular tasks.

Between specialists, barter was the most common form of exchange, and there is little evidence for the development of currency. However, among the

16 The Moche were seafaring people, as suggested by this vase painting depicting sailors with a boatload of pottery vessels.

Plate 10   nobility or karaka class, textiles and other fine arts fulfilled some of the functions that money serves today. Although fisherfolk and farmers exchanged produce, coastal señorios and parcialidades sought economic autonomy by expanding their territories to include both maritime and agrarian communities. As opposed to extensive mountain states with far-flung colonies, coastal states were more intensive and incorporated adjacent valleys to form continuous political dominions. Nonetheless, seafaring capabilities by kingdoms such as the Moche facilitated the establishment of distant coastal colonies.

The spatial separation of Maritime-Oasis and Arid Montane adaptations was not great. On a clear day fisherfolk could easily see aloof mountain-top fields. Separating these adaptations were the marked environmental contrasts resulting from extreme topographic relief that fostered different cultural developments with distinct economies. Yet in spite of economic division, the close physical proximity of mountain and coastal populations resulted in many shared beliefs about social organization and the cosmos in general. Andean traditions were significantly enriched by the not too distant Amazon and tropical forest adaptations. These lowland adaptations benefited desert oasis people because they could grow many of the crops that first originated in forested settings. Similar benefits did not accrue to the majority of Andean people because highlanders had to domesticate their own repertoire of uniquely robust plants and animals and to formulate their own verticality strategies in order to survive at high altitudes.

CHAPTER THREE

The Inca Model of Statecraft

In certain respects Inca statecraft differs from that of other ancient nations because institutions of rule were adapted to an unusual, multifaceted environment. The Inca and their political predecessors elaborated upon basic principles of organization that evolved first among local communities. Therefore, it is useful to review the organization of indigenous communities before describing the imperial institutions of Tahuantinsuyu and Cuzco.

The ayllu

Mountain agropastoralism, farming, and herding often require executing several tasks at the same time, but in different places. A married couple is the minimal unit of economic production, but working unaided, newlyweds lack the labor resources to erect adequate housing or convert unowned barren land into productive holdings. Nor can they efficiently cope with the agricultural cycle during critical toil-intensive times of plowing, planting, and harvesting. Thus, a couple – a nuclear family, a household – is a basic economic entity, but not an autonomous one. In the Andes the autonomous unit of production and reproduction is a group of related individuals and couples who exchange labor and cooperate in the management of land and herds. These kin collectives are called *ayllus*, and the well-being of a couple is proportional to the size and holdings of their collective.

An ayllu has a founding ancestor and contains a number of lineages divided among two 'moieties' (see below). Membership is determined by kinship that men tend to trace through male lines and women trace through female lines. Marriage partners are generally exchanged between sets of moiety lineages. This makes the ayllu an endogamous corporation that is reproductively autonomous. At birth a person inherits a set of relationships – responsibilities to others and claims upon them – that determine access to labor, land, water, and other resources. In selecting marriage partners individuals held in high esteem are those with the most kin, because relatives bring with them commitments to share work, resources, and their returns.

In addition to labor, pastureland and farmland are subject to ayllu management. Farmland must often be irrigated, and ayllus are commonly water-management corporations. They hold rights to lakes, springs, or rivers, and they maintain the canals. Although outlying land holdings are ideally scattered from high to low elevations, there is a spatial focus, or home territory for the ayllu. Generally this home territory is in potato and tuber growing elevations around 3,500 m. This is a strategic setting because puna pasturage lies slightly higher, allowing pastoralism to be readily combined with cultivation. Below the home territory irrigated land for growing maize and other important crops may lie within one or two days walk, depending upon topography.

The home territory of the ayllu often comprises a single community, usually of widely-scattered households because poorly developed highland soils require frequent crop rotation and fallowing. Today, most traditional villages of Quechua and Aymara communities are divided into two residential sections, an upper one and a lower one, corresponding to what were called the *hanan* and *hurin* duality in ancient Cuzco. Households in one section belong to a group of lineages that form one moiety, and a complementary moiety is formed by people in the other section. Women from one moiety marry men of the other and generally move to their husband's section of the community. However, women inherit land from their parents, and they retain full membership in their moiety of birth. This gives social and economic autonomy to married females, and it keeps labor and land exchange within the ayllu.

Rights and responsibilities

People sometimes marry into or are adopted into other ayllus if they are willing to meet the responsibilities of membership. Obligations are nested in the most precious of Andean essentials, labor and work, and responsibilities are based on the notion of reciprocity – the concept that when something is rendered, something of equal kind or value will be returned. The Aymara word *ayni* designates a service rendered with obligatory repayment of equal kind. The Quechua word *mit'a* designates a 'turn' of labor and the equal exchange of work. Ayni and mit'a allow a household to temporarily mobilize more labor than that for which it has workers, and this is essential for mountain agropastoralism. An individual's brothers, sisters, their offspring, nieces and nephews, comprise the nucleus of kin with which mit'a and ayni are exchanged for agricultural tasks, for house building, and for other jobs that a couple cannot do alone.

Ideally, the type of labor rendered is the same type of labor that will be returned. Strict accounting is involved. When male and female kin assemble to execute a job, such as plowing a relative's field, they do not work as a gang. Instead each couple works a different field row and then another. By clearly segmenting work the tasks that kindred render are clearly defined. Subdividing jobs into repetitive, modular tasks also characterizes large undertakings. When a number of ayllu are concerned with common endeavors, such as building churchyard or cemetery walls, each constructs and maintains a specified section.

Although work is carefully accounted for, among kindred it is often repaid with another type of service, or with goods resulting from other labor. Goods traditionally include textiles, and the time devoted to producing fabrics of a particular quality and size is well understood, but food is the commodity most

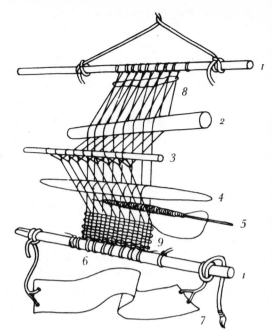

17 *A woman weaving with a back-strap loom. Textile production occupied more people for more time than any other Andean craft and fine fabrics served as a form of currency.*

18 *The components of a back-strap loom – an instrument still employed by traditional native weavers. (1) Warp beam, (2) shed stick, (3) heddle rod, (4) sword, (5) bobbin with yarn, (6) warp attachment, (7) belt or back-strap, (8) warp threads, (9) weft threads.*

frequently exchanged. When people render mit'a, they expect to be fed, and it is the obligation of those who are receiving labor to feed those who are rendering service. Beyond this, certain types of service are regularly repaid with staples. The exchange of food and other commodities ensures the redistribution of staples and dietary elements, and redistribution is vital to the autonomy of the ayllu.

Because ayllu rights and responsibilities form the indigenous basis of corporate organization, Andean society has often been characterized as a communal one. However, although ayllu members share kin and community ties, everyone is by no means equal. Some individuals inherit, marry into, or garner far more resources than others. There are wealthy couples, families, and lineages, and many very poor ones. Ayllu-like communal organization extends far back in the archaeological record, but even among simple societies of great antiquity some people were better off than others.

Cargo systems
Among ayllus the nature of decision making and authority has undergone great transformations since the Spaniards' arrival. Today communities may operate under governors and authorities who are outside appointees, but beneath this overlay two more traditional hierarchies of offices often survive. One chain of command comprises civil offices. Each moiety often has a series of posts, some of which roughly translate as clerk, constable, vice-mayor, and mayor. The other hierarchy entails posts of a religious nature. The responsibilities here are

for the observance of a series of annual ceremonies relating to patron saints and major church holidays.

The offices of both civil and religious hierarchies are rotational, and ideally, during the life of an individual he moves through both hierarchies and then retires as a respected community elder. A hierarchy of rotational offices is called a 'cargo system' by anthropologists, and they are widespread among native peoples of Latin America. Today Andean females do not generally hold civil offices, but they may hold religious posts. It is noteworthy that cargo offices are not revenue generating, but posts of public service. Holding an office entails substantial outlays of time and resources, as well as serving prodigious quantities of food and drink on formal occasions. Therefore, only the well-to-do, who can draw services and resources from many kindred, can assume a post and move through the office hierarchy to achieve respected retirement. As prosperous men and women move through the cargo system their expenditures serve to redistribute wealth and resources from the more fortunate to the less fortunate.

Governance based upon formal offices through which people rotated, but did not inherit, may go back to the very foundations of Andean civilization. One of the distinguishing features of traditional Andean cargo systems is that each hierarchical post is associated with a distinct ceremonial staff. Beautifully made, and often ornamented with precious metal, the office holder parades these hallmarks of position and authority on all formal occasions. Staff-bearing individuals are frequently depicted in ancient iconography and it seems reasonable to interpret these individuals as office holders. However, they need not have been cargo posts because offices could also be inherited in the past.

Karakas

When Pizarro's forces arrived ayllus were governed by hereditary rulers known as *karakas*. There were generally two, one for each moiety. The karaka of the dominant or more powerful moiety was called the *principale* by the Spanish, and his counterpart the *segunda persona*. Often moieties were subdivided into two, four, or more sections, and there was a hierarchy of four or more lords. These lords were generally males, but there were also female karakas. Karakas claimed closer descent from the ayllu's founding ancestor than the subjects they oversaw, and local lords and those of larger polities formed a separate class of people who married among themselves.

Karakas and kings ruled as intermediaries between heaven and earth, interceding with the cosmic forces on behalf of their subjects' well-being. When disaster struck, they were accountable. Fempellec, a powerful potentate in Lambayeque, was put to death when a great El Niño devastated his homeland. Karakas were managers of ayllu resources. They mediated quarrels over land and water and made sure individual households had field and pasture allotments sufficient for their needs. The lords supervised the agricultural and herding calendar and made sure plowing, planting, and harvesting were initiated at the proper times. In return, ayllu members tilled the fields, tended

19 A staff – the symbol of high office and authority – is carried by a winged figure in this Huari textile motif.

20 Staff emblems of authority probably evolved from clubs as wielded by this early Cerro Sechín figure incised on a monolith.

the herds of their leaders, wove cloth for them, and rendered other mit'a. In a symbiotic manner, karakas were expected to be generous and hospitable, and on formal occasions this meant feeding people and providing great quantities of maize beer for purposes of ritual intoxication. At a more basic level, leaders were expected to reciprocate with gifts, food, drink, and coca for labor and service received from their followers. Although reciprocity was expected, more was extracted than returned. The Andean archaeological record indicates that the evolution of leadership saw the crystallization of formal offices and hierarchical posts long before such positions were co-opted by the emergence of an hereditary élite. Whereas cargo-like systems of governance seem to have great antiquity, karaka-like rule did not become prevalent until shortly before the beginning of the Christian era.

Ancestors

Common ancestors gave ayllus their ethnic identity, and karakas ruled by claiming close blood-ties to founding forefathers. Ayllus were often named after their founders, who were heroic figures, if not mythical ones, and could turn into stone or some special object. They secured lands for their people, established codes of behavior, and were models for proper life. Their corpses were worshipped, and were ranked among the ayllu's most sacred of holdings. If outsiders captured these vital relics, the ayllu could be held hostage.

For commoner and karaka alike, ancestor veneration was a fundamental institution of Andean society. Native concepts did not maintain a sharp division between the living and dead, and the deceased actively influenced the health and well-being of their descendants. People consulted and propitiated

21 Mummies of important ancestors were paraded about on ritual occasions: a sketch by Guamán Poma.

22 Llamas were sacrificed on ritual occasions. Here Guamán Poma depicts removal of the heart.

their progenitors on a regular basis. Forbears defined the lineage, moiety, and ayllu to which an individual belonged, and position within the hierarchy of life's relationships. With this went the practice of keeping ancestors close at hand, and of using graves or bodies to document rights and responsibilities among heirs. Employing the deceased as documents was accompanied by the notion that corpses should be conserved intact, and led to the development of artificial mummification of the dead more than 6,000 years ago. The tradition culminated with the potentates of Chimor and Tahuantinsuyu, whose mummies were richly clothed and carefully attended at special shrines. Inca royal mummies, regarded as quasi-alive, were regularly paraded about, and formally seated at important council meetings so that they might be consulted and guide the living.

Everyone venerated a variety of shrines, objects, and phenomena loosely known as *huacas*, but Spanish documents relating to huaca looting at the ancient site of Chan Chan indicate that native peoples distinguished two classes of sacrosanct places. One, called *huacas adoratorios*, comprised places for the adoration of supernatural forces. The other class, called *huacas sepulturas*, comprised shrines and burial places of important deceased. Ancestor veneration horrified Spanish clerics, who launched a vigorous campaign against it known as extirpation of idolatry, involving the destruction of huacas sepulturas, the burning of mummies, and the undercutting of the ancestral fabric of native society.

Supernaturals

The extirpation of idolatry extended to huacas adoratorios of which there were many because the landscape was viewed as alive with supernatural forces. Even today, the traditional Quechua and Aymara folk see nature as extremely animate, and the earth, mountains, and waters can cause ill health and fortune. The concept of a dynamic landscape is certainly appropriate to one with smoldering volcanos, frequent earthquakes, and recurrent El Niño crises. There are rich survivals of this Pre-Hispanic cosmology, the most widespread being the veneration of *Pacha Mama* (mother earth), who is offered coca leaf, chicha beer, and appropriate prayer and ritual on all major agricultural occasions by all who till the earth. Likewise, she is regularly toasted on every occasion entailing formal consumption of alcohol.

Mountains and major peaks, called *apu* in Quechua and *achachila* in Aymara, are (and were) also influential in the lives of their adjacent communities. Water, the blood of agricultural life, is seen to flow down from mountain lakes and springs, eventually reaching the ocean. From the ocean it is taken up by the Milky Way, or 'celestial river', and from the sky redistributed as seasonal rains that water the sacred apu and achachila. The sanctity of mountain peaks has great antiquity and Andean people have made offerings to them for millennia.

Libations

Alcoholism is uncommon among ayllu members, but libations of chicha beer, and ritual intoxication occur at all important ceremonial occasions. Etiquette demands toasting and drinking, and servers are appointed to ensure the proper flow of spirits to all. Liquor is the accompaniment for libations, and commemorative declaration and oration are the essence of Andean ceremony and ritual. People are seated, served, and speak in formal order, governed by status and position. Alcohol is not only consumed in truly stupefying quantities by everyone, but the drinking may endure over several days and nights depending upon the rite or ceremony involved. Furthermore, ritual intoxication is a very ancient Andean tradition to judge from the quantities of libation vessels found in prehistoric graves. It horrified Spanish clerics, who campaigned as fervently against apparent drunkenness as they did against idolatry.

Time and space

To schedule economic activities, people must predict annual cycles of weather and plant-growth in advance. This is not complicated in homogeneous environments such as Egypt's Nile Valley. It is quite complicated, however, in the Andes where ayllus exploit many ecological niches with different botanical cycles. Long ago people observed that changes in terrestrial conditions correlated with changes in celestial conditions and the movement of heavenly bodies. Western calendars have proceeded from the movement of close heavenly bodies, the sun in particular. Andean societies proceeded from a different starting point – the largest of heavenly bodies – the Milky Way. This celestial body is called *Mayu*, or 'celestial river', by Quechua speakers and its use in organizing time and space by a traditional community 25 km from Cuzco has been investigated by the ethnographer Gary Urton of Colgate University.

To observe the Milky Way is to observe the course of galactic rotation. Urton notes that this provides a very encompassing way to organize change in celestial and terrestrial conditions. The plane of galactic rotation is noticeably inclined from the plane of the earth's rotation by 26 to 30 degrees. Observed from the southern hemisphere the vast star-stream not only divides the heavens, but also and more importantly pursues a wobbly course slanting left to right half the year, and right to left the other half. During the 24 hours that it crosses zenith, Mayu forms two intersecting, intercardinal axes (NE–SW and SE–NW). These great luminous axial lines create a grid for the entire celestial sphere, dividing it into four quarters, called *suyu*. All other astronomical phenomena can then be plotted and characterized by the quarters in which they occur or travel across.

This galactic systematization allows tracking not only of heavenly luminaries but also of great stellar voids. These voids, called 'dark clouds', are still thought of as animal constellations. They include an adult and a baby llama, a fox, a partridge, a toad, and a serpent. The movement of the dark cloud constellations across the sky is used to predict zoological cycles on earth and to time fauna-related activity. The solstices of Mayu coincide with wet and dry seasons, and the celestial river is used to predict water cycles. To predict botanical cycles and schedule flora-related activity, celestial luminaries are employed. Solar movement is central to planning the agricultural cycle, but lunar phases dictate planting, and the Pleiades, other constellations and planets time crop development needs.

Systematizing astronomical observation on the basis of galactic rotation opens the orderly movements of multitudes of heavenly phenomena to potential correlations with multitudes of natural cycles. Keeping track of relevant corollary cycles is not difficult given the saw-tooth skyline of the Cordillera. All that is required are two fixed points. One is where the observer stands (today Urton has found that this point is some agreed–upon station in a community plaza); and the other is a fixed point on the horizon. Many *Plate 16* mountain peaks are regularly employed as sighting references for the appearance and disappearance, zenith and antizenith, or equinoxes of relevant heavenly bodies.

Long ago it was realized that keeping track of corollary data was aided by spatial associations, such that a celestial cycle in one area of the night-time skyline corresponded with a terrestrial cycle in the same region of the daytime horizon. In so far as the heavenly landscape was divided into four quadrants, a parallel division of the terrestrial landscape into four aligned quadrants provided an efficient means of systematizing predictive knowledge. Today the settlement and land holdings of certain traditional Quechua ayllu are not simply divided into hanan and hurin moieties. Rather, from some point such as the center of the village plaza, there is a quadrapartite division of the community and of its territory that corresponds to and physically aligns with the four great suyu of Mayu. The very name Tahuantinsuyu implies that the Inca played out these principles on an imperial scale.

The Inca fort of Sacsahuaman

12 (above) Crowning the heights of Cuzco, the great fortress of Sacsahuaman was completed in the fifteenth century only after decades of labor by a workforce of 30,000.

13 (below left) The imperial-style Inca architecture at Cuzco impressed the conquistadores.

14 (below right) Imposing polygonal masonry faced the great terraces of Sacsahuaman.

Inca architecture

15 (left, above) Fine masonry embellished the terraces and ornamental niches of Tampu Machay, site of a sacred spring where the emperor Pachacuti is said to have lodged when he went hunting.

16 (left, below) Built of superb masonry, most buildings at Machu Picchu were rectangular. Built atop a carved rock of special significance, the oval 'Torreon' (center right) was a sacred building, its trapezoidal window perhaps providing a viewpoint for astronomical observations.

17 (above) General view of Machu Picchu.

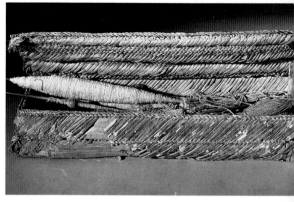

Andean textiles

18 (above left) A coastal native picks and cleans cotton. First cultivated for the manufacture of fishing-nets and clothing, cotton has dominated coastal textile traditions for 5,000 years.

19 (above right) Women were often buried with their weaving baskets, such as this one which contains spindles, thread, and loom implements.

20 (below) Paracas weavers 2,000 years ago produced ornate embroidered fabrics rich in iconography. The wool used for embroidering was dyed in a wide range of colors and was probably supplied by highland herders.

21 (right) This embroidered feline motif from a Paracas fabric depicts a costumed figure with a cat-like nose ornament and carrying a trophy head.

Inca ceramics

Opposite:

22 (top left) A classic Inca aryballoid vessel, displaying the distinctive shape and decoration of the imperial style.

23 (bottom left) After the fall of the city of Chan Chan to the Incas, Chimor's artisans toiled for their new overlords producing aryballoid vessels such as this, which is typically Inca in shape, but with ornamentation in the coastal Chimú tradition.

24 (center right) Holding birds, Inca women with shawls and long dresses are depicted in this late imperial style vessel. At Cuzco the style persisted into the initial decades of Spanish rule with increasing Hispanic influence as native artisans toiled under new rulers.

Inca metallurgy

25 (above) After sacking Cuzco, the conquistadores began looting ancient cemeteries for treasures such as this sheet gold funerary mask from Chimor.

26 (right) Inca silver figurine from Moquegua.

Farming origins: Guitarrero Cave

27 (above) Excavations at the mouth of Guitarrero Cave in the central Andes. Thomas Lynch found evidence here for the oldest cultivated plants in the New World, dating back 10,000 years.

28 (left) A stone scraper discovered at the site was wrapped in deer hide and secured with a cord binding.

Responsibility for scheduling economic tasks probably led local karakas to develop calendars appropriate to local conditions which varied between one ayllu and another. Because karakas held this fundamental knowledge in their heads, the Inca and earlier Andean polities found it incumbent to rule through local lords. Larger parcialidades, señorios, kingdoms, and empires must have had more comprehensive systems for predicting natural cycles in different settings. In addition, although the quarters of the Milky Way structured the Inca cosmos, solar cycles also figured prominently in the calendrics of Cuzco where Inti, the sun, was venerated.

Statecraft

The institutions of statecraft that culminated in Tahuantinsuyu were ancient ones employed by earlier states, drawn from the principles of ayllu and community organization. Taxes and tithes, in civil or religious form, are vital to government, but the paying of them is subject to considerable manipulation. Therefore, Inca imperial revenues are best reviewed in a general form, as the lords of Cuzco would have liked to have seen their income.

Money was rarely used in prehistoric Peru, nor were taxes paid in kind. Instead the imperial economy was based on extracting taxes in the form of labor. The local community was the basic unit upon which taxes were levied, and obligations were distributed among households by the karaka *principale* and his segunda persona down hierarchical lines. Labor taxation required accurate inventorying of people, resources, and conditions. When Tahuantinsuyu incorporated a new province into its realm, people were counted according to sex, age and marital status, along with their livestock, fields, and pastures. Topographic models of the region were made, and the corpus of data sent to Cuzco to be acted upon. Males and heads of households were graded by age and decimally organized. The smallest unit comprised 10 tax payers overseen by a foreman. In turn, 10 such units were overseen by a *Pachaka Karaka*, or Chief of 100, and continued in multiples of 10 to a *Hona Karaka*, or lord of 10,000, who reported directly to the Inca provincial governor. Through this organization three types of levies were extracted, which can be called agricultural taxation, mit'a service, and textile taxation.

Agricultural taxation
Agricultural taxation extracted work from both men and women. Commoners did not own land – it belonged to the ayllu. It was Inca practice to divide conquered agricultural land into three categories, ideally of equal size, all of which the peasantry was obliged to farm. The first category was dedicated to the support of the gods, including the imperial pantheon and huacas of local importance. These lands were cultivated first, before other categories of fields. Yields went to support religious functionaries, priests, and shrine attendants. Stores were also held to provide food and drink on holidays when particular gods, huacas, or ancestors received public veneration.

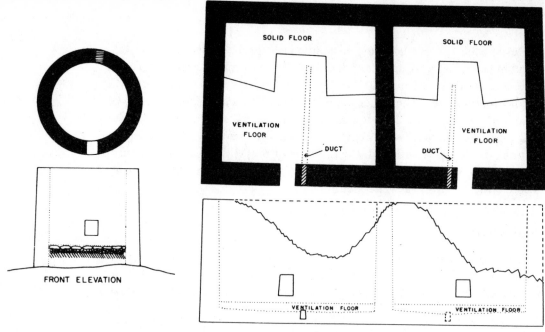

SOLID FLOOR

SOLID FLOOR

VENTILATION
FLOOR

VENTILATION
FLOOR

DUCT

DUCT

FRONT ELEVATION

VENTILATION FLOOR

VENTILATION FLOOR

FRONTAL ELEVATION

23 *Circular qollqa storehouses were often used for maize.*
24 *Rectangular qollqa buildings at Huánuco Pampa stored potatoes and tubers.*

The second category belonged to the Emperor, as head of state, who seems to have viewed ownership as his by divine right. Imperial fields were tended after religious ones, and yields went to support the royal court and the needs of government. Because the Emperor was the head of both state and the state religion, the majority of agrarian tax yields were under Cuzco's control. This was commemorated with a dramatic display of warehousing facilities, the most impressive of which comprised individual, one-room, masonry structures known as *qollqa*: circular ones were used for maize storage, and square ones for potatoes and other tubers. Both forms had ingenious ventilation systems that allowed air to enter through an underground channel in the floor and then escape through an opening at roof level. Designed for display, long rows of finely built qollqa were erected on hills and high places where they could be seen from great distances.

The third category of land was assigned to the local community for its support, redistributed annually to village members by the local karaka. This allotment was not in equal parts, but proportional to the size of a family and the number of dependents under each head-of-household. As households grew or shrank, their share of land changed. When an individual was absent working on a government project or attending official business, other members of the ayllu tilled his lands and fulfilled his agricultural tax obligations. Puna pasture lands, and llama and alpaca resources were organized in a similar three-fold manner. Systematic administration of pasture was critical because it encompassed more terrain than was under cultivation, and highland polities controlled immense herds for the production of wool and food. Thus, just as the highlanders were agropastoralists, so too was the tax system.

Mit'a service

While agricultural taxes extracted labor from both sexes, mit'a service was a draft levied annually on all able-bodied males. Mit'a service lasted for various lengths of time and embraced a wide range of activities from working on construction projects to participating in military campaigns. As long as some males remained at home to attend fields, the state was free to determine the numbers of draftees to be mobilized and their length of service. With millions of male subjects to draw upon, mit'a gave Tahuantinsuyu a very labor-intensive economy. This has vivid archaeological expressions in tens of thousands of kilometers of well-built road networks, vast irrigation and terrace systems, and great architectural monuments. The splendor of Cuzco, which so amazed the *conquistadores*, was impressive testimony to the toil of multitudes rendering mit'a. Thirty thousand men are said to have labored at one time simply building Sacsahuaman, the fort of Cyclopean masonry dominating the imperial capital.

Plates 12–14

It profits a government to expend the returns from one tax in a manner that will expand the returns from another. Revenue expansion among Andean states entailed transforming labor, an ephemeral item, into a productive commodity with tangible yields. To this end the Inca and earlier states invested mit'a labor in the acquisition of more agricultural land, which could then be taxed and yields stored in qollqa, thereby augmenting the imperial coffers. This strategy was pursued through both conquest and reclamation of formerly unfarmed land. Over many millennia reclaiming land required ever greater efforts, undertaken by progressively larger señorios and states that could mobilize mit'a from multiple communities. Beginning with Pukara and culminating in Cuzco, the major political centers of Andean civilization all organized large reclamation projects in their adjacent hinterlands. This work is dramatically

25 Inca forces storm a fortified hilltop pukara in this illustration by Guamán Poma.

Plate 2 expressed in the multitudes of masonry terraces surrounding Cuzco and lining the Urubamba Valley in its descent to Machu Picchu. The Inca not only resculpted their imperial heartland, but they also opened lands in other quarters of the empire, moving entire communities, known as *mitamaq* colonies, to work on newly claimed lands.

Using mit'a conscripts to acquire new land through conquest made Tahuantinsuyu the largest nation of the hemisphere. The Inca maintained a professional officer core drawn from Cuzco's royal families, but it is not clear to what degree they maintained standing armies. Resistance to Inca expansion was often from fortified hilltop bastions called *pukaras*, whose high walls and dry moats were costly to take by storm. Attackers suffered far greater losses than defenders. Yet pukaras were completely vulnerable to long-term siege and the Inca were victorious because they could field forces for the many months needed to starve out defenders. Repeated use of siege tactics suggests that some imperial legions were comprised of standing forces.

Textile taxation

Textile taxation is very ancient in Andean society. Women and men were taxed by being required to spin, weave, and produce cloth and cord. To home-bound taxpayers, the government annually doled out specified quantities of raw fiber, cotton, or wool. Men made cordage and rope, while women spun and wove. Spinning was done with drop spindles and weaving was done on several types of looms. For example the vertical frame loom was preferred by residents of Chinchaysuyu's north coast, while Aymara people of Collasuyu regularly wove on a horizontal loom. The finished products were collected by the government for its use.

26 *A painting from a Moche ceramic vase of women weaving beneath a ramada.*

Plates 18–21 Pride in clothing one's family is a hallmark of Andean femininity, and clothmaking occupied more people for more time than any other craft. All women wove, from the humblest of peasants to the wives of kings. Queens and empresses wove as an Andean symbol of their femininity. Many grades of cloth were produced, and very fine fabrics were very highly esteemed, culminating in the most elegant of Inca fabrics, known as *qomba*.

What people wove and wore – decoration, iconography, and quality – established their ethnic identity and indicated their rank and status. Heads of state wore the finest of materials, rich in color and design, and often fashioned from exotic fibers such as vicuña wool, embellished with threads of gold and silver, or with bright feathers of tropical birds. As a commodity highly valued by all, cloth fulfilled certain functions analogous to currency. Cloth was the Inca reward for government service, and the army received regular allocations of textiles.

Plate 10

State expenditures

With millions paying taxes, Tahuantinsuyu had enormous revenues. In addition to labor, the agricultural and textile taxes were used to support two types of expenditure. The agricultural tax was used to provide people with food and drink, termed 'staple' finance. The textile tax was used to reward people with valued goods, termed 'wealth' finance. The two financial systems operated rather differently: the karaka and kingly élite sought to monopolize items of wealth, whereas commoners and masters expected sustenance when rendering state service.

The greatest bulk of Tahuantinsuyu's agrarian staples were budgeted for feeding the millions who worked for the state. Many more people worked for the government on a temporary basis than on a permanent one, and the largest expenditures presumably supported vast numbers of males rendering mit'a service. A small portion of the population, perhaps ten per cent, was permanently subsidized because it occupied the highest ranks of local and national government. There were two tiers: the upper, decision-making one was occupied with rule and administration, while a lower technical tier was occupied with the implementation of rule and the support of governmental institutions. At the apex stood the royal families of hanan and hurin Cuzco, then the people of the Cuzco Basin, who were Inca by appointment and honor but not by ancestry. From the royal families came the heads of state and the heads of Inti's imperial church. From the body of Incas by birth or honor came the military and gubernatorial heads of the empire, and, it is assumed, the heads

27 Building monuments, roads, and suspension bridges required technicians skilled in surveying, engineering, and architecture.

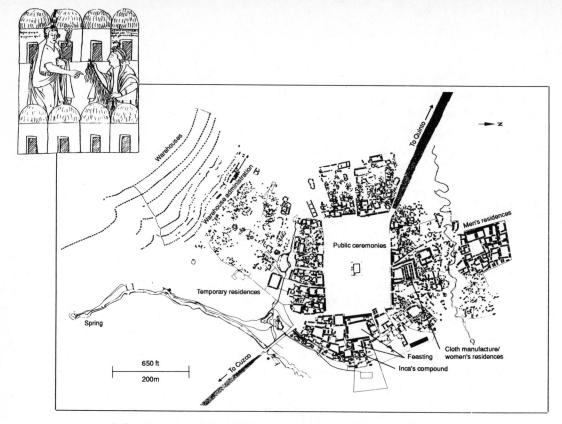

28 Standing in a complex of qollqa storehouses (above left), a noble reviews the quipu record of an accountant. The plan of Huánuco Pampa shows the hundreds of qollqa prominently displayed in ten hillside rows overlooking the site.

of all branches of the imperial bureaucracy. Allied with this apex by forced and voluntary allegiance, and by the exchange of sons and daughters in marriage, were the noble families and hereditary rulers of subject states. These ranks ranged from the conquered potentates of Chimor down to the karakas of formerly independent ayllus.

Beneath those enjoying great power and prestige was a significantly larger tier of people who were subsidized because of their occupations, hereditary knowledge or training relating to technical matters. The profusion of professional accountants, the *quipukamaks*, drew considerable attention from early chroniclers. Other technicians must have included agronomists, architects, surveyors, engineers, hydrologists, and the like. Another large body of support personnel comprised skilled artisans and craft specialists. Entire colonies of specialists – from ceramicists, through lapidarists, to metallurgists and jewelers – were removed from subject provinces and resettled in the Cuzco environs to serve the lords of the sacred city. These professionals were both numerous and important because 'wealth' finance, as opposed to 'staple' finance, depended not only upon textiles, but upon multitudes of other valued commodities culminating in finely wrought artworks of gold and silver.

At Cuzco's great rival capital of Chan Chan the vast majority of residents were artisans. Women were weavers of fine cloth, while men were predominantly metalsmiths and jewelers. By supporting tens of thousands of skilled craft personnel the government used staple finance to generate commodities for wealth finance, which made artisans essential to the national economy. Thus at Chan Chan artisans enjoyed the privilege of wearing earspools, albeit very simple wooden ones, a privilege otherwise reserved for the governing élite, who wore elaborate earspools as the hallmark of their status and rank. (Indeed, the Spanish referred to the Inca élite as *orejones*, or 'big ears', because of the large, round earspools that set them apart from the masses.)

Plate 51

Staple reserves

In spite of many outlays, the Inca state had surplus agricultural revenues that it banked in audaciously displayed warehouses called qollqa. Complexes of these one-room facilities were numerous and widely distributed in the highland provinces. Thousands surrounded Cuzco; and Cotapachi in Bolivia had 2,400. The provincial center of Hatun Xarza had an enormous complex, and 497 qollqa were arranged in rows along the hillsides overlooking the center of Huanuco Pampa. Excavations at the last two sites revealed locally produced agricultural commodities, showing that the government was not stocking exotic produce from distant provinces for redistribution to the local population.

In the Cordillera the storing of food surpluses was a critical adaptation at the household level, and a major component of risk management. Without reserves of charqui and chuño there would be no means of mitigating stress from frequent poor harvests in different ecological tiers. Storage was no less crucial at the imperial level in the mountains, where famine was not uncommon and disasters of tectonic or El Niño origin were recurrent, and could well trigger revolt. If bountiful harvests occasioned the replacement of older stock with fresh reserves the Emperor might order dispensation to local subjects. Yet, good harvests are less common than bad ones at high altitudes, and this may explain the grandiose nature of Inca warehousing. Excessive labor was lavished on the construction of qollqa, and their consistent placement in highly visible locations was not necessary for mundane storage. Qollqa were designed, constructed, and positioned to impress people, and it seems that the state wanted to reassure its subjects that it could adequately manage the risks and uncertainties common to mountain agropastoralism.

Staple reciprocity

The taxation system did not entail a unidirectional flow of labor from commoners, and of its fruits to the government. There were fundamental beliefs that both karakas and kings had reciprocal obligations of hospitality and generosity, particularly with food and drink. Staple finance was critical to the symbiosis between the ruled and the rulers and allowed the latter to schedule activities within a framework of public celebrations. In civil or religious guise, fiestas provide a major release from the somber drudgery of peasant life. Past rulers sponsored such festivities to coincide with plowing, planting, harvest, canal cleaning, and other labor cycles, so that work proceeded on a voluntary rather than a coercive basis.

29 (left) A Moche Phase V stirrup-spout libation vessel.

30 (above) A Tiwanaku keros beaker from Moquegua.

Plates 46,59

Toasting and libations with chicha beer were integral and ancient aspects of Andean ceremonialism and festivities. Seating, serving, swilling, and speaking order were no doubt hierarchical, as today. Status was indicated by an individual's drinking vessel: the lowly used gourd bowls, the well-to-do drank from finer containers, while gold and silver were reserved for the highest echelons. During the first millennium BC, different forms of ceramic libation vessels became firmly established in different regions. For example the lords of Chimor toasted from 'stirrup-spout' goblets that were traditional to the north coast, while the nobility of Cuzco drank from beaker-shaped *keros*, vessels indigenous to the Titicaca Basin, and used by rulers of Tiwanaku a millennium earlier. As markers of status and rank libation vessels regularly accompanied people to the grave.

Wealth reciprocity

Reciprocity to the masses largely entailed food and beverage, but the élite required more. Anticipating rewards appropriate to their rank, administrators confronted government with a hierarchy of reciprocal obligations. Military troops received cloth, but officers expected better cuts.

Carefully graded by quality, textiles were the most common reward for service. But for yet higher ranks the rewards included superb ceramics, lavish libation vessels, woodwork, lapidary arts, and splendid metalwork. Thus fine arts critical to wealth finance were the end returns of an élite investment strategy that used mit'a labor to gain agricultural lands. In turn the land was taxed and the staple revenues were used to subsidize skilled artisans who produced commodities to satisfy reciprocity among the élite. This system of transforming the fruits of unskilled labor into fine durable goods was an ancient one at least as old as the emergence of the karaka class.

Arts and crafts

Reciprocity based on valued goods placed fine arts and skilled crafts in direct service of the state. Artisans and tradesmen were subsidized, and their products were geared to serve corporate ends. As a result, aesthetic canons, design motifs, and iconography were dictated by the political and religious organizations supporting the artisans, commissioning their work, and controlling its distribution, creating 'corporate styles' that were characteristic of particular polities, religions, and organizations. In modern society, national coinage and currency convey such styles, depicting political founders, past rulers, heroic figures, totemic animals, and emblems appropriate to a nation. Postage stamps and church art convey similar corporate symbolism.

In the Andes there were two levels of economic organization: the self-sufficient community or ayllu, and the imposed señorio or state economy. Likewise, there were two levels to the production of arts and crafts, and to architecture. The base level comprised the ayllu and their folk traditions. These tended to be simple, conservative, and long-lasting. Above these were the corporate styles, the canons and composition of which conformed to particular political or religious dictates. Their duration depended upon the rise and fall of the corporate bodies they served, and they changed more frequently than did the basal stratum of folk traditions.

The great art styles of the Cordillera were all corporate styles, but the nature of the organizations that underwrote them varied in terms of political, religious, and social composition. Inca corporate arts and architecture illustrate a number of basic characteristics of such styles. First, the styles emerged well after the corporations that they identify came into existence. The Inca established their ethnic identity and their homeland generations before Pachacuti decided a corporate style was in order and rebuilt Cuzco as its architectural hallmark. Second, once a corporate body was established, a corporate style could be put together rapidly, either newly created or borrowed. Third, critical to the creation of a corporate style was the amassing of artisans and specialized technicians. Transforming peasant farmers into skilled craftsmen was not easily done. In later prehistoric times complicated technical expertise generally passed from parent to child and was therefore kin-based, with artisans forming guild-like kin corporations. The lords of Chimor not only subsidized cadres of kindred artisans, but sought to monopolize the production and circulation of precious metal. Upon conquering Lambayeque, metallurgists from the region were resettled at Chan Chan. In turn, when Tahuantinsuyu subjugated *Plate 23* Chimor, tens of thousands of craftsmen at Chan Chan were moved to the environs of Cuzco to serve new rulers. To the degree that fine arts constituted the coin of the realm, Chan Chan was thus stripped of the mint it needed to finance revolt.

Fourth, corporate styles generally spread as far as their supporting reciprocity systems reached. But reciprocity was not uniform. For example, the Inca exploited Ecuador more intensively than central Chile, and elements of Tahuantinsuyu's corporate style are more numerous and sharply defined in its northern holdings than in its southern. Fifth, stylistic unity at the corporate level had little relation to ethnic homogeneity or cultural cohesion at the folk level. The lords of Cuzco imposed widespread artistic cohesion over much of their empire, but this did not reflect a fundamental rise in ethnic unity among the diverse populations of the realm. Sixth and finally, change in corporate style and replacement of one by another did not necessarily reflect population change or the replacement of one ethnic group or cultural group by another. Conservative folk styles were more sensitive indicators of population dynamics, but these traditions also changed without entailing ethnic change.

The most dramatic expressions of Inca corporate style are new cities, towns, and installations erected where none had previously existed. Tumi Bamba, Wayna Capac's incipient Ecuadorian capital, closely cloned the imperial masonry and architectural styles of Cuzco, as did other new settlements founded along the great highway system radiating out of Cuzco. Inca imperial buildings were power emblems intended to impress, if not intimidate, and were generally executed in close accordance with Cuzco's canons. The urban administrative centers of Huanuco Pampa, and Hatun Xarza are well-studied new Inca cities, whose fine masonry and buildings, élite pottery and status goods conform to Cuzco patterns. Yet, close scrutiny of these materials indicates that most were produced by local personnel working under state overseers rather than imported from the capital.

Imperial heartland

The capital of Tahuantinsuyu was not large because the Inca royal families were the only people who resided in the metropolis. The chronicler Cristobal de Molina says that when the Spanish first entered the area Cuzco may have contained up to 40,000 souls, whereas some 200,000 resided within 10 to 12 leagues. Large numbers of technical personnel, artisans, and other people who worked for the government, but were not Inca by birth, lived in suburban communities near the capital. Great labor was expended upon agrarian reclamation and transformation of the imperial heartland into a park-like landscape. Magnificent terraces sculpted the hillsides, which irrigation kept verdant and luxurious. Here the nobility had sumptuous estates, and hundreds of huacas and shrines graced the scenery.

Cuzco and its environs were the quintessence of Inca corporate construction and architecture. Only the finest stonework was used, employing precisely carved blocks that fitted together without the need of cement. There were two *Plates 13,14* styles: one consisted of fine ashlars laid in even horizontal courses; the other was of bold polygonal blocks. Each multi-sided stone was a unique work laboriously cut to a special size and faceted shape that would fit the angles of adjoining blocks. The two styles of masonry were used for two different classes of

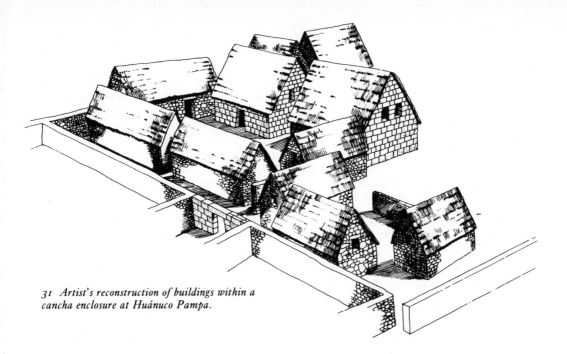

*31 Artist's reconstruction of buildings within a
cancha enclosure at Huánuco Pampa.*

structures: polygonal blocks for solid structures, such as terraces and
platforms; and ashlar blocks for buildings with freestanding walls and open
interior space, often surmounting solid structures. The doors, windows, and   *Plate 16*
niches of Inca buildings were distinctly trapezoidal, being wider at the bottom
than at the top. Roofs were gabled and of thatch. Typical of the Andes, roofed
buildings were usually one-room structures. If two or more rooms shared a
roof, they were treated as separate structures, each room having an outside
entrance but no interior doorways between compartments. Covered buildings
ranged from vast assembly halls, or *kallana*, to small rectangular quarters called
masma and *wasi*. The masma form was U-shaped with one side of the building
left open. They were rare, but perpetuated an ancient tradition of erecting U-
shaped ceremonial buildings.

The most common form of quarters was the one-room wasi, with a single
entry. Wasi were the houses of people and the lodges of idols and gods. They
were erected alone, in clusters, or in groups within large *cancha* – enclosures
built of stone blocks. A principal door led to the open interior of the cancha
where a number of wasi were grouped around patios and courts. People
generally worked out of doors near their small dwellings, and the surrounding
enclosure defined their private space. The cancha–wasi architectural pattern
was an ancient one that still persists among llama and alpaca herders today.

Although Inca architecture and masonry drew on earlier traditions, the lords
of Cuzco added their own corporate stamp, transforming their imperial
heartland into a majestic parkland.

Navel of the universe
Cuzco was among the greatest wonders of the ancient New World. For the Inca
it was literally the sacred center of the universe. Accordingly they lavished
enormous resources on opulent construction and extravagant embellishment.

From each of the distant four quarters of Tahuantinsuyu a great highway converged on the central plaza. The navel of the universe, the *capac usnu*, was a multifaceted dais of finely hewn rock with a vertical pillar and a carved seat, which stood within the plaza. The jutting pillar was a celestial sighting point for tracking heavenly luminaries and dark constellations in the quarters of the universe. The sculpted seat was a stone throne where the emperor, the 'son of the sun', maintained terrestrial order. The lord of the realm ascended the dais to review processions, to toast the gods, and to placate the ancestors. Copious libations of chicha were poured into the 'gullet of the sun', a regal basin of stone sheathed in gold resting at the foot of the usnu. Nearby towered the tallest of all edifices, a grand spire of exquisite masonry that cast no noontime shadow at zenith. The coming of zenith was precisely foretold from a tower window by observing sunrise over a marked point on the distant horizon.

The center of the imperial universe was intimately connected to a marvelously complex cosmos that has long defied western decipherment. The organizing principles of Cuzco were largely misunderstood by the *conquistadores* who left but five short, eye-witness records of the capital before it was consumed by flames during the native rebellion of 1535. These accounts are often contradictory and scholars differ in their interpretations of them. The Spanish thought native rule was similar to the Castilian monarchy, and that the Inca crown passed from father to son in dynastic manner. They recorded a list of ten Inca emperors and considered it a ten-generation succession of rulers. In a monarchy the great hero Pachacuti would have been crowned in 1438 before retiring in 1471, when son Topa Inca inherited the reins of state. Yet, with its hanan and hurin divisions, Cuzco was clearly structured by principles of dual organization. Rather than monarchy, diarchy or dual rule prevailed: hanan Cuzco was no doubt headed by a lord similar to a karaka principale while a counterpart or segunda persona led the hurin moiety. Therefore the Spanish list of emperors is subject to several very different interpretations. One is that figures such as Pachacuti and Topa Inca were not father and son, but senior and junior co-regents. If this was the case, the king list spanned but five generations, and dynastic history is truncated and compressed. Another interpretation holds that the list is not of individuals, but of imperial offices that operated concurrently and were held by the heads of royal kin groups. Split between the hanan and hurin moieties, ten royal clans, or *panaqa*, resided at Cuzco. Therefore, what the Spanish construed as dynastic history is likely to have been little more than a fictional kinship charter, which allowed ten ayllu to form a ruling alliance.

Inca lore associates the transformation of Cuzco into a monumental capital with the name of Pachacuti. Although the name could designate either a ruler or an office of rule, the lore outlines a three-fold succession of events that seems historically plausible. First, the Inca consolidated their homeland. Second, they expanded into the Titicaca Basin. And third, their sacred city was remade in imperial corporate style. The time span of this sequence is debatable. Initial political consolidation probably spanned a number of generations. The Inca

32 With Sacsahuaman as the head, the outlines of a great puma are traced on E.G. Squier's early map of Cuzco.

homeland did not have a tradition of fine stonework, and architects and masons were therefore probably drawn from conquests in the Titicaca region. Thus, the Inca corporate architectural style emerged only after a political base was in place to support it.

As the Ríos Huantanay and Tullamayo converge, they frame the triangle occupied by Cuzco. The narrowest section of the city, between the elongated confluence of the two rivers, was known as the *Pumachupan*, or puma's tail. Some scholars argue that the imperial metropolis was designed and laid out in plan as a vast puma. Others deny this. What the Inca had in mind is not clear, but the outline of a great cat seen from the side can be imposed over the architectural tracery of the Inca city. The main plaza creates an open space between the uphill front quarters of the cat, and its rear legs and down-hill tail. Forming entire city blocks, vast cancha–wasi compounds of the royal panaqa occupied the upper hanan and lower hurin sectors. Each sector apparently contained a palace compound appropriate for dual rule.

The head of the cat was formed by the largest and highest edifices, called Sacsahuaman. Perched atop a high hill, one side of the complex ran along a cliff with a commanding view of the city. The opposite side of the hill was relatively low and encased by three successively higher zigzag terraces. Each wall

Plates 12,14

employed the finest and most impressive of Inca polygonal masonry, including individual stone blocks weighing from 90 to more than 120 metric tons. In plan Sacsahuaman is suggestive of an elongated animal head topped by the great terraces. A marvelous complex of fine ashlar buildings crowned a flattened hill, including tall towers, and circular and rectangular structures. Excavations have revealed a complex system of finely cut stone channels and drains suggesting ritual manipulation of water. Cieza de León says that Pachacuti intended Sacsahuaman to be a temple that would surpass all other edifices in splendor. Garcilaso de la Vega relates that only royalty could enter the sacrosanct complex because it was a house of the sun, of arms and war, and a temple of prayer and sacrifice. Construction supposedly employed 30,000 workers who labored for several generations.

Cuzco's most extraordinary temple, the Coricancha, was located in the puma's tail. It was a grand cancha with a single entry, enclosing six wasi-like chambers arranged around a square courtyard. One chamber, richly bedecked with gold, was dedicated to the sun and held Inti's image; a second, clad in silver, belonged to the moon and held her image. Other structures contained images or symbols of Viracocha, *Illapa* the lord of thunder, *Cuichu* the rainbow, and various celestial bodies. In addition to the Inca pantheon, the Coricancha also housed sacred objects from conquered provinces. In an attempt to integrate their heterogeneous empire and to promote symbolic integration, the Lords of Tahuantinsuyu required kings and karakas of subject populations to spend several months a year in the Cuzco area. A hallowed huaca from each population was also required to be in perpetual residence, although the objects in it could be changed annually.

The Inca and other Andean societies employed a radial organization of space. Thus the boundary lines of the four quarters of Tahuantinsuyu radiated out of the main plaza of Cuzco and four grand highways departed along intercardinal routes approximating the intercardinal axes of Mayu. Within the plaza the pillar of the usnu and the towering Sunturwasi were used to sight outward to distant horizons where mountains and shrines provided points for tracking heavenly movements. The Inca also erected distant masonry pillars and stone pylons to sight upon the sun and to predict planting times at different elevations.

The Coricancha was the sighting center for a remarkable system of radial organization. A sun dial is perhaps the nearest analogy, but the grand temple was more akin to the hub of a cosmic dial for tracking multitudes of celestial phenomena and correlating them with terrestrial phenomena. Radiating out of the Coricancha, 41 sighting lines, called *ceques*, stretched to the horizon or beyond. Along these rays, or adjacent to them some 328 huacas, pillars, and survey points were arranged in a hierarchical manner. Astronomer Tony Aveni of Colgate University notes that the 328 stations represent the days in 12 sidereal lunar months. Given the importance of irrigation, it is not coincidental that one-third of the ceque points comprised the major springs and water sources of the region.

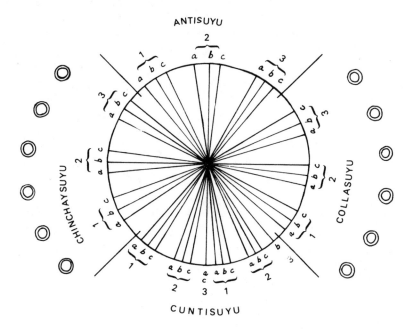

33 *The sighting lines known as ceques radiating from Cuzco's Coricancha temple. The ethnohistorian Tom Zuidema suggests that they were grouped according to the Inca four quarters, Chinchaysuyu, Antisuyu, Collasuyu and Cuntisuyu.*

The ethnohistorian Tom Zuidema of the University of Illinois suggests that the ceques were grouped into upper and lower sets and into four quarters. The upper set was associated with hanan Cuzco, Chinchaysuyu and Antisuyu, the lower set with hurin Cuzco, Collasuyu and Cuntisuyu. Significantly, at least one dividing line separating the four quarters was related to the intercardinal Milky Way, and to the southernmost point of Mayu's movement. Each quarter was in turn subdivided into three parts by ceque lines, and each third was again divided by three more lines. Owing to terrestrial and celestial realities, the angles of arc between lines varied. Particular ceque lines and their huacas were associated with and administered by particular panaqa. In part the rays and huacas distinguished panaqa holdings, established responsibilities and defined daily through to annual activity schedules. Thus, various spatial and temporal reference points along the rays helped to organize land, water, labor, and the ritual activities and festive ceremonies that initiated and closed work cycles.

One cannot but marvel at the Coricancha, or all of Cuzco and its monumental parklands. The *conquistadores* were justly impressed with the navel of the Inca universe, and it continues to amaze all visitors. The chapters to come will probe the ancient foundations of Andean statecraft and ayllu adaptations that underlay the Inca achievement.

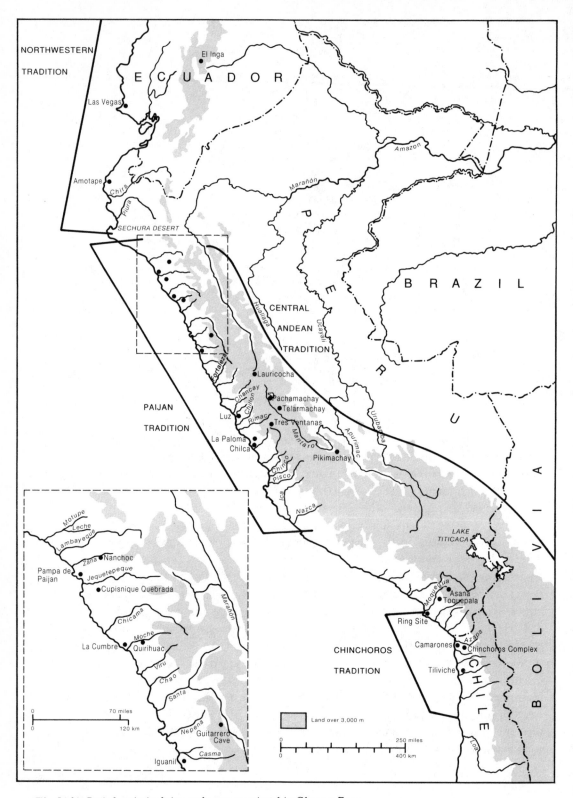

NORTHWESTERN
TRADITION

E C U A D O R

El Inga

Las Vegas

Amotape

Chira

Piura

SECHURA DESERT

CENTRAL

ANDEAN

TRADITION

Huallaga

Marañón

Amazon

B R A Z I L

P

E

R

U

PAIJAN

TRADITION

Fortaleza

Lauricocha

Chancay

Chillón

Luz

Rimac

Pachamachay

Telarmachay

Tres Ventanas

La Paloma

Chilca

Chinca

Pisco

Mantaro

Pikimachay

Apurímac

Urubamba

Ucayali

Ica

Nazca

LAKE
TITICACA

B O L I V I A

Moquegua

Asana

Toquepala

Ring Site

Azapa

CHINCHOROS

TRADITION

Camarones

Chinchoros Complex

Tiliviche

C H I L E

Loa

Motupe

Leche

Lambayeque

Zaña

Nanchoc

Pampa de
Paijan

Jequetepeque

Cupisnique Quebrada

Marañón

Chicama

Moche

La Cumbre

Quirihuac

Viru

Chao

Santa

Nepeña

Guitarrero
Cave

Iguanil

Casma

0   70 miles

0   120 km

Land over 3,000 m

0   250 miles

0   400 km

34 The Lithic Period: principal sites and areas mentioned in Chapter Four.

CHAPTER FOUR

Early Settlement of the Cordillera

Twenty thousand years ago, during the last Ice Age, the Andes were very different than they are today. The mountain peaks were heavily glaciated, and the world's sea level more than 100 m lower than today's. Throughout the Andes ecological zones were stratified at lower elevations. Tropical conditions extended into northern Peru, but the central Cordillera remained arid. Then, between 15,000 and 5,000 years ago, great processes began to change this Pleistocene environment to its present appearance. The glaciers melted, causing ocean levels to rise, shore lines to push inland, marine and meteorological currents to shift north, and natural habitats to move upward. In the same period Pleistocene animals became extinct and humans entered the Cordillera, eventually domesticating plants and animals. People developed adaptations for making a living in the various environments: tropical jungle, desert coast, sierra basins, and high puna. Adaptive specialization and the earliest plant cultivation are evident by 9,000 to 10,000 years ago. This period, the Lithic Period, ended around 5,000 years ago, coinciding with the stabilization of post-Pleistocene sea levels, and the establishment of the present-day climate and ecological zoning of the Cordillera, a major turning point in the physical and biological history of the continent.

The colonists

Scholars agree that the New World was colonized by a few small groups of people who crossed the Bering Land Bridge from the Old World and moved into unknown territory. Drawing upon linguistic data and data from the morphology of ancient human teeth, a recent interpretation proposes that three genetically distinct Asian populations crossed the land bridge into North America more than 10,000 years ago. Of these stocks only one reached Middle America where small numbers crossed the Isthmus of Panama into South America and the Andes. The proposition that the primordial colonists of the southern continent were few and came from only one stock of people is quite important for understanding similarities found among much later desert, mountain, and jungle dwellers. Geneticists note that if a pair of fruit flies with dark eyes are allowed to reproduce over many generations in a contained environment, most of their thousands of descendants will have similar dark eyes. This is called the 'Founder Principle'. Linguists employ analogous principles when they work back in time from contemporary dialects to reconstruct ancestral languages. We can be certain too that founding

35 *The atlatl or spear thrower probably armed the continent's first human colonists.*

populations influence the behavior, social organization and beliefs of their descendants.

The Founder Principle provides one way of explaining similarities found among the otherwise distinct populations living in different Andean environments and pursuing separate ways of life when the Spanish arrived. For example dual division of communities and moiety organization was widespread in Andean and Amazonian societies. Perhaps moiety organization was invented first in the highlands or lowlands and then diffused to other areas. But it is simpler to suppose that the continent's first colonists were moiety kin groups, and that this gave rise to the later prevalence of dual organization. There must have been individuals of ability who led with the consent of their kindred. It is also reasonable to suppose that there were shamans or healers whose practices gave rise to later religious emphasis on health and healing. The technology brought by the vanguard included spears – perhaps without stone tips – and probably the atlatl, or spear-thrower. In the tropical forests of Central America the use of stone probably diminished in favor of hardwoods and bone. Plant fibers were vital for bedding, cordage, and other artifacts; and it seems likely that looping, knotting and twining were known and used for bags, nets, and fabrics. Fire-making was known, probably by spinning and pressing a long, straight stick or 'drill' against a shorter, 'hearth' of wood.

The arrival

All authorities agree that the southern-most tip of the continent was reached *c.* 9000 BC by people using distinctive types of spearheads called 'fluted' points. Each flat side of the weapon has a long narrow flake channel, or flute, running from the base to the midsection, reducing the thickness of the projectile. Fluted points of similar antiquity are common in North America, and they mark the widespread dispersal of early Paleo-Indian populations in the New World. In spite of claims for even greater antiquity there is little compelling evidence that people were present before about 13,000 years ago. If they were in the Andes little can be said about them because stones claimed to be their artifacts are dubious and only vaguely dated. For example in the Ayacucho mountains of central Peru the basal deposits of Pikimachay Cavern produced remains of extinct cave-dwelling ground sloths dating between 12,000 and 20,200 years old. But it is not clear whether people were contemporary with the animals because most of the possible stone artifacts are of the same volcanic rock that forms the cave and may simply be pieces of stone that fell and fractured naturally.

Monte Verde

Better evidence for early human activity comes from Monte Verde in the subarctic pine forests of south-central Chile. Here a small group of people lived along the sandy banks of a small creek until it backed up and capped their settlement with a thin layer of peat that preserved dwellings, wooden artifacts and other tools, remains of plant foods such as wild potatoes, and animal bones including those of at least six mastodons – extinct cousins of elephants. Radiocarbon dates from 17 samples give a general date of c. 13,000 years old. Excavations by Tom Dillehay and his Chilean colleagues yielded numerous round rocks the size of an egg. Some may have been sling stones, but others were grooved for suspension as bolas stones. Grinding stones, hammer stones, choppers, a perforator and two long lanceolate projectile points were also recovered. Wooden artifacts included a sharp-pointed lance, digging sticks, three handles with stone scrapers mounted on them, and three rough-hewn wooden mortars.

Wood was used to construct two different types of structure. To form foundations for rectangular huts, small logs and rough-cut hardwood planks were laid on the ground and held in place by stakes. Next to these, vertical saplings were driven into the ground about every meter to form frames. On some fallen poles there are traces of what may be animal skin, suggesting that the walls were made of hides. The 12 excavated rooms each measured c. 3–4.5 m on a side and were joined at their sides to form two parallel rows. Inside the huts there were tools, plant remains, and shallow clay-lined pits that served as braziers. Cooking was apparently a communal affair and took place around two large hearths.

Separated from the dwellings, a second type of building was erected in an isolated setting at the western end of the site. This was a wishbone-shaped structure with a foundation of compacted sand and gravel. Fragments of upright wooden poles were present every half meter along both arms and served as a pole frame for a hide covering. A small raised platform protruded from the rear of the hut resulting in the 'Y' or wishbone configuration. The platform was about 3 m wide and almost 4 m long. The open front of the structure faced a small clearing or courtyard that contained small clay-lined braziers. The area yielded pieces of animal hide, burned reeds and seeds, and several species of medicinal plants, including leaves that had been chewed. Around the building and court there was a concentration of hearths, wood piles, tools, medicinal plants, and bones, including most of the mastodon remains found at the site. It is evident that this open-fronted structure was the focus of special activities that included the processing of game, if not ritual feasting, preparation of herbal medicines, and perhaps practice of shamanistic healing. The wishbone structure stands at the beginning of a long evolutionary tradition of special-purpose architecture that served corporate activities that we call ceremonial yet know little about.

The people of Monte Verde either scavenged or killed elephants and hunted camelids and small game in the countryside. Plant gathering was of equal, if not greater, importance. In addition to wild potatoes, botanical remains included edible seeds, fruits, nuts, berries, leafy vegetables, tubers and rhizomes. Plants were secured from nearby marshes, from inland forests, and from the Pacific coast, which produced algae and lagoon vegetation rich in iodine and salt. By exploiting widely dispersed ecological zones with different growing regimes the inhabitants obtained plants that matured during all months of the year and brought them back to their permanent settlement at Monte Verde. This evidence of residential permanence runs contrary to the notion that early foragers were always migratory. Although Monte Verde lies in the moist, cool forests far beyond the frontiers of Tahuantinsuyu, its occupation reflects adaptations that are Andean in general nature. Unfortunately, there is scant evidence of contemporary human occupation elsewhere in the Andes. The central Chilean sites of Taguatagua (dated 11,400 years ago) and Quero (dated 11,100 years ago) produced remains of mastodon and horse, stone flakes, and lithics thought to be unifacial tools, scrapers, and choppers. However, it is not until about 11,000 years ago that there is better evidence of human activity in the Cordillera, and by this time elephants were gone, but Pleistocene horse and ground sloth still survived.

Fluted projectile points

Horse was the most ubiquitous animal to have been hunted and remains have been found at a number of sites with different lithic technologies, including Pikimachay, Jaywamachay, Huarago, and Ushumachay in Peru and Los Toldos in Chile. In Tierra del Fuego, Junius Bird excavated horse, sloth and guanaco – wild relatives of the llama – remains associated with fluted points in Fell's Cave and Palli Aike Cave near the tip of Chile. Beneath deposits of later

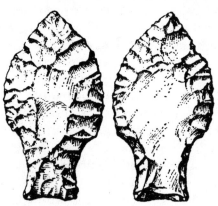

36 Fluted Fishtail points from Tierra del Fuego.

hunters, the lowest cave strata yielded dates of 9050 ± 170 BC and 8770 ± 300 BC, and produced simple stone tools and finely crafted spearheads called 'fluted fishtail points'. Similar in shape to a fishtail, the points expand slightly at the base and have a channel or flute on each side. Fluted projectiles are rare in South America and their distribution is limited to the Andes and southern plains, or 'pampas'. Occasional surface finds are reported from southern Brazil, Uruguay, and Los Toldos in Argentina. Near Quito, Ecuador, the highland site of El Inga yielded 21 specimens of fishtail projectiles in a shallow deposit mixed with later remains. These are not the remains of generalized hunters who mastered different environments, but they reflect an adaptation focused on the resources of the open grasslands and of people who avoided the tropical forests and the western desert, where there are but two surface finds of fishtail points in northern Peru. The occurrence of similar projectiles in Panama suggests that fluted points may represent a second penetration of South America by a small Paleo-Indian population.

Adaptive dispersal

Because the Andean landscape encompasses the environmental extremes of desert, high altitude, and tropics, human dispersal entailed early economic specialization. Distinct ways of life had evolved in desert, tropical lowlands, sierra, puna and altiplano by 8,000–9,000 years ago. To varying degrees these adaptations are associated with three types of stone tool assemblages called the Central Andean Lithic Tradition, the Paijan Tradition and the Northwestern or 'Edge-Trimmed Tool' Tradition.

Northwestern Tradition
Because rock is often scarce in the jungle, people living in tropical forests rely more on bone and various botanical resources. Stone is reserved for choppers, scrapers, and sharp flakes that can be used to produce other tools such as spears and arrows tipped with hardwood projectiles. The Northwestern Lithic Tradition is characterized by simple but variable stone artifacts, but no stone projectiles. Tropical adaptations of this tradition are found in coastal Ecuador on the Santa Elena Peninsula north of the Guayaquil Gulf. Here the Las Vegas culture is defined by more than 30 camps and settlements dating between 10,000 and 6,600 years ago. The type site is a dark midden about 1 m deep that accumulated during an early occupation and later served as a burial ground. People lived in circular houses c. 2 m in diameter with mud-plastered walls of cane or poles secured in a narrow trench cut below floor level. Small size suggests these were quarters for a couple and their offspring. With the exception of several axes, stone tools were simple and hunting must have relied upon weapons of wood, reed, and fiber. Land animals, particularly deer, accounted for about 54 per cent of the dietary protein, the remainder coming from fish and mangrove mollusks from the sea some 3 km away. Gathering of wild flora is reflected by midden pollen, which also indicates that people had

begun to cultivate the bottle gourd (*Lagenaria siceraria*) *c.* 7,000 to 8,000 years ago. Some 192 individuals were interred at the site in the form of secondary burials of disarticulated bones jumbled together some time after the flesh had decomposed or been removed. Secondary burial among tropical forest peoples contrasts markedly with central Andean peoples' concepts about the hereafter and it is evident that belief systems as well as economic systems diverged at a very early date.

During the Pleistocene warmer, moister conditions pushed down the Cordillera several hundred kilometers into northern Peru into areas that are now desert. Along the coast the Northwestern Lithic Tradition extended south to the Ríos Piura and Chira. Here it is represented by a succession of shallow or surface sites with occupations beginning some time between 11,000 and 8,000 years ago during the Amotape phase and then continuing through Siches, Estero, and Honda phases. During the early phases people hunted and camped along the shore, gathering shellfish from mangrove swamps, but about 6,000 years ago the mangroves disappeared as the northernmost coast reverted to desert.

At higher elevations a belt of montane forests extended southward during Pleistocene times, and survives today as relic stands of tropical trees and thorn steppes in the headwaters of the Zana and Lambayeque river drainages. People using the Northwestern Lithic Tradition settled the upper Zana by 8,000 years ago and their ongoing occupation left behind more than 47 prepottery sites situated along small streams or atop adjacent hill spurs. One site, Nanchoc, is of particular interest because it has a pair of small mounds. In plan the flat-top platforms are oblong, lozenge-shaped, and wider in the southwest than in the northeast. Roughly aligned, they are about 15 m apart, and measure 32 to 35 m in length and 1.2 to 1.5 m in height, in three tiers faced with fitted stones. The mounds were not all built at once, and radiocarbon dates from basal samples fall between 6000 and 5500 BC. Each consists of a series of superimposed floors separated by layers of artificial fill that gradually added height to the structures. This pattern of incremental building, in which periods of use and epochs of construction alternately succeed one another, is typical of later Andean platform mounds. From an organizational perspective episodic construction was an important means of reaffirming corporate identity by bringing people together periodically to work on an established symbol of unity. The excavators of Nanchoc, Tom Dillehay and Patricia Netherly, suggest that the twin mounds reflect dual social organization and the ceremonial architecture of moieties.

Most of the early Zana sites represent small residential areas about 35 m in diameter, defined by thin middens with hearths, carbonized plants, animal bones, and occasional secondary burials. Near some settlements there are traces of buried furrows and short feeder ditches that may date to the latter half of the Lithic Period. These are the earliest garden plots known to survive, although it is not certain what types of plants were cultivated. Lithics are limited to unifacial tools and grinding stones, but the discovery of part of a Paijan projectile and some marine shells indicates contact with the coast, less than 75 km away, where different adaptations were pursued.

Paijan Tradition

Sites in the Paijan Tradition have given numerous dates between 12,000 and 7,000 years ago. The tradition's hallmark is the long, slender Paijan point, averaging 10 cm in length. The piercing tips are exceptionally long and narrow, and they may be described as 'needle-nosed' projectiles. The noses rarely survive intact, and long broken tips have been mistaken for stone awls. The bases are characterized by long, narrow tangs indicating that the points were mounted in hollow shafts of cane or reed. The breakage tendencies of needle-nosed projectiles made them ineffective against large game with thick hides and they appear to have been designed for spearing fish, whose bones are found in inland middens. Yet, the shoreline sites where Paijan people presumably obtained much of their food were inundated long ago by rising sea levels. Thus, all that survives of this tradition are sites associated with secondary activities that drew people inland for brief periods.

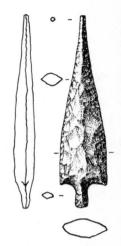

37 A Paijan projectile – the tip of the point is missing.

Three types of interior sites are known: stone quarries, lithic workshops, and short-term camps. Projectiles are commonly found at the first two, but rarely at the last, suggesting that the weapons were not used for hunting. Covering one square kilometer, the site of La Cumbre on the north side of the Moche Valley combined quarry and workshop activities and yielded more than 4,500 artifacts. Long, foliate, bifacially chipped pieces were the most numerous, and were probably preforms from which finished tools would be made, including projectiles, knife-like *limaces*, side scrapers, notches, beaks, denticulates, pebble scrapers, pebble tools, cores, and flakes or blocks modified by use alone. The base of a fluted point, fashioned from foreign stone, was found on the surface.

Further inland on the north side of the valley, a huge tilted boulder provided an overhang, known as the Quirihuac Shelter. Here a few Paijan people camped to collect land snails and left behind tool fragments, chipping debris, and burials of a child and an adult. These and other Paijan interments were primary burials of intact corpses. Bones of the adult were dated to 9,000 years ago; whereas the burial of the child was a millennium earlier. With the exception of one young date, assays of small bits of charcoal in the rockshelter ranged between 8,645 and 12,795 years ago.

Land snails appear in shallow camp deposits left by Paijan peoples in the Quebrada Cuculicote on the north side of the Chicama Valley. In addition to grinding stones for processing plant foods excavations show that people ate lizards, birds, and vizcacha (*Lagydium* sp.), a rabbit-sized mammal, as well as fish and crabs brought in from the sea. To the north, in the adjacent Cupisnique drainage, Paijan quarry sites, manufacturing sites, and camp sites have also been found. Although not rich in artifacts, two camps had midden deposits 20 cm deep. Charcoal associated with a human burial was 10,200 years old, and other midden remains produced dates of 9,800 and 7,700 years ago. Grinding stones were present, and, in decreasing order of importance, animal remains included land snails, fish, lizard, fox, and one deer bone.

The Paijan Tradition reflects a highly specialized adaptation with a sharply circumscribed geographic focus. The tradition is absent north of the Río Omo where more tropical conditions existed. It is also absent in the forested headwaters of the Río Zana where the Northwestern Tradition prevailed, but Paijan people were present at lower elevations on the coastal plain crossed by the Zana River. The primary focus of the Paijan adaptation was the wide coastal plain and broad continental shelf between the Ríos Omo and Santa where hundreds of needle-nosed projectiles have been found. As the coastline narrows to the south, the frequency of Paijan remains begins to diminish. Three surface sites near the Casma shore yielded a dozen or so needle-nosed projectiles, and several were discovered at high elevations in the Río Casma headwaters. The tradition is present during the Laz phase in the Ancon-Chillon area near Lima, and the most southerly occurrences of Paijan points comprise two surface finds in the Ica desert.

In overview needle-nosed Paijan points vie with fluted fishtail points as the most distinctive early projectiles on the continent. Paijan stands apart from other traditions in its circumscribed geographic focus, principally along the wide coastal plain of the north, with some southward penetration to Ica. It is curious that this wider distribution coincides with the later distribution of large architectural monuments along the coastal desert. The earliest of these monuments were erected by preceramic fisherfolk who relied on nets and hooks, but not harpoons. Paijan was certainly ancestral to these later developments but rising sea levels have submerged shoreline sites which would reflect their early evolution.

Central Andean Tradition

Fluted fishtail and Paijan assemblages are distinct yet repetitive, each probably representing people who pursued similar customs and spoke the same language. This is not the case with the Central Andean Tradition, which is a widespread, but generalized lithic technology shared by populations pursuing several environmental adaptations. It is characterized by projectiles that resemble willow leaves, with tapering points and rounded or blunt bases. The leaf shape is a simple configuration that constitutes a 'generic' weapon form, with minimal elaboration on the functional necessities of a projectile point. Leaf-shaped points are widely distributed from the Río Santa headwaters into Chile and Argentina and range in size from short, stubby blades to long, thin ones. There is such variation in leaf shape and associated tool assemblages, and they occur over such a vast area, that authorities do not agree on where the tradition begins and ends. It has been most often applied to northern and central Peru, but in a generic sense it encompasses much of the south central Andes as well. Leaf-shaped projectiles are associated with puna, sierra basin, and coastal adaptations. In the north each represented a separate way of life, but in the arid south impoverished resources led to combined adaptations.

Puna hunters

Except for the rich marine food chain, Andean animal life was most abundant in the high elevation puna grasslands of the north. The selective pressures of altitude kept the variety of puna wildlife small, but plentiful. The vicuña (*Vicugna vicugna*), a deer-sized wild relative of the llama, is frequently found along streams and creeks draining the grasslands. Vicuña live in two types of groups: bands and troops. Bands are reproductive groups consisting of one dominant male and an average of seven females that occupy a small, fixed territory. Troops are herds of up to 40 males that wander near the reproductive groups and are constantly being expelled from band territories by dominant males. The northern herds are not characterized by seasonal migration. These facts and the abundance of game have led John Rick to argue that if hunting bands numbered about 25 individuals sufficient vicuña could be hunted within a radius of 9 to 10 km to support puna occupation year round. Rick's interpretation has been based on excavations at Pachamachay Cave, surrounded by grasslands at an elevation of 4,300 m, and located *c.* 10 km from Lake Junin. The first two phases of occupation are dated at 10,000–7,000 BC, and 7,000–5,000 BC, and are associated with leaf-shaped points as well as with triangular and shouldered forms. Carbonized seeds indicate the collecting of wild grasses and other plants. Bone was common and no less than 97 per cent came from camelids. Phase 1 is thought to reflect the presence of relatively mobile hunting groups, who were in the process of formulating puna adaptations; but from Phase 2 onwards occupation was probably permanent by a small population that used the site continually for many millennia. To maintain a stable adaptation people had to limit their own numbers and avoid over-exploitation of the vicuña herds.

A number of other high altitude caves with stratified deposits reflect similar economic adjustments to the wet puna. They include the first two phases of occupation at Lauricocha Cave, 100 km northwest of Pachamachay. Located at an elevation of about 3,900 m, the site is in rugged terrain near camelid pasture as well as lower zones inhabited by deer. The earliest occupation dates to *c.* 7500 BC and is characterized by the presence of leaf-shaped projectiles that become longer in the Phase 2 occupation. The Lauricocha people were probably permanent residents and seem to have complemented their game diet with a remarkable variety of local edible roots and tubers.

Sierra basin foragers

At the time Paijan people occupied the Casma coast, highland people of the Central Andean Tradition pursued a very different living in the mountains only 80 km away. The sierra lifeway has been documented at Guitarrero Cave and at higher open-air sites in the Callejon de Huaylas by Thomas Lynch and his associates. The Callejon is one of the great Andean basins that drains from south to north, but it forms the headwaters of the Río Santa and is the only sierra basin to empty into the Pacific. At an elevation of 2,580 m, Guitarrero Cave overlooks the river and narrow floodplain a short walk away. The

Plates 27,28

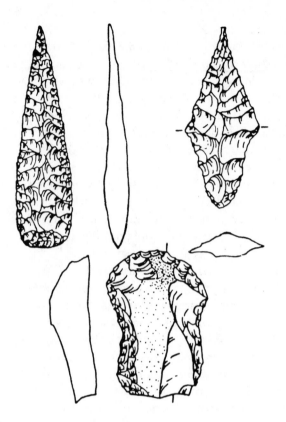

38 Projectile points and stone tools from Guitarrero Cave, shown actual size.

principal occupation of the cave – called Complex II – was short-lived and took place about 10,000 years ago. Lithic remains resemble those from higher local sites and those from Lauricocha and Pachamachay. However, the animal remains from Guitarrero are rather different. Here small rodents such as rabbits and rabbit-like vizcacha (*Lagidium peruanum*) are common, as are birds, including pigeon and tinamou. Larger game consisted principally of deer, which outnumbered camelid remains by seven to one. The bones reflect a sierra valley fauna which is more diversified than that of the higher puna, but less plentiful in numbers. Sierra game did not provide the hunting resources that favored year-round residency. The Callejon sites probably represent seasonal transhumance that brought people to the grasslands above 4,000 m when the sierra began to dry after the December to March rains. The recovery of only one marine shell at Guitarrero suggests limited contact with the coast. Thus, although only 80 km apart, marked differences in lithic assemblages and economic adaptations show that highland and lowland populations were already diverging culturally if not biologically.

Altiplano hunter-gatherers

The resources to support separate hunter-gatherer adaptations in the puna and sierra decrease as the Cordillera becomes higher and dryer. The turning point seems to be in the Ayacucho uplands of central Peru. Research in this region

39 Deer were never abundant in the arid Andes and by Moche times stag hunting had become a sport of the nobility. Wounded by an atlatl spear, a buck is dispatched by club in this ceramic painting.

suggests that from about 10,000 years ago successive phases of occupation reflect a relatively mobile way of life. The pattern of annual movement saw families congregating at mid altitudes in sierra drainages when the rainy season brought forth a rich bloom of plants attractive to animals and humans. Drier times necessitated a dispersal of people to other elevations, particularly to the higher puna hunting grounds.

The Lithic Period occupation of the Lake Titicaca basin is largely unexplored, but due west, in the Río Moquegua area, early sites from the dry puna down to the coast have been investigated. At an altitude of 2,000 m, the painted caves of Toquepala yielded radiocarbon dates as early as 9,500 years old. The long occupation of the cave was characterized by seasonal residence during the moister months between October and April. Painted and unpainted caves and rockshelters with Lithic Period occupations are common in the higher altitudes, but the open-air settlement of Asana in the high sierra is unique because of its architecture. Not far below the puna, it is situated on the banks of a Moquegua tributary at an elevation of 4,500 m. Its occupation spans the Lithic Period, with radiocarbon dates between 9,580 and 3,640 years ago. Beginning about 7,000 years ago the stratified deposits contain floor outlines of small circular dwellings that were apparently walled with brush, hide, or some other perishable material. From about 5,000 years ago they clustered around a larger, central ceremonial structure. Defined by a well-made clay floor 10 m in diameter, the structure may have been 'C' shaped in plan with an open front that was largely destroyed by a rock slide. The interior was kept clean and its most noteworthy feature was a cairn-like pile of rocks perhaps representing an altar. The excavator, Mark Aldenderfer suggests Asana was a wet season residential area for people who focused their efforts on exploiting the nearby puna much of the year and spent time camping in puna caves. The dry season affects both sierra valleys and higher grasslands, but the dry puna is dotted with seeps and springs that support moors, or *bofedales*. Contemporary pastoralists often channel the springs to irrigate and expand the lush bofedal vegetation. As a source of pasturelands where wild herds would congregate during the dry season, the moors were no doubt vital to past hunter-gatherers. Analysis of tools and the types of stone from which they were fashioned at Asana demonstrates substantial similarities in sierra and puna lithic assemblages, but marked differences with coastal assemblages.

From Lake Popo south the altiplano is enveloped by the Atacama desert. The salt puna and small sierra valleys of northern Chile become progressively more impoverished and this required greater seasonal mobility on the part of hunter-gatherers and a merging of what were separate adaptations to the north. A merger of highland and coastal exploitation patterns seems to have characterized the arid Cordillera from the Río Loa-San Pedro de Atacama region south. Here Chilean investigator Lautaro Nuñez postulates a pattern of transhumance with Lithic Period people utilizing coastal resources between May and September and then migrating high into the mountains for the remainder of the year.

Fisherfolk

Because the Pacific desert offers few terrestrial foods Paijan people were not the only folk to make early use of marine resources. From central Peru into Chile the narrow coast is characterized by lithic technologies with leaf-shaped projectile points of variable form. In the Ancon-Chillon area they comprise later replacements of Paijan points and are associated with lomas hunting during the Canario and Encanto Phases, which begin about 6000 and 4000 BC, respectively. However, south along the coast into Chile early leaf-shaped projectiles are contemporary with the Paijan tradition and down to the Río Loa region they are associated with coastal adaptations that were separate and independent of highland life.

Some of the earliest surviving evidence of maritime adaptations occurs in southernmost Peru and northern Chile. Near the Moquegua Valley shellfish from basal midden deposits of the Ring Site produced one date of 10,575 years ago, but most of the radiocarbon assays are several millennia younger. Nonetheless, by 7,000 years ago this large settlement was permanently occupied on a year-round basis by people who obtained their protein exclusively from the sea by angling and perhaps netting. Although largely destroyed by road construction, the midden was originally circular or ring-shaped in layout. The depressed center was apparently a plaza around which people lived and discarded shellfish and other refuse that mounded up to heights of more than 2 m.

In northern Chile very early reliance on sea foods is associated with the coastal occupations at Tiliviche and at Las Conchas Quebrada, which have yielded dates of 9,760 and 9,680 years ago. At Tiliviche there is evidence for the consumption of seafoods, as well as for inland hunting, which includes animal bones as well as projectile points of leaf-shaped form. Some points were fashioned from obsidian that must have come from the inland mountains. A

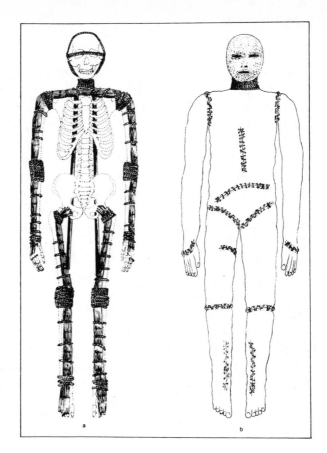

40 *After bracing the skeleton with reed supports (a), Chinchoros mummies were reassembled (b) and facial details were modeled in clay covering the head.*

greater focus upon marine foods is evident in the occupation of Las Conchas, where refuse deposits yielded fish-net fragments dated at 7730 BC.

By about 5000 BC the littoral of northern Chile was occupied by very sophisticated fisherfolk known as the Chinchoros culture. Although inland collecting and hunting contributed to the diet, fishing tackle underwent great elaboration. In addition to nets, harpoons and composite hooks, fishhooks were fabricated from sturdy cactus thorns, from shell, and later from bone. With growing abilities to harvest the sea, these fisherfolk increased their numbers and came to live in sedentary communities of modest size. Their beliefs about the afterlife included notions that the deceased should be physically preserved by means of artificial mummification – the earliest example of this practice in the world.

This remarkable cult of the dead focused on preserving the deceased in life-like form and technological concerns with mummification underwent gradual elaboration that climaxed during the third millennium BC, about the time ancient Egyptians began using embalming processes for similar ends. Chinchoros morticians perfected unusual skills: in disassembling bodies; in removing cerebral and visceral matter; in treating organs, structures, and skin to arrest deterioration; in reassembling the corpse components; in implanting cane or wood supports into the vertebral column, arms, and legs; in adding fiber, feather, clay or other fill to body cavities; in applying an exterior coat of clay permitting the sculpting and painting of facial details; and in replacing pelage with wigs and human hair embedded in clay. Infants as well as young and old of both sexes were mummified, but some corpses received much more elaborate treatment than others, and some received no treatment. This variation probably reflects social differences and inequalities. Mummified bodies were kept accessible to the living and curated for various lengths of time prior to being placed in the ground, evident from the fact that many were eventually interred as small discrete groups comprising children and several adults that may be interpreted as families.

Chinchoros folk were not alone in their concern with physically preserving the deceased. About 6,000 years ago corpses were salted to arrest deterioration at the settlement of La Paloma on the central Peruvian coast. In sharp contrast to secondary burial practices among tropical forest people these early coastal mortuary complexes reflect ancient and profound Andean beliefs that the deceased had to be physically intact to enter the afterlife and join the realm of the ancestors. Ranging from ayllus to the Inca state, Andean social formations were held together by kin bonds based upon veneration of tangible common ancestors, and mummies were the preferred symbols of founding fathers and corporate identity. Thus, the Chinchoros and Paloma mortuary complexes reveal an ancient inception of concepts and beliefs critical to the rise of Andean civilization.

Domestication

Andean civilization was based upon domesticated plants and animals that were extraordinarily robust and upon reclamation of inhospitable terrain for farm land. Yet, even with these adaptations mountain people lived on the brink of famine. Recognizing that plant and animal husbandry was not an idyllic way of life in a land of contrasting environmental extremes is critical for understanding the unusual evolution of Andean agriculture. Exploring agrarian origins begins with an important distinction that separates domesticated plants and animals from all other forms cultivated, tended, or wild. Under human care domesticates experience genetic changes that biologically distinguish them from their wild progenitors. Changes in behavior and morphology transpire over generations of tending and cultivation, but tending does not always result in domestication. To construct watercraft Andean fisherfolk have long cultivated bulrushes that do not exhibit genetic modifications qualifying them as domesticated plants. With ancient remains, it is difficult or impossible to tell if an organism was gathered wild or matured under human care, because there are no genetic or morphological signatures distinguishing between the two. The vital first step in the domestication process, human tending of wild plants and animals, is therefore elusive.

Theories
There is ancient evidence of cultivation and plant domestication at Guitarrero Cave and other Andean sites. Still, there have long been fewer facts than

theories about domestication. Pioneering insights about agricultural origins were put forth more than two centuries ago by the great nineteenth-century naturalist Alexander von Humboldt. As the first European scholar to systematically explore the Cordillera and to report upon the archaeological monuments of Latin America, he wrote voluminously about the flora and fauna of the hemisphere. Aware that tens of thousands of plants and animals thrived, but that fewer than one per cent were domesticated, a notion of risk lay at the heart of his ideas. Von Humboldt believed that early experiments with tending organisms and altering their behavior and characteristics offered far greater chances for failure than for success. Therefore, the origins of domestication would not be found among well-off people living in productive habitats because they had little reason to accept such risks. The motivation for tending wild resources would instead be found among the inhabitants of marginal settings and harsh environments. Here, confronted with low or insecure yields from nature, trial and error with the care of plants or animals offer acceptable risks as potential means of stabilizing or increasing food supplies. The Prussian scholar reasoned that people were gradually pushed into harsh settings conducive to experimentation as population growth filled in more favorable habitats. To this push we may add the climatic and environmental changes that accompanied glacial melting at the end of Pleistocene.

Von Humboldt saw necessity as the mother of invention, but his theory does not imply that people consciously sought to domesticate plants and animals. In the Andes the major route to domestication lay with experiments that encouraged plants and animals inhabiting one place or zone to live in another. The motivation for altering the distribution of wild resources may have been to increase their numbers, as herders do when they irrigate bofedal pasturage, or simply to bring useful organisms closer to where people lived. Moving potential domesticates entailed seeding in the case of beans and cereals, and certainly transplant of root parts or cuttings in the case of tubers. Distances between natural occurrence and human placement were probably short to begin with. Yet, in the rugged Cordillera living conditions change over very short distances and habitats can vary within a few hundred meters of elevation. Therefore, moving organisms and altering their placement injected both human selection and natural selection into the Andean domestication process.

Traveling the Cordillera, von Humboldt could see that the domestication process remained unending and that the harsh highlands were still undergoing agricultural and pastoral transformations in the nineteenth century, as they are today. Plants and animals are continually moved from tolerant to less tolerant settings. Cultigens are shifted laterally at their established elevation to new fields with different soil, moisture, or other growing conditions. However, the thrust of agropastoralism has long been into ever higher mountain regions where vast tracts of open land lie invitingly beyond the altitudinal limits of farming. This is a dynamic economic frontier that fluctuates up and down continually in response to short and long term changes in temperature and precipitation. The upward assault is spearheaded with a few varieties of exceptionally robust root crops, but nature defends her elevational boundaries with the greatest stress and highest agrarian risks in the continent. Crop failures, or poor yields, are recurrent and good harvests the exception. The battle is waged in small, scattered plots where a few farmers believe that microenvironmental conditions might be less hostile than average. These peasants suffer the risks of battling the frontiers of agriculture because they are the land-poor and economically marginal members of local communities and ayllu.

Many Andean domesticates and the majority of highland crops probably originated at different points along the eastern flanks of the Cordillera, where rich natural diversity occurs in narrowly stratified habitats. Botanists believe that the wild ancestors of upland or lowland cultigens came from many places and that domestication transpired in many different settings. For example, peanuts have their nearest wild relatives in Argentina and may have originated there. Wild potatoes in southern Chile are thought by some to be the source of certain types of domesticated potatoes. Still other types of potatoes probably derived from wild forms around the flanks of the Titicaca Basin. The higher basin section of the range is the probable origin area for tubers such as oca and ulluco, as well as for grains such as quiñoa and cañihua. Here we may also look to the puna grasslands for the hearth of llama and alpaca domestication. Alternatively, fruits such as avocado, chirimoya, and coca originated in the north where the range is tropical. Finally, the Amazon or Orinoco Basins supplied the important lowland root crop of manioc. Tropical forests are much easier to farm than bleak deserts that demand irrigation, or arid mountains that require irrigation and terracing as well as unusually robust cultigens. Thus, the evolution of Andean agriculture was not merely a matter of acquiring domesticates, but also involved the acquisition of land and water.

Early evidence

Dating to almost 10,000 years ago, the well-preserved botanical assemblage of *Plate 27* Complex II at Guitarrero Cave includes the oldest cultivated plants yet found in the New World. In order to assess the Guitarrero finds, it is important to recognize that native flora provided many more things than food. Medicinal plants were vital to health care, while so-called 'industrial' plants provided clothing, containers, weapons, bedding, and shelter. Therefore, plant tending need not have arisen exclusively from concerns with food. The dry deposits of Guitarrero reveal a plant assemblage dominated by wild vegetation that was not eaten, but used to make a variety of items ranging from beds to apparel. Furthermore, it was a technology emphasizing fiber over wood. Wood was used for weapon shafts, dowels, and fire-drills, but the bulk of the assemblage consists of fiber debris from hemp-like plants including *Tillandsia*, *Puya* and *Furcraea*. People slept on, wore, and made mats and mesh containers out of *Plate 28* fiber. Cordage was the basic element of production, and was used for textiles and netting. One fragment of an open mesh bag or net was recovered from the lower cave deposits while other fabrics were made by simple twining. The

Guitarrero assemblage stands at the beginning of a major Andean tradition focused on fiber technology that later incorporated domesticated plants (cotton) and animals (alpaca), and made textiles extremely important to statecraft.

Fiber-plant debris at Guitarrero was large in comparison with food-plant remains. Tubers and rhizomes were a major source of carbohydrate, and oca and ulluco have tentatively been identified among the remains. A number of Andean fruits were represented, including lucuma (*Pouteria lucuma*), pacae (*Inga* sp.), *Solanum hispidum*, and *Trichocerus peruvianas*. Because these fruits and tubers are native to the general region, they may have been gathered wild, or they may have been tended. Excavations yielded a few specimens of domesticated common beans (*Phaseolus vulgaris*) and lima beans (*P. lunatus*) and one specimen of chile pepper (*Capsicum* sp.). The beans and pepper represent cultivated plants because they do not grow naturally in the region; rather, their wild range was probably the eastern slope of the Cordillera. To occur at the cave the plants must have been tended perhaps in small plots near the river. If people were cultivating foreign plants they may well have propagated the local fruits, tubers, or industrial plants also. The Guitarrero cultigens were sturdy ones that could be sown and left unattended while seasonal hunting and gathering was pursued elsewhere.

Guitarrero Cave was not the only place in the Andes where early plant tending transpired. In the headwaters of the Chilca drainage, at an altitude of 3,925 m, Tres Ventanas Cave produced tubers thought to be ulluco and potato also dated to about 10,000 years ago. Fragments of gourd (*Lagenaria siceraria*) of comparable or somewhat greater antiquity have been reported from cave deposits in the Ayacucho region. We need not pursue further evidence to say that domestication began at a remarkably early date in the Andes but it did not usher in an agricultural revolution. Plant and animal tending in the Cordillera served a secondary role, complementing other ways of making a living, for thousands of years before it played a primary role as an economic mainstay.

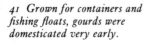

41 Grown for containers and fishing floats, gourds were domesticated very early.

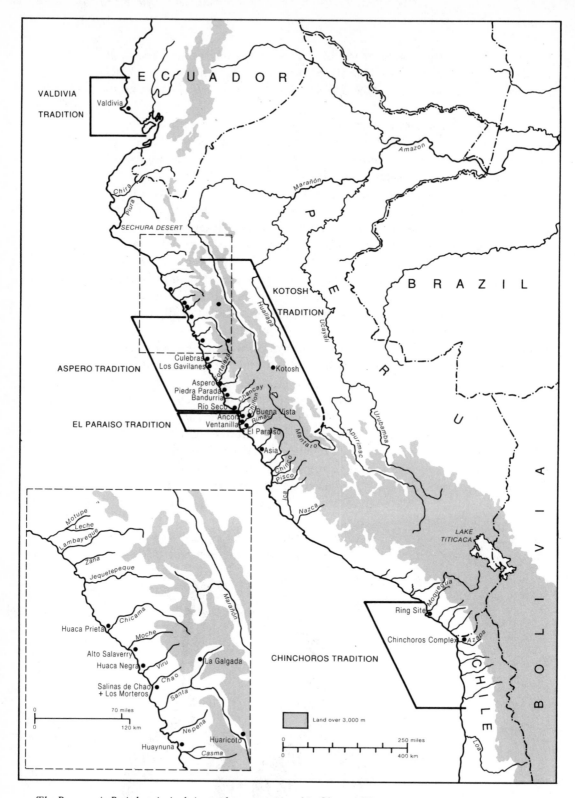

VALDIVIA
TRADITION

Valdivia

ECUADOR

Amazon

Chira

Piura

SECHURA DESERT

KOTOSH
TRADITION

BRAZIL

Marañón

Huallaga

Ucayali

ASPERO TRADITION

Culebras
Los Gavilanes

Aspero
Piedra Parada
Bandurria
Río Seco

Kotosh

Chancay

Chillón

Buena Vista

EL PARAISO TRADITION

Ancon
Ventanilla

Rimac

El Paraiso

Asia

Urubamba

Apurimac

Mantaro

P E R U

Chincha
Pisco

Ica

Nazca

B O L I V I A

LAKE
TITICACA

Motupe
Leche
Lambayeque

Zana

Jequetepeque

Marañón

Huaca Prieta

Chicama

Moche

Alto Salaverry
Huaca Negra

Viru

La Galgada

CHINCHOROS TRADITION

Moquegua

Ring Site

Chinchoros Complex

Azapa

Salinas de Chao
+ Los Morteros

Chao

Santa

Nepeña

Huaynuna

Huaricoto

Casma

C H I L E

Loa

0   70 miles
0   120 km

Land over 3,000 m

0   250 miles
0   400 km

42 *The Preceramic Period: principal sites and areas mentioned in Chapter Five.*

CHAPTER FIVE

The Preceramic Foundations of Civilization

Environmental change provides a convenient means of subdividing the long prepottery era into two periods: Lithic and Preceramic. The first coincides with the meltback of the last ice age. The second period begins with the end of glacial melting, when the environment entered its current regime, about 5,000 years ago. At this time sea levels stabilized near their modern heights, and marine and meteorological currents assumed their present configurations, as did ecological zones in the mountains. The survival of archaeological sites improved dramatically, providing fuller evidence of emerging civilization.

Dictionaries define civilization as a high stage of cultural development marked by advances in art, technology, and social conditions. I would add that these advances are underlain by beliefs that rationalize inequality and allow a minority to direct the activities of the majority. All ancient civilizations were based upon institutions that promoted integration, social fusion, and corporate unity. In the Andes, environmental diversity encouraged counter forces that fostered separation, fission, and autonomous activity, and thus ethnic heterogeneity. No doubt dialects, beliefs, customs and lifeways diverged during the Lithic Period. Therefore, tendencies for social fission evolved to counterbalance the formation of institutions forging organizational homogeneity.

Preceramic economies

Most authorities agree that civilization did not emerge before pottery came into use. Ceramics are broadly associated with societies that obtained most of their calories from farming. People in the tropical north and east began producing ceramics well before 3000 BC, but the use of pottery does not make its appearance in northern and central Peru until *c.* 1800 BC, and in the Titicaca Basin and northern Chile until *c.* 1400–1200 BC. If early pottery reflects reliance on agriculture, then both appeared latest in those settings most hostile to farming. In the central Andes, reliance on intensive agriculture was taken up along a two-fold path of least resistance. It came first to lower elevations where most cultigens grow well and later to high altitudes tolerated only by specialized domesticates. It also came first to self-watering lands where rainfall or seasonal inundation of river floodplains encourages plant growth. Later, canal irrigation opened dry land to agriculture, and only much later was

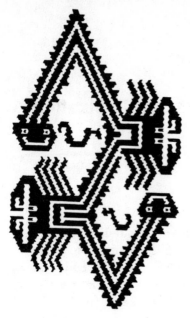

43 *The sea influenced the art and iconography of preceramic fisherfolk who depicted crabs and serpent-like fish or eels in this Huaca Prieta textile motif.*

irrigation combined with extensive terracing to reclaim steep, arid mountain slopes. Thus, the evolution of Andean agriculture was a long and arduous process.

On the coast people turned to marine resources early in the Lithic Period and then exploited the sea in ever greater numbers through preceramic times. The inability of the desert to sustain intensive agriculture without sizable irrigation systems restricted casual farming to river floodplains. In the sierra basins foragers of the Lithic Period depended on seasonal access to high grasslands. Access to the puna remained important, but growing reliance on cultivation caused sierra people to settle in lower elevations less hostile to plant tending. With larger populations living at mid-altitudes, mountain people were poised to begin exploiting still lower habitats, but true verticality adaptations awaited domestication of the llama.

Sierra uplands

As mountain populations decreased their dependence on wild resources and increased their reliance on cultivation, they were slowly drawn away from the higher elevations to lower settings where warmer temperature and milder conditions favored plant tending in the bottomlands of sierra drainages. A gradual downward shift in the locations of camps and residential sites is well documented during prepottery times in the quasi-tropical headwaters of the Río Zana, where the use of irrigation began at an early date. A parallel shift, perhaps a little later, is also evident in more arid drainages to the south, including the western Callejon de Huaylas and its eastern sierra counterparts formed by the headwaters of the Ríos Marañón and Huallaga.

In these mountain drainages the shared beliefs about ritual and special purpose architecture is called the Kotosh Religious Tradition. The type site of Kotosh, near modern Huanaco, is located on the bank of the Río Higueras, a tributary of the Huallaga river, at an elevation of *c.* 2,000 m. The climate is temperate and seasonal rainfall is limited but supports subtropical vegetation and scattered thorn trees. The site comprises two large platform mounds flanked by lesser constructions and a number of small structures on a nearby river terrace. Perhaps the twin mounds reflect moiety organization. With a basal diameter of almost 100 m, the largest mound was a mass of superimposed structures that reached a height of 8 m and reflected long building activity and ceremonial use. Deep trench excavations exposed ten superimposed constructions. The two lowest and earliest, called the Kotosh Mito Phase, are preceramic but lack radiocarbon dates. Subsistence remains included unidentified charred seeds, domesticated guinea pig, deer antler, and bones of camelids that may have been hunted or herded. Hunting is indicated by a chipped-stone industry with leaf-shaped points similar to those found in the Lauricocha caves. Crops could have been tended along the nearby river, or by irrigation, but there is no surviving evidence of cultivated plants. There are indirect suggestions that higher and lower ecological zones were exploited, perhaps adumbrating verticality adaptations. The camelid remains suggest hunting or herding in the puna. The mid-range elevation of Kotosh afforded access to lower habitats along the Amazon tributaries. The site produced ground stone axes that are typically Amazonian, and when pottery appeared at Kotosh it had many lowland characteristics.

Ornamental products from high and low altitudes have been found at the site of La Galgada, a complex of two ceremonial mounds and surrounding dwellings in the Callejon de Huaylas on the east bank of the Río Tablachaca, a major tributary of the Santa River. The drainage forms an east–west corridor for crossing the Cordillera and La Galgada is located at midpoint *c*. 80 km from the Pacific coast and an equal distance from the tropical reaches of the Río Marañón. The arid Tablachaca Canyon cuts through a highland plateau and the site lies at 1,100 m, below the elevation of seasonal rainfall. The architectural complex includes two large platforms and several smaller ones, plus numerous other small structures. Consisting of a mass of superimposed buildings, the largest mound has produced dates between 2200 and 1200 BC and is associated with preceramic and early ceramic occupations. Cultivated plants included beans, squash, fruits, chili peppers, gourd, and a great deal of cotton. Irrigation was needed to grow the plants and nearby remains of ancient canals are thought to be of preceramic origin.

The excavators of La Galgada believe the economy was based on more than farming, and see the site as a hub for the movement of goods between distant habitats. Funerary objects included marine shell beads and disks of coastal origins, as well as finely fashioned pins and ornaments of bone. There were also colorful feathers that may have come from Amazonian birds. It is unclear from evidence thus far uncovered at the site whether these foreign products were obtained by exchange, or by direct collection from the coast and Marañón. However, the foreign items are small and light because pack animals had yet to enter the economy.

Kotosh and La Galgada provide but fleeting glimpses of preceramic economies in the sierra uplands. At the same time vital developments were taking place within and without the Titicaca Basin. Cave sites in the grasslands above the altitudinal limits of farming continued to be occupied as herding gradually replaced hunting, but evidence of the processes that later linked puna herding and sierra farming to produce agropastoralism remains elusive for this early period.

Desert coast

After the appearance of pottery coastal civilization involved a close association of fishing and farming. Irrigation transformed the desert valleys into high-yielding oases, but only after the sea had long supported large numbers of people. In the late 1960s several American and Soviet scholars independently concluded that the 'neolithic revolution' could be initiated by more than one type of economy, and they proposed a maritime hypothesis for the coast. The theory holds that exceptionally rich, easily accessible marine resources provided preceramic people sufficient calories for sedentary residence, population growth, formation of large communities, and the rise of complex societies capable of building large architectural monuments.

Cold upwelling currents make the Peruvian coasts the richest fishery in the western hemisphere, but also create a temperature inversion which creates the world's driest coastal desert. Whereas all the littoral waters can be fished, very little of the desert can be farmed. Even with the largest irrigation systems in the Cordillera less than 10 per cent of the coast is arable; and self-watering river floodplains are few. The construction, maintenance, and use of coastal irrigation systems entail multitudes of corporately organized people. Conversely, the fishery is most efficiently exploited by net-harvesting from small craft with small crews. By 1970 Peru earned far greater foreign revenues from anchoveta fishmeal than from those mechanized coastal plantations that focused on international export crops. The reason is that commercial yields of anchoveta averaged 100 metric tons per year per square kilometer over the 2,000 km length of the near-shore fishery. The anchovy harvest alone could sustain more than six million people. Near the northern end of the anchovy belt, around 8°, 11°, and 15° South Latitude, there are fishery 'hot spots', called productivity maxima, with yields of 1,000 tons per square kilometer per year. It is significant that very large preceramic monuments only occur along the 600 km stretch of shoreline bracketed by these hot spots. Thus, the most complex maritime societies arose where the fishery was at its richest.

Dietary evidence. The coastal diet of transitional Lithic–Preceramic Period times has received intense scrutiny at Paloma, a small settlement behind San Bartolo Bay 15 km north of the Chilca drainage. Situated adjacent to lomas vegetation *c.* 4 km in from the littoral zone, the 15-hectare occupation area comprises thin, scattered middens with radiocarbon dates between 6,500 and 5,000 years ago, bracketing three phases of occupation. Initially Paloma served as a seasonal camp for relatively mobile people. Their descendants then became fully sedentary as economic conditions improved during the two subsequent phases. Over the course of time the local population may have averaged between 30 and 40 individuals. The Palomans lived in circular dome-shaped houses, more than 50 examples of which have been excavated. Providing about 11 sq. m of floor space, the structures were built in shallow, flat-bottomed pits roughly 40 cm deep. Cane was used as wall supports and reeds and grass as thatch. Over the span of one and a half millennia, many people died at Paloma and the larger midden is estimated to contain about 900 burials. The dead were interred in shallow pits in house floors and most structures held a number of burials that can be reasonably interpreted as family members of the same household. Keeping the deceased in their dwellings would later culminate with the mummified emperors of Chimor and Tahuantinsuyu being retained in their palaces. The ancient Palomans salted corpses to check deterioration, and the typical burial was placed on its side with the knees drawn up to the chest and the hands held in the pelvic or facial region. Most corpses were wrapped in a twined mat of reeds and apart from fragments of twined clothing, burial goods were scarce, most often accompanying men.

Well-preserved middens included plant and animal remains as well as bone fish-hooks and fragments of fish-nets. Mollusks, large fish, sea birds, and sea mammals are well represented, but the faunal remains are dominated by bones of small fish including anchovies and sardines. Small fish bones are the primary constituent of human feces at the site, but small seeds from wild grass were also present. Detailed analysis of the more than 200 burials by Robert Benfer, a physical anthropologist, also revealed this dietary dominance of small fish, and the ear structures of males reveals a high incidence of osseous damage caused by diving in cold water. Finally, chemical analysis of the bone showed exceptionally low levels of strontium, indicating a remarkably high protein component to the diet that must have come from the sea. Initially males consumed more protein than females, but this difference diminished over time. As the people of Paloma shifted to a sedentary way of life they enjoyed increased life expectancy. The physical stature of adults increased, while the incidence of anemia among children decreased. The community experienced growth in population. At the same time Palomans apparently sought to control their numbers by social means, including later marriage to delay the age of reproducing and disposing of new-born baby girls – female infanticide. Female diet and infanticide reflect sexual discrimination and inequalities. While female protein consumption improved over time, some individuals and some families continued to enjoy better diet than others, clear indication that at Paloma everyone was not equal.

Although not abundant, remains of cultivated plants, including squash, beans and gourds, were found in the midden and must have been sown in the Chilca stream bed after its annual flooding. Traces of squash and beans have also been found in the stomach contents of some burials. The presence of domesticates was predictable given the great antiquity of plant tending in the Andes and it was also expected because there is good evidence that the

Palomans were in contact with distant areas where farming was becoming important. This evidence includes obsidian from the highlands, a tropical forest monkey, no doubt kept as a pet, and a *Spondylus* shell from Ecuador.

Farming was not more important to the people of Paloma and their preceramic successors because early cultivation was limited by a lack of the technology needed to grow suitable plants in quantity using extensive large canal systems. We could also ask, if fishing could adequately feed people, why farm? Although the Paloma population depended on marine foods, their inland residence adjacent to lomas vegetation is a basic reminder of the importance of terrestrial resources. The rich Andean fishery can sustain multitudes, but it does not yield cooking fuel, nor provide clothes and shelter. Neither does it supply fiber for fishing line and netting, net floats nor materials for watercraft. Thus terrestrial resources provide the infrastructure for successful fishing, because the marine- and land-based components of littoral economies were interdependent and change in one could effect changes in the other.

The Paloma data indicate a decrease in the size of firewood over time and point to deteriorating lomas conditions, either from over-exploitation or from natural causes. When plant communities sustained by coastal fogs gradually failed local demands, the pressure to develop alternative resources may have attracted people to the narrow ribbons of wild vegetation growing along seasonal streams and rivers, and thus to a setting conducive to plant tending. Contemporary with the later phases of Paloma, a community of very similar nature, called Chilca I, arose on the banks of the Chilca stream bed about 3 km inland. During the occupation 5,500–4,500 years ago, people collected or tended junco reeds (*Cyperus* sp.), gourds and perhaps beans. If fisherfolk were increasing their reliance on wild and cultivated plants over time then the flood plains of streams and rivers must have assumed growing importance.

Feeding more people. The Paloma and Chilca occupations reflect growing numbers of people, and over time early littoral communities expanded in size and number along the coast. Feeding this growing population was sustained by increasing maritime yields, done in several ways. In Chile, Chinchoros diversified their fishing technology, and used different types of tackle to bring in a wider range of marine life. Along the fishery hot spots of Peru, preceramic populations intensified their technology and focused on producing more nets and small craft to bring in greater harvests of small fish. By 2000 BC fragments of net with small mesh for capturing small fish represent the most ubiquitous tackle found at littoral communities. Increasing marine yields to support increasing populations required the production of ever greater amounts of net, line, floats, and watercraft and eventually wild plants alone could not accommodate the expansion, so people began to grow the necessary plants for their equipment. In Peru the period between 3000 and 1800 BC is often called the 'Cotton Preceramic Period' because this plant becomes ubiquitous at littoral settlements. It is a time when archaeological specimens of edible

44 *An enduring tradition of embellishing gourd containers with incised designs made its first appearance at Huaca Prieta.*

domesticates are far outnumbered by the remains of industrial cultigens: cotton for net, line, and textiles; gourd for floats and containers; and reeds for watercraft and mats.

Coastal adaptations were affected by variations in marine resources. North of the Río Santa upwelling currents and the anchovy belt veer far out to sea as the shoreline becomes one of sandy beaches. In this region, at the mouth of the Río Chicama, lies the preceramic type site of Huaca Prieta, excavated in 1946 by Junius Bird. Here the residents tended beans, squash, fruits, the root crop achira (*Canna edulis*), and capsicum peppers, as well as many industrial cultigens. Seafood was the principal component of human feces and came largely from net-fishing and mollusk-collecting.

Hook and line tackle was not found at Huaca Prieta because it is associated with fishing from rocky promontories, not sandy beaches. South of the Río Santa mountains push out into the sea, creating a broken coastline with long stretches of rocky headlands framing desert bays or sandy beaches at valley mouths. Dangerous for watercraft, the headlands plunge into deep waters inhabited by larger fish that can be taken by hook and line from the shore. In addition to supporting abundant rock-perching invertebrates, the headlands provide nesting for millions of marine birds, as well as breeding grounds for sea-lions and marine mammals. Easily approached at night and dispatched with clubs, prodigious quantities of headland game were consumed by early fisherfolk.

Resources are different along the sandy shores of protected bays, where women and children collected clams and seaweed. Here, casting hook and line beyond the surf is difficult, but launching watercraft to fish by net fishing is not dangerous, and small fish school in the bays on a regular basis. As part of the process of increasing maritime yields preceramic populations gradually moved off rocky headlands and settled along sandy stretches of the coast in ever greater numbers. Thus, the largest littoral communities and the biggest preceramic mounds arose in settings favorable for net fishing.

Plant foods. Edible plants grow in the sea and they have been consumed for generations. North of Lima on the edge of the now dry Ventanilla Bay, excavations at the small preceramic midden of Camino indicate that it was a specialized site. Net fishing was practiced, but the primary activity centered on collecting and processing kelp seaweed. Air bladders, plant stems, and root holdfasts were found in exceptional quantities, but kelp leaves – the edible portion of the algae – were rare. In addition to marine flora, coastal preceramic populations consumed cattail roots, and other wild plants, as well as cultivated plants.

It seems that maritime people favored domesticated plants that could grow with little care and not interfere with fishing. Cultivated plants represented by high frequencies of unusable and inedible plant parts occur in coastal midden sites far from rivers, indicating that after harvesting in river floodplains the crops were carried back to shore-line communities where they were processed and the waste discarded. Some communities were closer to riverside land than others and this probably contributed to the marked variation in food plants found at different sites. Variation may also reflect differences in outside contacts. *Zea* maize has its only littoral occurrence at a few preceramic sites in a desert pocket bounded by the Ríos Culebras and Supe. Here it may have reached the coast from the adjacent sierra. Maritime communities at Ventanilla and Ancon Bays, north of Lima, produced limited evidence of interaction with sierra populations in the form of comestible tubers that included three specimens of oca (*Oxalis tuberosa*), two of ulluco (*Ullucus tuberosus*), and one of so-called white potato (*Solanum* sp.). These highland cultigens could not grow or would not do well on the coast and perhaps were exchanged for marine products such as the seaweed processed at Camino. Evidence of economic interaction with sierra is important because it is to the highlands that we must look for the early development of the irrigation technology that would open the desert valleys to intensive agriculture.

The Tank Site at Ancon Bay has stratigraphic deposits that bracket the close of the preceramic Gaviota Phase and the introduction of pottery and new agricultural products. Here basal strata produced abundant industrial cultigens, plus peppers, guava fruit, beans and squash. Overlying preceramic strata included the addition of lucuma (a fruit) and half a dozen tubers, including sweet potatoes (*Ipomea batatas*). A marked increase in tubers is associated with the first ceramics – 18 sherds. The next stratum, with 415 sherds dating to *c.* 1750 BC, produced even more abundant root crops and fruit, as well as peanuts (*Arachis hypogaea*) and *Pacae* fruit. The Tank Site is more than 25 km from the Río Chillon, and a fishing economy persisted here, while other people began farming the desert valleys. Whereas early maritime sites contain debris from processing crops after harvest, this type of evidence tends to disappear with the advent of pottery and irrigation, indicating that littoral populations now obtained processed plant foods from agriculturalists, and that fishing and farming were separate ways of life.

Social formations

Some authorities estimate that maritime societies on the central coast experienced a 30-fold increase in their numbers during the Preceramic Period. Estimates vary, but populations certainly grew in the sierra as well. There were probably more small, scattered homesteads than large centers such as Kotosh or La Galgada. Littoral resources may have supported larger residential aggregates and by late preceramic times fisherfolk lived in moderate-sized communities spaced along the coast at intervals of around 10 km or so.

There were some very sizable maritime communities, such as Río Seco, situated in the desert behind a sandy beach, 10 km north of the Río Chancay. The occupation covered 11.8 ha, where 1–1.5 m accumulation of dense refuse was interspersed with compacted floors of small dwellings which were probably mat or thatch covered. The deceased were interred within the area of occupation. The total mortuary population is estimated with considerable certainty at 2,500 to 3,000 individuals. Río Seco also has twin platform mounds 2 to 3 m high, providing circumstantial evidence for dual organization.

Erecting platform mounds required corporate organization and a chain of command with positions of authority that allowed a minority of individuals to direct the activities of the majority. In the context of dual organization, the chain of command would be ranked and two-fold. I suspect that corporate authority and decision-making was vested in offices similar to those of 'cargo systems', in which capable individuals rotate through a formal hierarchy of leadership positions, rather than in karaka rule because there is little mortuary evidence of an élite class or of chiefs who inherited their offices.

Early mortuary practices indicate that everyone was not equal, but this is expected where there is dual organization and lineages of different status. Infant mortality was high and the very young were frequently disposed of without grave goods in shallow pits scattered randomly through middens. It seems that children had to live for a certain length of time before they were formally recognized as social beings. Older juveniles and adults generally went to the grave with at least a cloth garment and a mat wrapping. People were buried both in areas of occupation and in separate exterior cemeteries, and three times as many males as females were interred within the occupation areas of the Asia site near the Olmos drainage and at the Culebras site adjacent to the Río Culebras. This might reflect female infanticide, as at Paloma, or perhaps that ancestor veneration entailed keeping male kin closer at hand. Other evidence of social discrimination at Asia is in the form of eight severed heads, all mat wrapped and accompanied by textiles and additional items. These remains appear to be an expression of the 'trophy head cult', which involved the ritual *Plate 21* display of crania and persisted in modified form among tropical Jivaro peoples

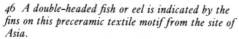

45 *Condors descend to the coast to feed upon fish and inspired this Huaca Prieta textile motif.*

46 *A double-headed fish or eel is indicated by the fins on this preceramic textile motif from the site of Asia.*

famous for shrinking the heads of their adversaries. Finally, social bias at Asia is also evident in the distribution of 133 cloth accompaniments among 28 normal interments. Most individuals had two to four textile offerings, but a few individuals received two to three times the norm. The person receiving the most fabrics, 12, also had gourd containers, bone tools, wood tubes, a sling, a slate tablet, a comb, and other goods. This unusually rich grave was that of a young male who may have achieved high status either through personal deeds or by being born to a prosperous family.

Arts

Developed arts are another criteria of civilization, and preceramic people laid enduring aesthetic foundations. Prepottery media included stone, shell, bone, baked clay, gourd, wood, basketry, bark cloth, and fabrics. Textiles were by far the most important. From garments to wraps and bags, textiles served many purposes and are a prevalent artifact at preceramic sites. People lived in, sat and slept on, and went to the grave in twined mats of reed. At Huaca Prieta, La Galgada and elsewhere, twined baskets and looped satchels of reeds and sedges fulfilled the need for containers, as did gourd vessels; but the greatest time and care was lavished upon twined textiles of cotton. Twining with spaced wefts and exposed warps was the most common construction technique, but looping, knotting, and simple weaving were also employed.

Plates 20,21   The lattice-like structure of the fabrics imparted geometric undertones to the arts, which have an angular quality, emphasizing symmetry and interlocking elements. The roster of design elements falls into two classes – abstract and representational. Stripes, diamonds, squares, and chevrons make up the former, and occur individually, as repetitions, and in combinations making up more complex patterns. Representational designs depict people, birds, serpents, crabs, fish, and other animals. When used individually such

47 Double-headed 'serpent' motifs persisted in Paracas textiles and later coastal arts.

motifs are often repetitive and interlocking. They also appear in compositions showing several creatures. Frequently attributes of two animals are combined to form composite beings. In one case, perhaps showing the heraldic overtones of an insignia, a large bird, perhaps a condor, with spread wings is depicted from the front, while on the chest or in the stomach a spotted serpent or elongated fish is shown. In other cases, artisans crafted preternatural beings. One Huaca Prieta fabric depicts a double-headed serpent with a pair of rock-crabs appended to its elongated body. A double-headed bird with a serpentine body was engraved on the cap of a gourd bowl.

Double-headed serpents and birds, and composite beings with animal, avian, reptilian or invertebrate features persist into later Andean arts. As with griffins and unicorns, these composite creatures were surrounded by lore and beliefs that made the iconography intelligible to the general populace, and preceramic motifs were the building blocks of symbolic communication that came to dominate the later corporate styles.

Monumental architecture

During preceramic times the largest architectural monuments in the hemisphere were erected on the desert coast and in the adjacent sierra of the central Andes. These corporate works are called ceremonial facilities because they were settings for formal activities and ritual observances. They were probably both civic and religious in nature and the seats of cargo–like systems of administration.

By the third millennium BC distinct forms of ceremonial buildings crystallized in tropical, sierra, and desert settings. In the forested north, Ecuadorian populations using Valdivia pottery and relying on farming often resided in houses arranged around an oval or circular central plaza. Within plazas they built two types of oval, dome-shaped structures atop low mounds of piled-up earth. One type, called the 'Fiesta' house served feasting and drinking, and has ethnographic analogies with the 'Men's' house in tropical communities. 'Charnel' houses, the other type, were used in the preparation of corpses for secondary burial. The modest size of the plaza houses suggests that they were built and used by local villagers who lived around them.

In the central Cordillera some preceramic ceremonial centers drew labor and participation from many different settlements while others were local undertakings of individual communities. Early Peruvian centers were frequently built of distinctive materials to differentiate them from mundane buildings, and were also distinguished by being kept very clean. In the arid environment roofs were generally restricted to small structures and a great deal of ritual activity transpired in open courts. There was a long-standing concern with demarcating entryways and passages, culminating in the elaborate gateways at later centers such as Chavín de Huantar and Tiwanaku. Concern with the sanctity of entrances cross-cut the different traditions of ceremonial architecture that arose on the coast and in the mountains, traditions also cross-cut by manners of construction and by beliefs about sunken courts.

Platforms. Due to their size and solid nature, platform mounds are the most common and conspicuous of preceramic corporate works. They reflect the basic notion that elevation conferred status and segregated extraordinary from ordinary space. Perhaps mounds were meant to emulate mountains. On the coast and in the sierra preceramic platform mounds exhibit a number of recurrent canons. With isolated exceptions, there are always two or more platforms of different size at a site, expressing pluralism within pantheons and within the constructing societies. Where there are only two mounds, as at Río Seco, La Galgada and Kotosh, propositions of dual organization are reasonable. What greater numbers mean is open to question, but distinctions in size and elaboration point to differences in status. Many platforms began as ground level buildings and rooms that were later filled in to create an artificial eminence. Final size was always a product of 'temple interment' entailing multiple construction stages interspersed with periods of maintenance and use.

In Chapter Three, we reviewed the fact that Andean people keep very close account of their labor when working on group or corporate undertakings. Creating a mound by burying earlier buildings required substantial quantities of architectural fill. Rather than midden, freshly quarried rock was the preferred fill, and rubble was hauled from quarries in large open mesh satchels called *shicra*, made of coarse sturdy reeds and capable of holding as much as 26 kg of stone. At the construction site the bag was not emptied, but rather satchel and fill were deposited intact. This conferred no apparent engineering benefits and used up multitudes of bags, but reflects the segmentation of corporate work into repetitive tasks, and provided a means of accounting for labor expenditures.

Preceramic platforms on the coast were rectangular, while in the sierra corners were often rounded, later leading to more oval shapes. Mounds were both free-standing and banked against hill slopes. When banked they could rise as a single eminence, or one structure could be stacked behind another to form a larger terraced platform. The inclined sides of mounds were faced with rounded boulders or angular quarry stone set in mud mortar. The masonry was sometimes tiered or stepped and often plastered with adobe, increasingly so after ceramics came into use.

The most obvious feature of early platform mounds is that they were designed with ritual display in mind. There was a vertical spatial hierarchy in which platform summits were occupied by walled structures, including courts and smaller rooms that could accommodate relatively few participants. Access was by a central flight of stairs or by a ramp that could be recessed into the mound, or project slightly outward. Generally spacious, the stairs or ramp very likely served as stages for ritual display to the multitudes assembled in forecourts in front of the mounds. In the summit buildings, however, the ritual activities were hidden from the masses in the courts below. On terraced platforms, higher courts were smaller than lower ones and the basal forecourts were largest. Thus, there was an elevational progression to the numbers of people that mounds accommodated, with few on top and many at the bottom. It took far larger numbers to build platforms than could fit on their terraces and summits and we may conclude that hierarchical accommodations related to differences in status.

Sunken courts. In the Andes vertical discrimination of space was three-fold. It included ground level or neutral planes, elevated or positive planes represented by platform mounds, and pits or negative planes represented by sunken courts. Most sunken courts had two aligned flights of steps on opposite sides, one for descent and the other for ascent. Thus, they were designed for ritual procession into and out of negative space. The earliest sunken courts are circular and occur in preceramic contexts in central and northern Peru. In ceramic times there was

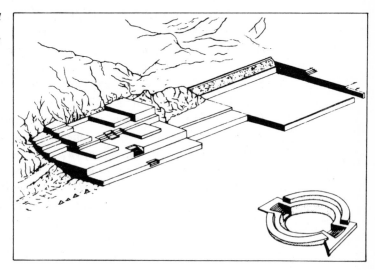

48 The circular sunken court and terraced platform at Salinas de Chao are aligned in this idealized reconstruction.

a transition from circular to rectangular forms at Chavín de Huantar in the sierra. Rectangular sunken courts then persist in the Lake Titicaca region until the demise of Tiwanaku. Because the architectural history of sunken structures spans at least three millennia it is evident that ancient Andeans developed and maintained important and persistent notions about recessed ceremonial planes.

In coastal preceramic contexts a small circular sunken court was found alone without other monumental architecture at the Alto Salavery maritime community in the Moche Valley, but more often courts were positioned directly in front of platform mounds, as at La Galgada. Initial Period examples also occur on platform wings and in lateral positions. Later, in the Titicaca region, sunken rectangular courts most often occur atop elevated platforms. Thus, because sunken courts occurred in variable contexts that cross-cut regional fashions in ceremonial architecture we may infer that they were associated with a set of beliefs or a cult that cross-cut religious traditions.

The emphasis on sunken sacrosanct space brings to mind Andean origin myths in which humanity ascends from an inner world to the outer world that it now occupies. Perhaps the pits were places for re-enacting the dawn of creation when people emerged from the inner earth through caves, springs, and holes in the ground. Alternatively sunken courts might pertain to the widespread reverence of Pacha Mama, mother earth. When pits occur in front of platforms the stairways of both structures are generally aligned, indicating that ritual processions moved in a linear manner from the neutral surface of land level, to the negative plane of the sunken court, to the positive plane above it. One must wonder if this was not a cosmological pathway from the earth's interior to the heavens above.

The Kotosh Tradition

In the northern highlands, preceramic ceremonial architecture emphasized discrete, one-room buildings. Kotosh is the type locality for these widely used chambers, which varied in form and elaboration with the circumstances and prosperity of the people who built and used them. The structures were often limited to their bare essentials, as at the site of Huaricoto, and allow us to recognize their most important features. Situated in the Callejon de Huaylas at an elevation of 2,750 m, Huaricoto was used for two millennia as a ritual center by people who erected many chambers but few larger works. Here detached, small one-room structures with a single entry, a carefully plastered floor, and a central hearth were the most elemental of sanctuaries. Exhibiting intense use, hearths were heavily burned, often replastered and remodeled, while clay floors were kept clean and in good repair. These essential features indicate that the sanctuaries were designed for secluded, private rituals, to accommodate small congregations – probably kindred – and focused on rituals relating to fire and burnt offerings. Remains of marine shell and animal bones were recovered from one of the latest hearths at Huaricoto, but the nature of earlier burnt offerings is mysterious. Preceramic refuse outside the chambers included bones of deer and large camelids, probably guanaco, as well as sea shells and fish bones from coastal contacts. Although a number of chambers were in use simultaneously, many sanctuaries were not intended for prolonged service because their walls were made of wattle and daub, which fares poorly under seasonal rainfall.

Beginning about 2260 BC and extending into Chavín times, the Huaricoto chambers evolved along lines characterized as much by variation as by standardization. Nonetheless, a relatively standardized form of sanctuary emerged at other preceramic sites and at Huaricoto following the introduction of ceramics. Rectangular or square in form these chambers were of masonry with an entry that could be tightly closed. Plastered floors were split-level: a higher surface created a wide bench for an audience, surrounding a recessed rectangular floor housing the central hearth. Outside air was fed to the fire by a slab-lined ventilator which passed beneath the bench to the chamber exterior, thereby allowing the sanctuary to be sealed during ceremonies.

Preceramic Mito Phase construction at Kotosh saw the initial construction of twin platform mounds that were terraced with wide tiers, and episodes of use and renewed building extended into the Initial Period. The platform terraces and summits were surmounted by numerous chambers that define the Kotosh ceremonial tradition. The most elaborate preceramic chamber of standardized form was uncovered on the middle terrace of the larger platform. Measuring about 9 m on a side and built of cobbles set in mud mortar, this sanctuary had thick, plastered walls with rows of ornamental niches inside. The wall opposite the entry had a central, over-sized niche flanked by smaller niches. Below each of the two smaller niches there were clay friezes depicting sets of human arms crossed at the wrists, causing the excavators to dub this the 'Temple of the Crossed Hands'. Mitos people later filled in this structure to elevate the underlying platform, and then erected a similar chamber, the 'Temple of the Niches', which had ornamental wall recesses but no friezes. It is noteworthy that niches and friezes make their appearance in the sierra and on the coast in preceramic times and persist into Inca times as symbols of high status architecture.

Situated in the Río Santa drainage, La Galgada is the best preserved of the early sierra ceremonial centers, and one of the most elaborate. There are two substantial mounds at the site, each supporting a Kotosh-type chamber. Oval in shape, the larger platform was faced with fine masonry and fronted by a circular sunken court. Mound construction began before 2200 BC, and periods of use were interspersed with more than three episodes of enlargement in subsequent centuries. Sanctuaries on the platforms also had rounded corners imparting an oval shape. The well-built structures were of stone set in mud mortar, then clay plastered, painted pearly white, and always ornamented with rows of symmetrically arranged interior niches. Roofs of logs were capped with clay. Each sanctuary had a single narrow entrance generally opening to the west, the front of the mound. A horizontal ventilator shaft passed beneath the door to feed a single hearth centrally positioned on the lower surface of a split-level floor or floor and bench arrangement. White, orange, and green downy feathers of tropical birds and deer antlers were encountered on some floors.

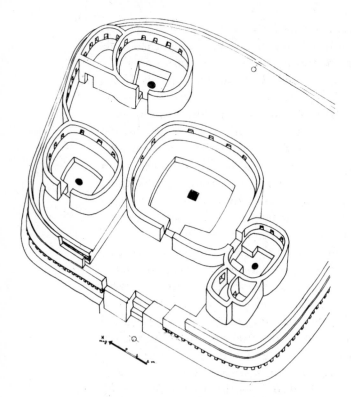

49 *The isometric view of mound-top chambers at La Galgada reconstructs the hearths, benches, and niched walls of the ritual sanctuaries but not their roofs.*

Plant remains, particularly chili peppers, were found in firepits. Burnt offerings of chili would certainly have brought tears to the eyes of the ritual participants!

It is noteworthy that after serving the living, these chambers served the dead as tomb vaults before being filled in and covered by later construction phases. Men, women, and children, with a variety of offerings, were placed in the vaults and interred in the underlying mound. The mortuary component at La Galgada seems to be a local innovation added to the Kotosh tradition, and represents an important transformation in the use of ceremonial architecture. Presumably the sanctuaries were erected as huacas adoratorios for the adoration of metaphysical powers, and their subsequent use as crypts, possibly ancestral shrines, adumbrates the later practice of building sacrosanct structures specifically designed as huacas sepulturas.

Ceramics make their appearance during the two final episodes of platform construction at Galgada, and they are associated with significant changes in architecture and art, including the introduction of heddle loom weaving. The first episode of Initial Period building saw a reorganization of summit space on the platform. The mound top was now dominated by a single, centrally placed structure comprising a large rectangular chamber with an over-sized fire basin. An adjacent mound suggests a similar transformation. The enlarged central chambers were capable of accommodating audiences of 50 or more and thus mark a shift from compartmentalized private rituals to larger, more integrated ones. Unique to La Galgada was the late construction of internal galleries to house burials. This phase was also associated with a slate and shell mosaic disk depicting a feline in a manner similar to much later Chavín art.

An even bolder transformation transpired with the final phase of construction, when the summit assumed a U-shaped configuration with three elevated platforms surrounding a lower central court opening to the front of the mound. The court lacked a hearth but could accommodate a much larger audience than any of the previous structures. The last two construction phases at La Galgada produced radiocarbon ages falling between 1700 and 1200 BC.

The Aspero Tradition

During the second and third millennia BC the largest architectural monuments on the continent were erected along the arid coast between the Ríos Chao and Chillon. Preceramic sites with noteworthy corporate works include El Paraiso, Río Seco, Bandurria near the Huara Valley, Piedra Parada and Aspero in the Supe drainage, Culebras and Huaynuna near Casma, and Salinas de Chao and Los Morteros near the Río Chao. With the exception of El Paraiso, the coastal monuments can be assigned to the Aspero Tradition of ceremonial architecture, which emphasized flat-topped mounds as stages of ritual display for large audiences assembled in front of the platforms. This is a more public-oriented doctrine of ceremonialism than that in the Kotosh Tradition of small private chambers. Yet, other than platforms of variable form, the Aspero Tradition is not defined by many other standardized architectural features.

The platforms at Río Seco, Bandurria, Culebras and Huaynuna are associated with midden deposits and domestic remains of sufficient size to suggest that the monuments could well represent corporate undertakings executed by their local communities. This is more questionable for Salinas de Chao and Los Morteros, where big populations are less evident. In the case of El Paraiso there are few indications of large residential populations, implying that the monuments were built by people who lived elsewhere, thus initiating the emergence of corporate institutions that integrated multiple communities. This raises the probability that some sites, such as Aspero itself, by combining large populations as well as numerous sizable monuments, may have drawn support from and served both resident and non-resident populations.

With half a dozen large mounds surrounded by 15 ha of dark midden, Aspero occupies a shallow basin surrounded by hills that jut into the sea at the north end of a long sandy beach formed by the mouth of the Supe Valley. The valley margin in front of the settlement is swampy today and would have been suitable for tending reeds and providing potable water from shallow wells. Max Uhle discovered the complex in 1905, noting that 'from a distance, the settlement appears black, like an old foundry site.' Dark midden with a high carbon content is typical of many preceramic maritime settlements and makes them stand out. The large platforms are more subtle because they were made of stone and orange-colored fill quarried from the nearby hills, which they resemble.

In addition to 11 smaller mounds each 1 to 2 m high, the site has 6 major platforms. The free-standing mounds range up to more than 4 m in height, and to over 10 m where the structures were banked against or set upon hills. Alignments varied within a 20° angle, with some platforms facing out into the valley and others back into the basin. Flanking the mounds, low terraces, with and without stone facing, were used to define an assortment of court and patio areas, and some terraces may have served as residential areas. Excavations by Robert Feldman focused on two of the larger mounds, Huacas Idolos and Sacrificios. Huaca de los Sacrificios was a free-standing platform and excavations on the summit were limited to the last phases of construction and use, which produced radiocarbon assays that averaged to 2857 BC. Basal dates would certainly be earlier and construction of this huaca probably began and ended earlier than at other mounds. Many of the walls were built of basaltic blocks rather than of rounded boulders. Some exhibited 'H' type masonry, in which long blocks were stood up to form the uprights of the letter H and smaller stones were laid horizontally between them. This method also occurs in other preceramic and early ceramic ceremonial structures. Ascent to the huaca summit was by an eastern stairway that led to a large entry court flanked by an irregular grouping of smaller compartments. In the center of the court lay a hemispherical fire pit about 50 cm across and 25 cm deep. It showed repeated use, both by multiple ash layers and by several replasterings of the interior walls, which were burnt to a light-orange color. Perhaps burnt offerings were made in the hearth, which produced charcoal dated to 2533 BC.

Huaca de los Sacrificios derives its name from the two burials, an infant and an adult, that were found 3.5 m apart on the same floor level of a summit compartment. The poorly preserved adult corpse was very tightly flexed and some joints may have been cut to force the body into a cramped position. At one time the individual was either bound or wrapped with cloth and the only accompaniment was a broken gourd. This contrasts with the two-month old infant, which was slightly flexed and placed on its right side facing west. The head was covered with a cap or hat adorned by 500 shell, plant, and clay beads and the body was completely wrapped in a cotton textile. Along with a gourd bowl, the bundle was placed in a basket, which was itself textile wrapped. A cane mat was rolled around the bundle and tied with strips of white cloth. This

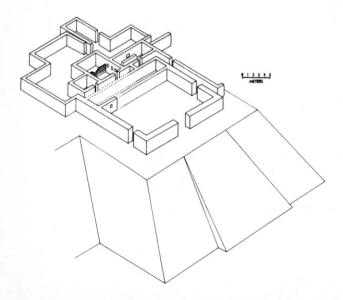

50 A summit entry court on Huaca de los Idolos leads to the interior compartments without roofs. In one room an altar-like bench sat in front of a wall niche. Another room with niches was partitioned by a low wall with a frieze of horizontal adobe bands.

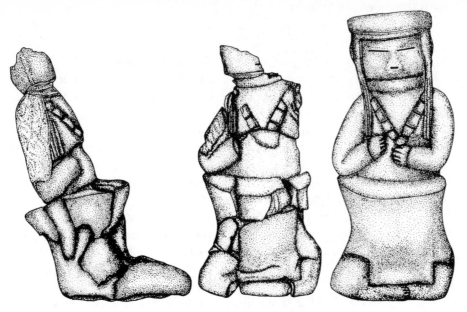

51 Figurines of unbaked clay were deliberately broken and buried at Huaca de los Idolos. This fragmentary figure, 16 cm tall, is shown in side, front, and reconstructed view.

was placed on the ground with two large pieces of cotton cloth wadded together. The assemblage was then covered with an inverted basin carved from stone. The stone basin is one of the finest preceramic objects ever found. Carefully crafted from a single boulder, it has four legs, stood 9 cm high and measured 38 × 44 cm. The upper surface had been used for grinding and traces of red pigment adhered to the inner lip. The infant burial was obviously one of exceptional importance.

Perched against a small hill, Huaca de los Idolos is one of the higher platforms. Summit structures cover an area of 20 × 30 m. Feldman's excavations penetrated the upper third of the platform revealing only its later architectural history, and which produced radiocarbon dates of 2558 and 3055 BC. Three major construction stages were identified. From ground level, a wide slightly projecting ramp led to the summit and to the gateway of a high-walled entry court. This spacious reception area was the largest summit structure, and smaller courts and rooms were irregularly arranged behind it. The most important of these was a centrally located compartment, measuring *c.* 4 × 5 m, on the main axis of the platform. Each interior wall had a row of three small rectangular niches at chest level and the niched compartment was, unusually, subdivided by a thin wall, faced with a geometric adobe frieze consisting of horizontal bands of raised plaster. The ornamented wall had a distinctive 'T' shaped central doorway that was wider at the top than at the bottom. Another important summit structure abutted the north side of the niched court, and was reached by a separate hallway system. On the rear wall, aligned with the single entry, there was a single recessed niche. The bottom of the niche was level with the top of a centrally positioned altar-like bench built against the center of the rear wall. The overall configuration of the niche and bench impart a shrine-like impression, but how the structure was originally used is uncertain.

Huaca de los Idolos derives its name from the human figurines of unbaked clay found in the summit compartment with the altar-like bench and niche, where a small alcove had a cache of objects spread over its floor before it was filled-in to support a new, higher floor. The cache included twined baskets, matting, plant material, animal fur, and at least 13 figurines, all broken, but seemingly the work of a single artist. The figures ranged from 5 to 14 cm in height. Eleven represent females, four of them possibly pregnant. Portrayed in a seated position with crossed legs, the figures held their arms against the torso, bent at the elbows so that the hands meet at the chest. Eyes were represented by narrow slits; the mouth by a shorter, wider slit; and the nose by a slightly raised triangular ridge. Some wore turban-like hats with flat tops. Necklaces of square red beads were occasionally indicated, and two such beads were found elsewhere at Aspero. Thigh-length skirts covered the lower body, but no footwear was shown.

The Aspero cache is the largest group of early clay figurines known from Peru, although others are known from Río Seco, Bandurria, El Paraiso, and Kotosh. Production of figurines continued in Peru, but they never became as prevalent as in the tropical north. Tropical people used figurines in curing ceremonies where shamans transferred the ills of the patient to the effigy, which was then disposed of. A piece of *Spondylus* shell from the Aspero midden indicates that the residents were in contact with Valdivia people.

Other preceramic sites indicate that over time bilateral symmetry came to characterize the arrangement of courts and compartments atop coastal platforms. For example, the small terraced mound at Huaynuna had equal-sized rooms and courts on either side of a central access structure that ran from the base to the top of the platform, which was banked against a low hill. Midden from the associated maritime community produced late dates between 2250 and 1775 BC. This Casma settlement is noteworthy because it produced an example of a Kotosh ceremonial chamber. It is not clear if this was built by sierra people visiting the coast or by fisherfolk converted to mountain beliefs, but it certainly points to interchange. Circular sunken courts could be another feature that spread by interchange. Some authorities postulate that they originated on the coast, but the few preceramic examples with associated radiocarbon assays seem to date later than the sunken court at La Galgada.

By the end of the Preceramic Period three major types of structures figured in the coastal architectural tradition: platform mounds, rectangular courts, and circular sunken courts. These elements could occur individually, but more often several were erected in association. The most elaborate pattern of association is expressed by the main monument at Piedra Parada in the lower Supe Valley, 2.5 km inland. Here the tripartite pattern consists of a terrace platform symmetrically fronting a large rectangular forecourt housing a smaller circular sunken court. The low-walled forecourt is square in plan and measures 40 m on a side. The centrally positioned sunken court is 20 m in diameter, faced with boulders and plastered, and had passageways on two sides. These were aligned with the central axis of the forecourt and the terraced platform. About

10 m behind the forecourt, the first boulder-faced terrace rose to a height of more than 5 m and was 80 m long by 65 m wide. A central stairway provided ascent to an entry court that was 26 m wide. On either side of this, there were two additional courts each 20 m wide. The three summit courts were in turn subdivided into front and back halves by a single wall running the length of the terrace. An entrance connected each half, but the rear compartments were higher than the front ones. The second terrace of the platform rose about 5 m above the first. It was also 80 m long but only 20 m in width. Similar to the lower surface there was a three-part, two-level division of the summit court space. The rear of the platform stood about 75 cm above ground level because it was built against a hill to give the terraces imposing height. Piedra Parada may be of late preceramic or early ceramic age, but nonetheless reflects the development of more standardized ceremonial architecture.

The Paraiso Tradition

El Paraiso is the largest preceramic monument in the western hemisphere. *Plates 29,30* More than 100,000 tons of stone were quarried to erect nine masonry complexes that occupy 58 ha of the Chillon Valley, 2 km from the sea. The buildings survive as jumbled rock piles reaching three stories in height. The two largest ruins are elongated complexes that form the wings of a giant 'U'. Each wing is more than 50 m wide and more than 250 m long. They frame a spacious 7 ha plaza and the base of the U is partially closed off by several smaller ruins, while other masonry complexes are scattered around the periphery. The orientation of El Paraiso is exactly the same as later U-shaped ceremonial centers in the region, but the uneven layout of the site suggests a piecemeal pattern of growth.

The masonry complexes are platform mounds that were erected in multiple stages by piling fill-in mesh bags into interconnected rectangular courts, rooms, and corridors with thick walls, often standing more than 2 m high. Hills nearby were quarried for rock that was set in mud mortar for walls, which were then plastered with adobe. Excavation and restoration of one complex at the base of the U indicates that it was more or less square, measuring 50 m on a side and standing about 8 m high. Two separate flights of stairs led to the summit. The main entry was the larger, more elaborate flight of stairs to the west. The rooms behind the entry are more or less aligned with it, and include a reception court that was painted red and had a sunken central floor area measuring 4.5 × 4.25 m. The finely made clay floor had been burnt to a bright orange, and had a dark oval stain in its center. Square in form, the depression made the higher, outside floor area rather bench-like. Here there were four large circular pits, each 1 m in diameter, symmetrically positioned behind each corner of the sunken floor. They contained charcoal to a depth of 0.8 m. This unusual court certainly involved rituals relating to fire, as did the summit court of Huaca de los Sacrificios at Aspero and chambers of the Kotosh tradition. The other summit compartments of the Paraiso complex were highly compartmentalized and could be reached from the court.

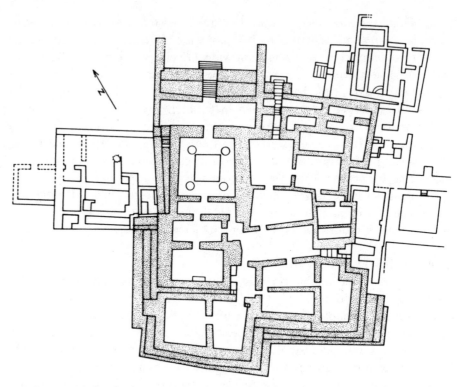

52 A court with four fire basins and a sunken floor lay behind the main entry of the restored complex at El Paraiso.

Explorations of other complexes demonstrate that they also consist of interconnected courts and rooms, but were without hearths or evidence of residential activities. Artifacts included stones used to grind red pigment, figurine fragments of unfired clay, brightly colored bird feathers, and sticks and branches of fruit trees. The largest deposit of trash, about 80 cm in depth, is scattered to the north of the restored complex. In addition to abundant seafood, including small fish remains, there were industrial cultigens, plant foods including fruits, achira and perhaps squash, and jiquima (*Pachyrizus tuberosas*) tubers. Although some residential debris is present at El Paraiso, there is nothing approaching the scope of domestic midden found at either Río Seco or Aspero. Thus, we can conclude that the vast monument of El Paraiso was largely the product of workers who did not live at the site.

El Paraiso is located next to 150 ha of river flood plain that could be irrigated by the construction of small ditches, and which were probably monopolized for growing cotton and other crops. Near the coast terrain suitable for flood–water farming or simple ditch irrigation must have been in short supply by the close of the Preceramic Period and it is not surprising that preceramic sites appear more than 40 km up the Río Chillon by the time El Paraiso was founded. Radiocarbon assays indicate that building was underway by 2000 BC. One third of the assays fall after 1800 BC, when pottery appeared in the area.

Thus, El Paraiso is a very late site and raises the possibility that preceramic maritime adaptations persisted for a century or so after ceramic-using people began irrigating the desert valleys. Constructing canal systems to create desert oases could have been undertaken by either of two populations. Inland people, such as those living at La Galgada, may have expanded downstream, gradually radiating into the coastal valleys. Alternatively, some segments of the maritime population may have forsaken fishing and turned to farming, although transforming fishermen into farmers would be a complex process because fishing is governed by tides and lunar cycles whereas coastal farming is scheduled by solar cycles and seasonal rainfall in the mountains. The risks of each adaptation are also dissimilar: fishermen worry about sharks and turbulent seas, farmers about insects and droughts. (Today these dissimilarities result in divergent beliefs where fishermen and farmers pray to different saints and observe different religious holidays.) Perhaps both inland and coastal peoples were involved in canal development.

Where does El Paraiso stand in the transformation process? The ceremonial center could be the product of imitation, and thus built by preceramic maritime populations copying the U-shaped centers of contemporary farming societies. Some authorities suggest that sunken courts, and other forms of ceremonial architecture were passed from pottery-using farmers to preceramic fisherfolk during a period when the two coexisted as separate cultures. While granting coexistence, I would suspect changes in technology to precede changes in ideology. If El Paraiso assumed its U-shaped configuration by about 1900 BC, then it would represent something very different. Architect Carlos Williams proposes that the masonry complex represents the first phase of a long tradition of U-shaped ceremonial centers that subsequently dominated the inland valley bottoms, where they were associated with irrigation agriculture. El Paraiso and later U-shaped ceremonial centers literally turn their back to the sea to face the mountains, with their great arms reaching out to the rising sun and the mountain sources of desert water. In so doing they graphically express the ideological and organizational transformations that opened the desert to agriculture. Thus, El Paraiso is certainly the architectural expression of an impending new era.

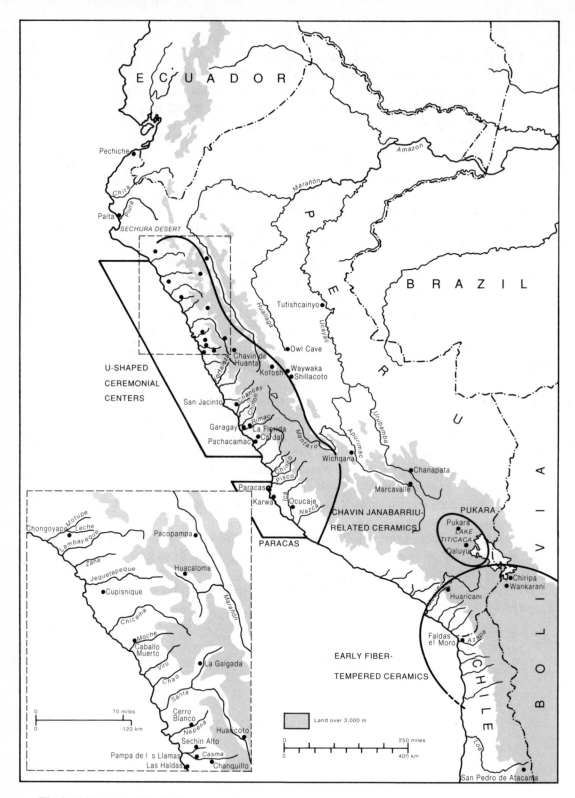

ECUADOR

Pechiche

Chira

Paita
Piura
SECHURA DESERT

U-SHAPED
CEREMONIAL
CENTERS

San Jacinto

Garagay
Pachacamac

Chavín de
Huanta
Kotosh
Fortaleza
Chancay
Chillón
Rimac
La Florida
Cardal

Marañón

Huallaga

P
E
R
U

Tutishcainyo

Owl Cave

Waywaka
Shillacoto

Ucayali

Urubamba

Apurimac

Wichqana

Mantaro

Chincha
Pisco

Paracas
Karwa
Ocucaje
Nazca
Ica

PARACAS

BRAZIL

Chanapata

Marcavalle

CHAVIN JANABARRIU-
RELATED CERAMICS

PUKARA
Pukara
LAKE
TITICACA
Qaluyu

Chiripa
Wankarani

BOLIVIA

Huaricani

Faldas
el Moro
Azapa

EARLY FIBER-
TEMPERED CERAMICS

CHILE

Amazon

Chongoyape
Motupe
Leche
Lambayeque
Zaña
Jequetepeque
Cupisnique
Chicama
Moche
Caballo
Muerto
Viru
Chao
Santa
Cerro
Blanco
Nepeña
Sechin Alto
Pampa de l s Llamas
Las Haldas
Casma
Chanquillo

Pacopampa

Huacaloma

Marañón

La Galgada

Huaricoto

0   70 miles
0   120 km

Land over 3,000 m

0   250 miles
0   400 km

Loa

San Pedro de Atacama

53 *The Initial Period and Early Horizon: principal sites and areas mentioned in Chapter Six.*

CHAPTER SIX

The Initial Period and Early Horizon

Lasting more than a millennium the Initial Period was an era of profound change that accompanied the growth of populations nourished principally by domesticated plants and animals. Beginning about 1800 BC the gradual spread of intensive farming promoted systematic exploitation of previously settled areas as well as the colonization of new habitats. Because much of the Cordillera was inhospitably high or dry, the favorable occurrence of water, land, and climate in sierra basins and desert valleys transformed these areas into evolutionary nodes where domesticates supported increasing numbers of people. With population growth the mountain and coastal poles of Andean civilization began to crystallize. Arid Montane adaptations supported the largest of high altitude populations in the south where upland basins are the biggest. Alternatively, Maritime-Oasis adaptations sustained the densest coastal populations in the north where desert rivers are the biggest.

New concerns with the cosmos and with religion accompanied the economic and social transformations which swept the Andes. The Initial Period witnessed an exceptional spate of monumental construction. Highland ceremonial centers became widespread. In the coastal pole of civilization more large mounds were erected in many valleys than at any other time in Andean prehistory. By 1400 BC work was under way on one of the largest of all early monuments in the Americas – Sechín Alto, a colossal, stone-faced platform *Plates 31–34* that stands some 40 m high. Measuring 300 m in length by 250 m in width, the

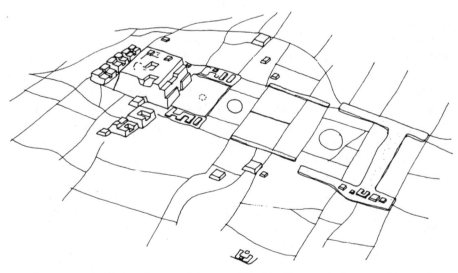

54 By 1200 BC the U-shaped ceremonial center of Sechín Alto was the largest architectural monument in the New World.

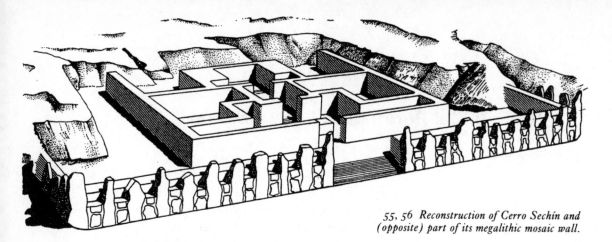

55, 56 Reconstruction of Cerro Sechín and (opposite) part of its megalithic mosaic wall.

enormous mound formed the base of a vast U-shaped center. Aligned plazas held circular, sunken courts while flanking mounds framed a core area of 600 by 1,100 m. Erected on the Sechín branch of the Casma Valley, the gigantic U anchored a 10.5 sq. km sprawl of structures and platforms that comprise the Sechín Alto Complex. For its age this is the biggest early architectural complex in the Western Hemisphere, but Sechín Alto is rarely mentioned in archaeological texts because its antiquity and significance were overlooked for decades.

Plates 31–34 Julio Tello explored the Casma complex in the 1930s and noted that the Sechín Alto platform ranked among the five largest architectural works in the ancient Andes. His excavations focused on Cerro Sechín, a small building enclosed by a macabre megalithic wall of carved monoliths. The monoliths form a giant mosaic that depicts a procession of armed men interspersed with dismembered humans rendered as severed heads, limbs, torsos, and viscera. The mosaic exhibits some stylistic attributes that Tello also encountered when excavating at Chavín de Huantar in the nearby sierra. The sierra monument is but one-tenth the size of Sechín, but it yielded an exceptional corpus of fine stonework embellished with a rich and powerful iconography. Tello considered the more ornate, but smaller site of Chavín to be the fountainhead of ancient civilization and therefore the inspiration for Sechín's art and architecture.

The notion that Sechín was an insignificant derivative of Chavín persisted until it was recently belied by radiocarbon assays. Cerro Sechín dates to 1290 BC, while other architectural works in the Casma and adjacent valleys have even greater antiquity. Radiocarbon dates now anchor in time an extraordinary era of monumental construction on the coast. Well under way by 1700 BC, it was remarkably precocious. It was also exceedingly prolific in filling the desert landscape with multitudes of small, sizable, and often stupendous ceremonial centers. The extraordinary era came to a seemingly abrupt end some time before 500 BC.

In contrast, critical evaluation of radiocarbon assays from Chavín de Huantar leads Richard Burger of Yale University to propose that early occupation and modest construction at this center only began around 800 BC. More importantly, Chavín was not enlarged, nor did its style exert outside influence until some four centuries later. The regional spread of Chavín

iconography and ideology around 400 BC was well after the collapse of the older coastal centers. Chavín was certainly symptomatic of a new era and a new order of beliefs, but the site was not the primordial fountainhead of civilization that Tello and others thought it to be, and archaeologists are now reassessing the roles of Sechín, Chavín, and other early centers. This is an exciting story in the making that we will probe on the coast and in the mountains before concluding with Chavín itself.

Irrigation agriculture

The Initial Period is associated with the florescence of farming economies. The average date for the appearance of ceramics on the central coast is 1800 BC. Although agricultural economies emerged at different times in different settings they generally appeared in conjunction with pottery and heddle weaving: ceramics were vital for storing, cooking and brewing agrarian comestibles; farming and herding led to increased cotton and wool supplies; and heddle weaving allowed for the mass-production of cloth. South American root crops were the primary staples, complemented by beans, legumes, squash, and fruits. Although present in the highlands, maize growing and llama herding remained rare or absent in early coast settings. The arid mountains and rainless coast made irrigation an integral aspect of the new economic order, and irrigation influenced where and how people worked.

Canals. Herders irrigate bofedal pastureland and the basic concepts of channeling water to plants are not complicated. The sierra uplands receive sufficient rainfall to support high elevation tuber and quiñoa farming. In somewhat lower zones, irrigation works (fed by mountain springs and streams) allow other plants, including squash, beans and maize to be sown earlier and harvested later than nature would otherwise allow. With artificial watering it is possible to plant and reap several times a year and irrigated land is valued for its high yields. Steep mountain slopes must be terraced if they are to be irrigated. *Plate 2* Below this the sierra basins provided limited bottomlands that are relatively flat and enjoy favorable growing conditions. These lands were reclaimed first, and in the upper reaches of the Ríos Zana and Santa channeling runoff to crops was underway in preceramic times if not earlier. These activities drew mountain people into lower elevations both permanently and seasonally. By opening the sierra bottom habitat, below and separate from higher rainfall farming, mountain irrigation contributed to verticality.

On the coast irrigation supported human dispersal into an otherwise inhospitable ecological niche – the desert. Pacific drainages exhibit three relationships between river water and arable land. First rivers descend narrow canyons; here steep gradients allow short canals to reach arable land, which is scarce and occurs in isolated pockets. Second, they pass through the necks of coastal valleys that fan out to the sea. Necks are prime canal locations because short leadoff channels supply canals that open outward as the V-shaped valleys do and thereby irrigate a great deal of land. Third, rivers slow down as they near the sea, and relatively long canals must be built to irrigate modest amounts of land, which can suffer salinization or drainage problems due to high water table conditions near the sea. In many valleys it seems that irrigation developed along the path of least resistance, and most canal systems were situated well inland. Development began in canyons and valley necks where river gradients are relatively steep, and these areas generally have substantial numbers of Initial Period monuments. Reclamation then advanced downstream where shallow gradients required greater investments in canal construction. In many valleys land immediately behind the coast was either never irrigated or only reclaimed very late. Because canal irrigation pulls farmers inland the Initial Period is marked by split patterns of residence, with fisherfolk living along the littoral and farmers settling inland.

Fishing can go on almost any day of the year, but farming is structured by the seasonal runoff and weather. Coastal rivers discharge more than 75 per cent of their runoff between February and May, after which smaller drainages are dry. Annual variation in discharge is dramatic: the flow of large rivers can vary between 500 and 2,500 million cubic meters within a ten-year period. Such a great source of uncertainty to farmers must have fostered the prominent development of rites and rituals intended to placate the life-blood of irrigation.

Construction. On the coast intensive agriculture gives the surprising impression of rapid implementation. Irrigating the New World's driest desert with runoff from its most rugged mountain ranges is a taxing undertaking and more than 90 per cent of the land in production today is corporately worked in one way or another. Initially, canals may have been built by independent farmers as well as by corporate groups. But less than 5 per cent of the desert that is farmed today could be easily reclaimed by individual effort, and this condition certainly worked against the rise of independent farmers during the Initial Period.

Preceramic economies supported the evolution of corporate organizations capable of executing large building projects. The ability to build sizable canals by collective labor favored corporate reclamation of land. And as easily irrigated land became scarce the collective had greater resources for reclaiming additional land than did the individual entrepreneur.

Numbers. Given water, almost every canal can operate independently, and therefore support an independent group of people. Most rivers sustain several canal systems that maintain a number of agrarian collectives. In some cases a

Plate 5

single canal is associated with a single group of people, but the Spanish also encountered groups that operated more than one canal and cases where several kin corporations shared the same channel. Nonetheless, coastal irrigation has always been segmented by separate canals able to support autonomous groups of people. Therefore, early reclamation fostered the development of segmented agrarian populations. The Initial Period is characterized by exceptional numbers of inland monuments, and these early ceremonial centers probably commemorated the rise of numerous autonomous groups sustained by independent canal systems.

In the Moche Valley early land reclamation supported three independent ceremonial centers in irrigated pockets of canyon land. Further downstream there was an additional large cluster of big platforms – the Caballo Muerto complex – on the main valley neck canal. Finally, there was a separate ceremonial mound in mid-valley. In succeeding millennia new ceremonial centers were built downstream, in fewer numbers, and eventually the entire valley was dominated by a single vast center, Huaca del Sol, and later Chan Chan. This suggests that irrigation underpinned the rise of independent corporate groups with separate ceremonial facilities long before the populations fused into larger political formations.

Plate 39

Plates 56,99

Initial Period monuments reflect significantly larger populations than in preceramic times, and irrigation certainly brought about a demographic revolution. Reclamation of relatively accessible land supported growth of larger work-forces capable of opening more difficult desert terrain. Once under way, the expansion of reclamation and population was probably self-propelling. Growth could continue for a long time before limitations on water and land would outstrip the labor, organizational and engineering capabilities needed for further reclamation.

Organization. The number and size of Initial Period monuments reflect not only more people but new orders of organization. Canal builders generally monopolize the land and water they bring into production. If reclamation was undertaken by collectives of kindred then the means of agrarian production were always corporately controlled and owned. Individual farmers were similar to sharecroppers, and access to the means of making a living was based on kinship and ancestors, and paid for by contributing to corporate undertakings. In Inca times peasant farmers did not own the land they tilled, and it is unlikely that they ever did.

It cannot be proven, but it is reasonable to presume that agrarian corporations of the Initial Period were similar if not ancestral to the ayllu-like organization found by the Spanish on the coast. However, the early corporations were not ruled by karaka. In nascent form similar kin groups no doubt structured earlier maritime and mountain societies. However, intensive agriculture and irrigation in particular fostered a new order of collective monopolization. Farmers prospered and increased their numbers, but under a rather totalitarian yoke of the larger kin collectives into which they were born.

Monumental architecture

The Initial Period was the great age of ceremonial architecture, and monuments were more widespread and numerous than in preceramic times. Coastal agriculture supported construction of large works in areas as far north as the La Leche Valley and as far south as the Mala Valley. Even in later times sizable coastal monuments were seldom erected south of the small Nazca drainage due to the southward decline of agrarian potentials as the Cordillera becomes higher and drier. Initial Period monuments are so numerous, variable, and little explored that they defy easy summation. Most are vaguely dated on the basis of architectural morphology, and their associated ceramic arts have yet to be sorted out after decades of being treated as Chavín-derived.

Most forms of preceramic architecture persisted and were elaborated. Mesh bag construction fill, temple interment, and H-type masonry continued. Irrigation built up soils suitable for producing mud bricks, and adobe construction became more common employing hand-made bricks of conical, *Plates 101,102* cylindrical or bullet shape. Adobe friezes, a truly monumental art, and often painted in rich polychromes, frequently ornamented ceremonial courts and chambers. Applied to the exterior faces of great mounds, they created dazzling *Plates 35,36* façades of enormous size designed to impress huge audiences. With many centers vying with one another, ostentatious display was certainly a conscious concern of corporate power and policy.

Coastal traditions

As yet there is little evidence that Initial Period mounds were designed and built to house élite tombs. We may presume that the early platforms and their attendant buildings were similar to later huacas adoratorios, and they no doubt also served civil and political ends, with governance taking place in the name of the gods. A variable and pluralistic pantheon would help explain their marked variation. In Inca times different parcialidades maintained shrines and huacas dedicated to local doctrines and deities, and similar practices may be inferred for early kin corporations. Local beliefs were cross-cut by broader cults and creeds associated with ceremonial structures of repetitious form, such as sunken courts, Kotosh chambers, and U-shaped centers. To judge from architectural variation, interpretation of these cults and creeds was flexible. For example, sunken courts could differ in numbers and placement relative to other structures. Ceremonial structures that occur together in a group are rarely of equal size, and creeds and congregations may have been of different status or rank.

At least three Initial Period traditions in ceremonial architecture, with overlapping distributions, can be recognized on the coast. In the north between the Ríos Jequetepeque and La Leche, a variable tradition emphasized low, wide, rectangular platforms, often aligned with rectangular forecourts. Rogger Ravines located 30 such monuments in the middle Jequetepeque drainage, with a majority of them occupying the canyon flanks at an elevation of 400 and

El Paraiso: a Preceramic monument

29 (right) With nine complexes of collapsed stone buildings, El Paraiso was the largest New World monument ever erected by people who neither made pottery nor relied principally on agriculture. The two largest masonry complexes parallel one another, similar to the arms of later U-shaped ceremonial centers.

30 (below) A small, restored masonry complex at El Paraiso is more than two stories high.

Cerro Sechín: an Initial Period site

31 (left) A severed body and severed head incised on a monolith at this important site, dating to 1290 BC, near the Sechín Alto complex on the north coast.

32 (above left) A club-wielding figure on an incised Cerro Sechín monolith.

33, 34 (above right and below) The iconography of these Cerro Sechín severed heads reflects a concern with conflict and dissonance.

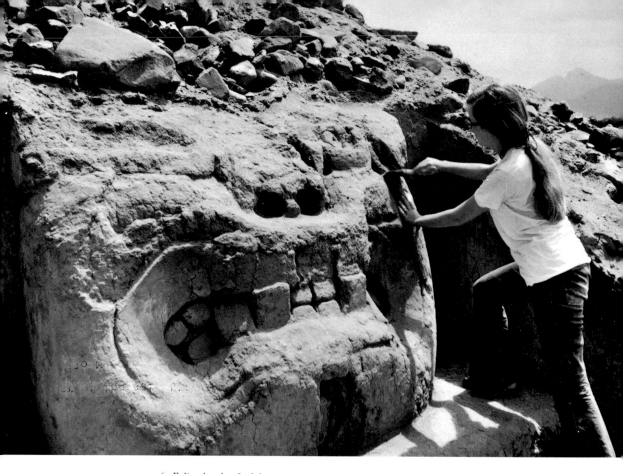

35, 36 *Feline heads of adobe ornamented the façade of Huaca Los Reyes in the Caballo Muerto Complex, Moche Valley.*

37, 38 *The north coast Cupisnique style, contemporary with Huaca Los Reyes, had early prominence in the Viru, Moche, and Chicama valleys. These Cupisnique ceramic vessels portray (above) an aged individual and (right) a woman and child.*

39 (below) *An aerial view of Huaca Los Reyes, its U-shape clearly visible. Above the main huaca sits a smaller platform in a separate court. A later prehistoric canal course lies uphill. In the desert beyond (center left), two parallel lines are traces of an ancient road leading to an outlying mound.*

Huaca Los Reyes

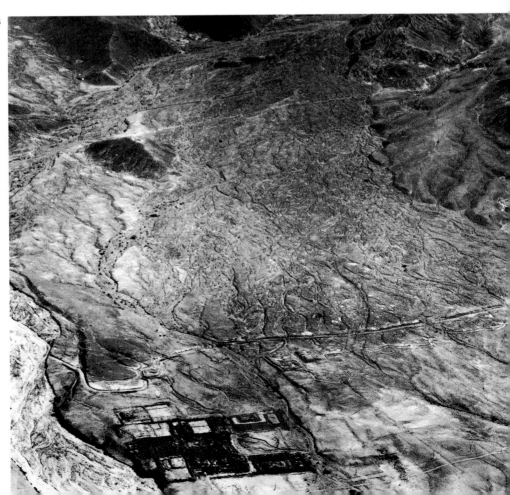

Pukara: an Early Horizon center

40 (left) A Pukara stone figure holding a trophy head.

41 (above) A Pukara-style incised polychrome vessel fragment with a feline head.

42 (below) Occupying a broad terrace, the sunken court at the site of Pukara, northwest of Lake Titicaca, was surrounded on three sides by detached one-room buildings built of stone blocks.

Opposite:

43 (above) General view of the Castillo façade at Chavín de Huantar, the magnificent site in the northern highlands whose rise in the first millennium BC defines the onset of the Early Horizon.

44 (left) An incised vessel of the coastal Paracas culture, with a feline motif, attributed to Chavín influence.

45 (below left) An incised polychrome Paracas vessel.

46 (right) A coastal stirrup-spout vessel with incised decoration probably influenced by Chavín.

The Chavín style

Chavín de Huantar

47 (above) Stone heads with human and animal attributes were once tenoned into the façade of the Chavín Castillo, and are now stored for their protection in an interior gallery.

48 (below) A New Temple anthropomorphic tenon head from Chavín, with exaggerated canine teeth.

49 (right) Head of the so-called Lanzón stela in an inner chamber at Chavín.

450 m. In addition to U-shaped complexes and sunken courts, there were isolated platforms, ones with forecourts, as well as terraced mounds with and without summit structures. The associated ceramics exhibit many elements of styles found at adjacent highland centers, such as Huacaloma in the Cajamarca basin. Thereafter strong linkages between coast and sierra persist up to the time of Spanish arrival.

Between the Ríos Santa and Huara, architect Carlos Williams recognizes more of a defined tradition emphasizing circular sunken courts in front of rectangular platforms, possibly derived from the style at preceramic sites such as La Galgada. There are some 30 pit-platform combinations in the Supe Valley that probably date to the Initial period, and even larger numbers in the adjacent Patavilca and Fortaleza Valleys. With a hundred or more examples altogether, the three drainages were the nexus of pit-platform construction.

Williams postulates an evolutionary sequence for the Supe Valley structures, in which the pits were at first physically detached from the platforms, as at Piedra Parada. Next, sunken courts were connected to mounds, and wide, flat collars built around the pit. Collared structures had upper court walls above ground level that were widened as causeway-like connections with platforms. After this fusion of the two structures, pits became much larger relative to pyramids and this trend culminated in complexes where the sunken court was the dominant structure. Finally, the structural proportions reverted to earlier norms, but platforms were low and square rather than tall and rectangular. This sequence suggests that for a time rites in sunken courts became more important than those on associated platforms.

The Paraiso Tradition

Sanctuaries built in the shape of a U are the most enduring form of ceremonial architecture in the Andes. Their evolution spans four millennia. During the Initial Period U-shaped complexes on the coast were the largest and most elaborate of all early monuments in the Americas. Over time their size was reduced, but not their importance. The lords of Chimor ruled from open-fronted throne rooms called *audiencias*, and U-shaped masmas served Inca potentates.

Plate 100

Contemporary Aymara people near Lake Titicaca worship in a mountain-top shrine that is U-shaped. The one-room stone structure is open to the sky. An interior altar of slabs projects from the middle of the rear wall and there are three exterior altars, one against the center of each outside wall. All are blackened and ash-covered from burnt offerings. The sanctuary serves a powerful mountain spirit that influences meteorological phenomena and the shrine is employed for rain-bringing rites to benefit crops. In a similar vein an intimate association with agricultural concerns characterizes the ancient U-shaped centers on the coast. These monuments almost always face inland mountains, opening their ceremonial wings to the mountain headwaters of desert rivers.

Carlos Williams considers the preceramic ruins of El Paraiso to be the starting point of the U-shape tradition, and the inland orientation and general shape of the ruins make this a reasonable typological argument. But the Paraiso economy was more maritime than agrarian. Origins are also uncertain because a U-shaped configuration was found to be superimposed atop La Galgada when pottery and Chavinoid arts appeared at this Santa center about 1900 BC.

Monuments of the Paraiso tradition have an Initial Period coastal distribution between the Ríos Jequetepeque and Mala. In terms of numbers, they were most common between the Huaura and Lurin Valleys where more than 25 centers were erected. However, the north includes both the biggest complex, Sechín Alto, and one of the most elaborate, Huaca Los Reyes, a member of the Caballo Muerto Complex.

Plate 39

Located more than 25 km inland, Los Reyes yielded dates that begin early in the Initial Period and span more than six centuries. Over the course of generations, the complex grew to a final size of 200 m by 200 m. Architect William Conklin envisages eight phases of building that started in a two-fold manner. A small platform, with a U-shaped summit was erected at the rear of two aligned courts facing up-valley to the east. This little mound was never modified again. At the same time, to the south, work began on the rear buildings of what later became a higher, dominant platform. In phase two the platform was elevated and became a two-tiered huaca, the added lower frontal mound with a central entry court. The façade of the lower mound was

Plates 35,36

ornamented with six large niches, each framing an enormous cat-like head of adobe executed in high relief. Proceeding outward from the mound, later episodes of construction added detached lower wings framing a spacious court in front of the central platform. In the fourth phase the builders began to erect colonnades of square pillars in front of wing platforms and later on the main

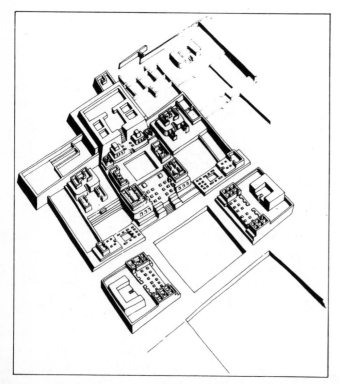

57 *A reconstruction of Huaca los Reyes. The smaller, presumably older temple sits in a separate court at the top.*

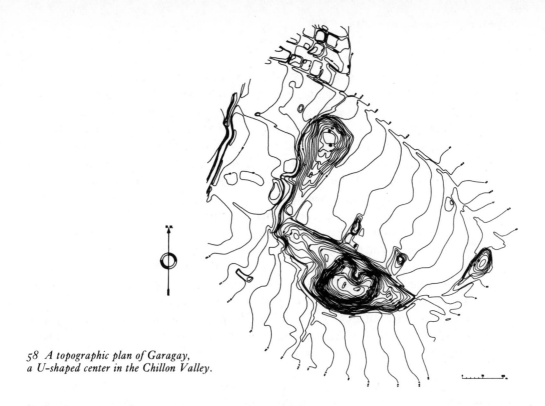

58 A topographic plan of Garagay,
a U-shaped center in the Chillon Valley.

mound. The colonnades became more grandiose over time and pillars were transformed into frieze panels, each depicting a large human-like figure facing forward toward audiences assembled in the center of the U-shaped complex. Colonnades and monumental friezes made Los Reyes more ostentatious and ornate than most other centers.

No two centers of the Paraiso tradition were exactly alike and their friezes are not standardized. Nonetheless, the direction of orientation, ground plan, and spatial organization of U-shaped complexes were broadly repetitive. As huacas adoratorios, they invite analogy with cathedrals and mosques in terms of recurrent structural canons and sacrosanct character. Commemorating the initial flowering of civilization, the magnitude of early U-shaped complexes is often astounding. Including Sechín Alto, there are at least ten cases where size equals or greatly exceeds the Early Horizon complex of Chavín de Huantar. The Ríos Chillon, Rimac, and Lurin each contain two centers larger than Chavín, as well as one or more smaller complexes of nearly equal dimensions. One estimate calculates that the monuments in these three valleys represent in excess of 12 million man days of work.

Based upon architectural considerations, Williams has proposed a six phase sequence of development. Following El Paraiso, there was increasing standardization and size. Size increased especially from Phase 3, with complexes such as La Florida. Florida is located near Lima, dates from between *c.* 1750 and 1650 BC, and is estimated to have required 6.7 million man days of labor to construct. Garagay, the largest of the Chillon complexes has a projected labor expenditure of 3.2 million man days. Yet, in all such cases work was interspersed with long episodes of use spanning centuries. Emphasis on size persisted into Phase 5, when the largest of six U-shaped Chancay centers was completed at San Jacinto, which was three times the size of Chavín. Size then decreased at the end of the sequence, at centers such as Cardal.

Large populations are implied not only by the labor needed, but also by the design, which seems oversized in relation to human scales. For example Cardal, one of the smaller centers of four in the Lurin valley, has a 3 ha court. By today's architectural formula for standing room, it was designed to accommodate an audience of some 65,000 people – more than six times the population that has traditionally resided in the lower Lurin! Excavations at Cardal by Richard and Lucy Burger indicate that occupation and construction began relatively late, at about 1100 BC, and ended about 850 BC. It is intriguing to note that two circular sunken courts were cut into one of the wing platforms of this U-shaped center, while a third was placed between the main mound and the other wing. Each of the unroofed courts could accommodate a small standing audience of 150 or so. Walls exhibited traces of red, white, and black paint. Except for a central hearth with ash, floors were clean, but beneath one a votive offering was found consisting of a child's cranium.

Clearing the central façade of the main mound revealed a polychrome clay frieze depicting a giant mouth of interlocking triangular teeth and large canines each a meter long. Painted cream, yellow, rose, and black, the band of great teeth had seen long exposure and was renovated at least four times. The imposing frieze was centrally positioned on both sides of the entry to the summit atrium, so that one stepped into the fanged aperture to reach the top of the mound. Seen from the court of the U, the great size of the artwork was certainly intended to impress. Cardal's builders may have drawn on work forces that did not live at the site, but the monument was not a vacant ceremonial center because adjacent excavations revealed small domestic dwellings and refuse consisting of cultivated plants and sea foods. It is significant that construction and use of Cardal overlapped with similar activities at the nearby U-shaped centers of Manchay Bajo, 1 km away, and Mina Perdida, 5 km away. As in the Moche Valley, the concurrent operation of multiple ceremonial centers suggests that they served different audiences and, by inference, different kin corporations.

Political formations

In the center of Cardal's summit atrium there were burials of both sexes. The burial location suggests these were important individuals, but they were not wealthy people. Other than common pottery, grave accompaniments were few. The most noteworthy burial was an old man adorned with a necklace of sea lion teeth and earspools fashioned from porpoise vertebrae. These were probably emblems of status that the elder achieved through service and not symbols of rank that he inherited. Elsewhere there is little Initial Period evidence of huacas sepulturas, personal wealth, or hereditary rule, with a possible exception at La Galgada. This leads most authorities to think that decision-making and governance were vested in offices that individuals either rotated through, as in cargo systems, or did not bequeath to their heirs, as in western church systems.

The Vatican is an apt reminder that powerful institutions can flourish without inherited rulers, and it seems likely that the early integration of Andean populations occurred in religious and ritual guise. The most common unit of this integration comprised discrete kin corporations, each of which commemorated its identities by building its own ceremonial facility. The plethora of monuments suggests that local groups vied with one another over construction, but at the same time used similar elements indicative of shared beliefs. Higher orders of early integration took several forms. If Huaca La Florida was a regional center, then dominance of the site by one enormous monument points to relatively centralized organization. Alternatively, the Caballo Muerto Complex, with multiple mounds, denotes multifaceted organization.

The Sechín Alto Complex falls between these extremes. The U-shaped center is colossal, yet the larger complex includes other monuments of exceptional size, such as Sechín Bajo which is U-shaped, and Taukachi-Konkan which is not, and the elaborate shrine of Cerro Sechín. Less than 10 km away in the Casma branch of the valley there is still another assemblage of imposing monuments, the Pampa de Las Llamas–Moxeke Complex. It is dominated by two large, rectangular platforms about 1 km apart, that are aligned and centrally situated on either side of a spacious square court measuring more than 350 m on a side. Numerous small low mounds and domestic dwellings flank the court. When Tello investigated the larger platform, Huaca Moxeke (c. 25 m high and 165 m square), he found the façade ornamented with giant niches framing high relief friezes painted in red, blue, white, and black. Two depicted human faces, two illustrated richly garbed individuals facing forward, and one showed the back of a person with arms bound at the rear in a manner similar to later Moche renditions of prisoners. The lower Llamas platform (12 m high and c. 130 m square), was excavated by Thomas and Shelia Pozorski, who studied many of the smaller buildings in the complex. The platform had two entrances. One, facing Moxeke, led to a long central corridor connected to the other entrance, or exit, which faced a circular sunken court. Three rows of symmetrically arranged courts and rooms occurred on both sides of the corridor, which were possibly used to store foodstuffs.

The Casma is a small drainage that has traditionally supported less than 7,000 people. Given the labor expended on Initial Period construction, the Pozorskis postulate that it was the authoritative center for six drainages from the Ríos Chao to Huarmey. The Sechín Alto and Moxeke–Pampa de Llamas complexes may have been the centers of complementary moieties. If this was the case, the plans of the two complexes indicate ideological differences: Sechín Alto emphasized the U-shaped tradition complemented by sunken courts, whereas Llamas emphasized rectangular platforms, with only one ceremonial pit.

The Pozorskis suggest that three other sites may also have been centers of regional authority. One area stretched between the Ríos Lurin and Chancay

Plates 37,38

and was characterized by U-shaped centers. Another, Supe, lay between the Ríos Huaura and Fortaleza where pit and platform centers were common. And Caballo Muerto presumably held sway between the Ríos Viru and Jequetepeque. The existence of such regional 'polities' is speculative, but alliances between valleys were probably fostered by cooperation and competition. Rites and rituals for coping with agricultural uncertainties and disasters of El Niño or other origin may well have bonded people together. Yet, competition for land and water could also foster confederations for defense. Iconographic, if not ideological, concerns with dissonance are expressed by the macabre megaliths

Plates 31–34

of Cerro Sechín, where men in arms with pike-like clubs parade among dismembered corpses. One must wonder if the pikes were not emblems of authority that later evolved into staffs of office. Yet who actually wielded the power that brought forth the most colossal of early American monuments is a fascinating puzzle that future generations must solve.

Highland developments

In the highlands Initial Period settlements and monuments were widely dispersed between northern Peru and the Titicaca Basin. Built of stone and adobe, ceremonial centers were elegant but generally smaller and more widely scattered than on the desert. The more widely scattered distribution of highland centers reflects larger but more dispersed populations engaged in agropastoral pursuits. Domesticates vital to these pursuits came into use during the Initial Period, but, as we have seen, their evolutionary origins are poorly understood. Herding did not replace hunting at Pachamachay Cave until about 1600 BC, yet, less then 100 km away at Telarmachay Cave, the transition is dated shortly after 3800 BC.

Plates 4,11

Llama and alpaca domestication opened the highest of economic zones, the puna, to controlled exploitation while irrigation opened sierra bottomlands to farming. As highlanders increased their dependency upon plant and animal husbandry they increased their reliance upon domesticates that prospered at different altitudes. If nature operated in the past as it does at present, then yields of different crops in different habitats varied and counterbalanced each other year by year, and encouraged reliance on a range of domesticates adapted to different altitudes, or verticality.

Northern frontiers

In the north and east where the Cordillera is low and forested, people pursuing tropical adaptations engaged in rainfall farming long before agropastoralism emerged in the mountains and irrigation transformed the desert. Altitude set boundaries on tropical agriculture because its major crops, such as manioc, fare poorly above 1,500 m. Similarly, its southward spread along the coast was inhibited by the prerequisites of large-scale irrigation. With the later rise of powerful states, such as Moche and Chimor, the frontiers between Andean and Amazonian spheres of influence were pushed northward from an ancient divide at the Sechura desert that had persisted into the Initial Period. In coastal Ecuador Valdivia farmers were producing pottery by 3000 BC. Yet, more than a millennium passed before ceramics and agriculture spread the 400 km down the desert coast where intensive farming required irrigation and land reclamation. Dating between 1800 and 400 BC, early ceramic phases in northernmost Peru include Santa Rosa and Pechiche in the Tumbes Valley, Paita in the lower Chira and Piura drainages, and Encantada in the upper Piura. These assemblages are Ecuadorian in affiliation and they are associated with settlements of moderate size, but not with large monuments.

Mountain adaptations prevailed in the highlands east of the Sechura Desert. Situated at an elevation of 2,410 m in the Chamaya Basin, Pacopampa is among the most northerly of early Peruvian ceremonial centers. Initial Period and Early Horizon corporate architecture covers some 10 ha, and the habitation area is probably more extensive. The crest of a natural hill was modified to create a series of terraced platforms that were faced with massive masonry walls and fronted spacious courts, lined with stone colonnades and a modest number of stone carvings.

Early sierra adaptations are also evident in the Cajamarca-Crisnejas Basin at the ceremonial centers of Huacaloma and Layzon. Each center consists of one or more rectangular platform mounds that were generally terraced, stone-faced and sculpted from a natural hill or eminence. Huacaloma is the type site for the Early Huacaloma Phase, which dates between c. 1500 and 1000 BC and is characterized by ceremonial chambers of the Kotosh Religious tradition. These were covered during the Late Huacaloma Phase, c. 1000 to 500 BC, to create masonry platforms embellished with polychrome paintings. Camelid and llama remains increase sharply during the Layzon Phase of 500 to 200 BC, when sizable platform construction was undertaken at the nearby center of Layzon. Huacaloma was also remodeled with the significant addition of two stone-lined, stone-roofed canals to one of the mounds. One channel was straight, but the adjacent one was serpent-like and rather impractical. Elaborate stone conduits are a recurrent feature of early ceremonial architecture in the highlands. Some were certainly drains. Others were inefficiently designed and over built for useful ends, and probably served as conduits for the ritual manipulation of water. People apparently thought natural rainfall and runoff could be influenced by the ceremonial maneuvering of water flow.

Although Cajamarca was Andean, the basin was flanked by relict stands of tropical forest in the upper Lambayeque and Zana drainages. Sandwiched between the Pacific desert and the high sierra, the Zana held a southern enclave of people who pursued more tropical adaptations well into the Initial Period. To the east, lowland forest envelops much of Peru and here human development remains elusive until the introduction of pottery resulted in durable artifacts. Near the jungle city of Pucallpa on the Río Ucayali the site of Tutishcainyo has early ceramics with an estimated date of 2000 BC. The pottery is associated with a sedentary farming community that presumably emphasized manioc cultivation and perhaps maize tending, while lake and river fish supplied protein. Similar ceramics occur at the Río Huallaga site of Owl Cave near the mountains. Along the mountain fringes tropical adaptations probably gave way to Andean ones at elevations around 1,500 m.

At Kotosh, in the upper Huallaga drainage, the Initial Period opens with the Waira-jirca phase. Waira-jirca pottery is well made and shares attributes with the Owl Cave assemblage less than 100 km away. Similarities are expectable if Waira-jirca people descended into the lower montaña to grow crops or procure tropical produce. Movement into the high mountains is attested by a significant increase in domesticated camelid remains at the site. Ceremonial construction focused on the elaboration of earlier platform mounds, but ritual chambers of the Kotosh religious tradition were no longer built. Beliefs may have changed as the local economy changed. However, a very large chamber was built nearby at Shillacoto, and the Kotosh tradition persisted at other sites including Huaricoto.

Across the mountains to the west, at La Galgada, irrigated farming of scant canyon lands persisted. The Initial Period saw the addition of a few new crops, but herding is not in evidence. In preceramic times Kotosh-type chambers had served first as seats of ritual and then as burial crypts, but they ceased to be built. When pottery was introduced the summit of the main platform was remodeled into a U-shaped configuration. This new design was accompanied by internal construction of long, narrow galleries within mounds and platforms. The slab-lined sanctuaries were then used as repositories for corpses. Some mummies were accompanied by textiles and jewelry that rank among the finest of Initial Period grave goods yet recovered. The latter includes shell disks with engraved birds and a stone disk mosaic with a cat-like face that are rather similar to later Chavín artwork. The grave goods are highly suggestive of personal wealth and status, while the gallery crypts are equally suggestive of sepulchral huacas of later-period nobility. This is by far the best early evidence for élite individuals and kindred who inherited wealth and status, thereby adumbrating the later karaka class. Yet, parallel developments are not evident elsewhere in the Cordillera for more than a thousand years! If karaka rule is considered a social adaptation, then La Galgada suggests that local adaptations often flowered but failed because conditions were not conducive to their spread or evolutionary perpetuation.

Central highlands

In the Ayacucho region Initial Period settlements have yielded pottery assemblages, called Andamarca and Wichqana, with limited decoration and few suggestions of tropical influence. The Wichqana site has a ceremonial structure, reputedly in the shape of a U, associated with the buried skulls of decapitated women. In the nearby Andahuaylas Valley excavations in the Muyu Moqo sector of the Waywaka site produced a 3,440-year-old stone bowl containing metalworking tools and gold beaten into thin foil. This is the earliest evidence of precious metalworking in the Andes.

Some 250 km to the east, in the Cuzco Basin the valley-bottom settlement of Marcavalle was occupied as early as 1300 BC. Continued use over almost half a millennium produced dense midden around dwellings with thin walls built of adobe. In addition to plain utilitarian containers, Marcavalle pottery includes painted vessels, some of which were decorated with metallic pigment. Thousands of years later Inca residents of the region looked to Lake Titicaca for their mythical origins. Thus, it is of interest that Marcavalle is not the only Initial Period pottery to appear in the Cuzco region. John Rowe identified examples of a second ceramic complex, known as Qaluyu after its type site on the northern shore of Lake Titicaca. The most common forms were open vessels such as bowls and plates, often decorated with incised geometric designs or painted with black and red motifs on cream-colored surfaces. Dating to *c.* 1300 BC, the site of Qaluyu is a low mound of habitation debris covering about one ha. Superficial explorations suggest that it was a long-lived community supported by farming, herding, and a collection of lacustrine resources. After abandonment the site was taken over later by Pukara people who resculpted the mound into the shape of a catfish. Although not the earliest ceramic complex in the region, Qaluyu attests to ancient links between the lake area and Cuzco. The persistence of links in tangible and mythical form through to Inca times simply reflects the fact that agropastoralism transformed the vast Titicaca Basin into the demographic and cultural nexus of high-altitude civilization.

The Titicaca Basin

The bounty of Lake Titicaca and the water's mitigating effect on climate have long supported densely packed populations adjacent to the hundreds of kilometers of shoreline. The transformation of the basin landscape by agropastoralism was a gradual one that draws into archaeological focus as people began to farm and herd.

Chiripa

Dating between 1400 and 850 BC, large quantities of fish, waterfowl, snails, and aquatic plant remains were recovered from early deposits at the site of Chiripa on the southern shore of the lake. Excavations by David Browman also produced tatora rushes, which were probably used for reed watercraft, as is the practice today. Wild camelid and domesticated llama and alpaca bones were used to fashion instruments for producing textiles. Small seeds and tubers may represent cultivated quiñoa and potatoes. Thus, food remains point to the early integration of lacustrine and agropastoral resources.

Plate 8

Chiripa pottery occurs at a number of settlements on the Bolivian side of Lake Titicaca. It is well made and sometimes includes vegetable matter as temper. Utilitarian vessels, such as cooking ollas, were left plain, but open bowls with flat bottoms and vertical sides saw frequent decoration. Designs were first outlined by thin incision and then painted in polychrome emphasizing red, cream and black. Further embellishment included appliqué felines, animal heads, and human faces. Potters also produced ceramic trumpets that rank among the earliest musical instruments found in the Andes.

People resided at Chiripa for a number of centuries before erecting a platform mound about 1000 BC. During its long use the structure underwent several construction stages before brief abandonment was followed by extensive remodeling and use by Tiwanaku peoples who brought it to a final height of 6 m and dimensions of *c*. 55 m square. The platform was initially stone faced, and the summit seems to have had a square sunken court surrounded by small rectangular buildings. This basic configuration was enlarged upon during a second major phase of remodeling and use between 600 and 100 BC. At this time the stone-faced sunken court measured 23 m square and 1.5 m in depth. Carved stone plaques were set in the masonry walls of the court and ornamented with serpent, animal, and human motifs, beginning a stelae and stone carving tradition in the Titicaca Basin that persisted for millennia.

Atop the Chiripa mound 16 small, rectangular buildings ringed the court and opened to it. The facilities were symmetrically arranged and apparently comprised a row of three aligned structures on each side of the court, and one building diagonally placed at each corner. Each building was similar and built of earth and adobe. They were double-walled, the exterior walls forming an outer shell while parallel but detached interior walls created a smaller rectangular chamber. Long narrow cells separated the two sets of walls. Niche-like interior windows provided access to the cells, which might have stored ceremonial paraphernalia. Walls were stuccoed and painted with terracotta and green pigment, forming a chevron design in one case. Opening to the court, each building had a single rectangular entrance that was 'stepped': the exterior wall entry was wider than the interior wall entry. The appearance was of a smaller doorway set within a larger one. The entries were fitted for a sliding door that could be pulled back into the wall. Finally, plastered door jambs were stepped in a two-tiered manner reinforcing the door within a door appearance.

Architect William Conklin cogently argues that Chiripa features mark the onset of Titicaca architectural traditions, which lasted into Inca times. The door within a door entries provide antecedents for the monolithic gateways at Tiwanaku which are similarly tiered. The single entry, detached, one-room structure eventually evolved into the Inca wasi. Interior wall niches, sunken courts, and structures arranged around a central court also persist as architectural themes. Karen and Sergio Chavez have studied the art, stone carving, and buildings at Chiripa and other early ceramic sites in the Titicaca Basin. They conclude that by about 500 BC local populations producing different types of ceramics had come to share beliefs about ceremonial procedures, iconography, and architecture. Called the 'Yaya-Mama Religious Tradition' many of these beliefs persisted for a very long time, as did the forms of Chiripa ceremonial architecture.

Chiripa and Qaluyu pottery belong to a family of early ceramic complexes that differ in decoration, yet share forms and, to varying degrees, employ vegetable matter as temper. Other complexes include Huaricani in the middle

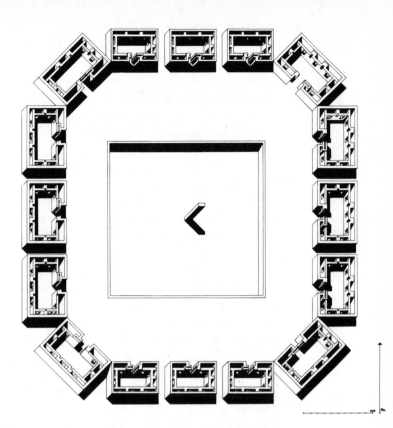

59 *A reconstruction of the Chiripa mound-top buildings and sunken court. Emphasis on detached one-room buildings persisted through Inca times.*

Moquegua Valley, Faldas el Moro in the lower Azapa drainage, and Wankarani in the Lake Popo highlands. Similarities among these assemblages are probably due to the diffusion of ceramic technology out of the Titicaca Basin. West of the basin the long preceramic occupation at Asana in the Río Moquegua headwaters indicates that scarce resources in the arid high sierra encouraged seasonal movement to the dry puna. Opening the sierra to year-round occupation required creation of an artificial niche based on domesticated plants and animals as well as on irrigation. This was a gradual transformation that pulled people into lower settings favorable for crops. Beginning in the first millennium BC, the Huaricani complex is represented by valley-side settlements in warmer elevations around 2,000 m. Here stone outlines of rectangular one-room dwellings are scattered above traces of ancient canals. Adjacent to some sites there are cemeteries where seated, flexed burials were interred in cylindrical pits lined with stone. This pattern of interment is typical of the Titicaca region, and it supports propositions that the lower sierra was reclaimed by highlanders.

The coast had a long occupation by maritime folk such as those of the Chinchoros tradition of northern Chile. Here archaeologists see ceramics, woven textiles, and irrigation agriculture as introductions from the outside that were adopted by local people by 1200 BC. The introductions are thought to be from the Titicaca Basin because the pottery, called Faldas el Moro, has highland similarities. However, some crops came into use that were not of highland origin, and squash, cotton or gourd may equally have diffused down the coast from one valley to another.

The far south

Lake Titicaca drains south to the more arid region of Lake Popo, where early ceramics, with general similarities to those of Chiripa, are represented by the Wankarani complex. Defined by Bolivian archaeologist Carlos Ponce, this complex may have arisen as early as Chiripa, and then persisted into Tiwanaku times as a conservative agropastoral adaptation to a harsh environment. The Popo region and drier reaches of the southern Cordillera lack elaborate ceremonial architecture, and there are few expressions of corporate construction other than defensive walls enclosing settlements. Walled and open Wankarani villages consisted of circular adobe houses that were probably thatched. The number of households ranged from 15 to one extreme case of over 700. Metallurgy is in evidence in the form of copper-smelting slags that radiocarbon assays date between 1200 and 800 BC. This marks the beginning of a southern Andean metallurgical tradition, emphasizing copper, tin, and brass, that developed independently of a more northern tradition, associated with copper-arsenic ores and gold-working. Some eastern Wankarani villages occur at lower altitudes near the Cochabamba Valley. These settlements may have been established to exploit temperate maize growing lands, and if so, they represent an early expression of verticality on the eastern slopes of the Cordillera.

In arid Chile Nuñez and Dillehay propose that altitudinal movement of people and produce was somewhat different than in northern verticality adaptations. The southern salt puna and hyperarid reaches of Chile are where hunter-gatherers probably pursued seasonal transhumance between the coast and puna. Agriculture came late to this harsh environment, appearing in the last century BC in the highland oasis of San Pedro de Atacama and in the Río Loa desert valley. Here farming and herding seem to have been independent pursuits managed by different groups of people. Widely separated communities of sedentary farmers arose in highland oases and small coastal valleys. Apparently farmers did not travel up and down the mountains to obtain distant resources, but relied for the transport and exchange of goods on herders, who moved their herds between high and low pastures on a seasonal basis. Herders did not cultivate the produce they transported, nor were they colonies of the communities they connected, but their symbiotic relationship with farmers served the same ends as verticality did in the north.

THE EARLY HORIZON

Discussion of Chilean adaptations has carried us beyond the framework of the Early Horizon. This is an era of some debate. Technically, the horizon is a unit of time that begins when artistic influence from Chavín de Huantar first appears in the ceramic arts of the Ica Valley. Beginning dates between 1400 and 800 BC were once assigned to the horizon. But, as we have seen, radiocarbon assays from Chavín itself indicate that the site was not occupied until 800 BC and did not become influential until about 400 BC. Here let us simply review developments during the latter half of the first millennium BC as 'Early Horizon' while realizing that a beginning date has yet to be agreed upon. In general this important period saw further consolidation of the northern and southern poles of Andean civilization. Let us briefly examine developments in the south before turning to Chavín which was largely a northern phenomenon.

The southern sphere

Chiripa reflects the beginning of Arid Montane adaptations in the Titicaca region. Populations probably differed ethnically, but similar ways of making a living promoted shared technology and ideas, including the beliefs that underlay the Yaya-Mama Tradition of ceremony and ritual. In the south, where mountain populations were vastly larger than coastal ones, verticality presumably contributed to the coastal spread of highland influence. A southern sphere of loosely shared traditions appears first in ceramic technology, and then in art and ideology.

Pukara

Drawing on the Yaya-Mama Tradition corporate styles began to emerge in the Titicaca region *c*. 400 BC or shortly thereafter. They included Pukara and Tiwanaku at opposite ends of the lake. Both were associated with nascent states and Pukara assumed regional prominence during the last centuries BC. Located 75 km northwest of Lake Titicaca the modern town of Pukara lends its name to the nearby sprawl of ruins demarcating the ancient political center. It is *Plate 42* associated with élite ceramics of a corporate style that was complex and beautiful. Motifs were outlined and subdivided by incision to demarcate intricate zones of color. Vessels were then slip-painted in red, yellow, and black which firing transformed into harmonious tones. The style passed through several phases of development combining stylized and realistic motifs. The latter include birds, llamas, felines, and humans. Human and cat heads were *Plate 41* often modeled in relief on flat-bottomed open bowls. Richly ornamented keros beakers were used as libation vessels and music was played on delightfully decorated ceramic trumpets. Drawing on aspects of the Yaya-Mama tradition, Pukara stone carvers created both full-round and flat-relief sculptures. Incision and excision techniques were used to fashion low-relief carvings on stone slabs and stelae, depicting felines, serpents, lizards, fish, and people. Sculptures *Plate 40* carved in full round tended to emphasize relatively realistic humans, often accompanied by trophy heads, which also figure prominently in the few surviving examples of Pukara textiles.

   Pukara is spread over several kilometers, banked against a range of hills. Elegant corporate works and finely built élite quarters were erected on massive hillside terraces. Faced with large boulders and rock slabs, the biggest terrace had centrally positioned masonry stairs. The spacious summit was occupied by a rectangular sunken court with well made stone walls. On three sides it was *Plate 42* enclosed by a series of detached, one-room structures, creating an arrangement very reminiscent of the court-and-room complex at Chiripa. The central complex consisted of flanked plazas and other structures with dressed stone foundations supporting adobe walls. An extensive residential zone spread across the plain below the elevated civic center. Although little explored, the residential flats, which are covered with ceramics and surface tracery of small houses, suggest a population of urban dimensions.

The nature of Pukara rule is poorly understood; however, it did entail substantial investment in agricultural works, including ridged fields and *cochas*. Rainfall in the region is seasonal and uncertain, and had to be assisted by the construction of enormous, shallow ponds called *cochas*. Connected by canals and ditches, the ponds filled seasonally and as they gradually dried up crops were planted along their banks and eventually in their bottoms. This increased agricultural yields by allowing farming to go on over a much longer time than rainfall alone would support.

The political focus of Pukara was the northern limits of the Titicaca Basin, but its arts made sporadic appearances much further afield. Several specimens of Pukara textiles from the Azapa coast, and occasional Pukara ceramics in the Moquegua Valley point to distant western contacts. In the mountains examples of Pukara stone sculpture are known from the department of Cuzco. These widely scattered remains are suggestive of economic interactions rather than imperial hegemony. There is little evidence that Tiwanaku, at the southern end of the lake, was politically incorporated by Pukara. The first two phases of the Tiwanaku occupation produced radiocarbon dates ranging between 400 BC and AD 100. It was thus contemporary with Pukara, but seems to represent an independent course of development. The two corporate styles share certain similarities, but this is thought to reflect common ancestry in earlier stone carving and artistic concerns of the Yaya-Mama Tradition.

Paracas
Luis Lumbreras cogently argues that Pukura polychrome wares and early painted pottery at Tiwanaku exhibit affinities with contemporary Paracas pottery and textiles found in the coastal valleys of Pisco, Ica, and Nazca, and at the famous coastal necropolis of Paracas. The artistic affinities between this coastal area and the Titicaca Basin are of a rather generic nature, but still *Plates 44–46* affiliate Paracas with the more southerly sphere of civilization. The ceramic

60 *A Paracas vessel depicting a feline face attributed to Chavín influence.*

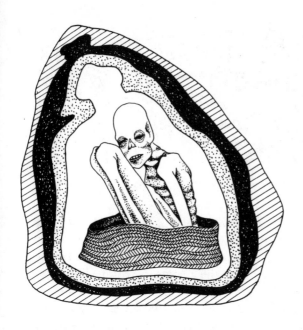

61 *Schematic reconstruction of a Paracas mummy bundle.*

62 *Paracas underground burial vaults included 'Cavernas'-type pits (top) and 'Necropolis'-type masonry crypts.*

tradition includes both monochrome and polychrome wares. Framed by incised lines, polychrome motifs were rendered in resin paints applied after firing. Richly ornamented libation vessels have squat bodies with two short spouts connected by a bridge. Hereafter, such double spout and bridge bottles remain a preferred drinking vessel in the region.

In the Ica Valley, the Paracas style has been subdivided into a ten-phase sequence, designated Ocucaje I through X. By Ocucaje III and IV times, if not earlier, local potters occasionally produced stirrup-spout libation vessels ornamented with relatively realistic depictions of feline heads, and there are no Paracas antecedents for such vessels. These vessels are attributed to the Chavín influence which marks the opening of the Early Horizon. Subsequently, Ocucaje ornamentation became simpler and more naturalistic. During Ocucaje IX and X there seem to have been close ties with the highlands and Pukara.

The seaside Paracas necropolis was not a simple fisherfolk cemetery, but included numerous well-to-do mummy bundles with remarkable finery. Many of the excavated bodies showed evidence of cranial surgery, known as trepanation, where depressed skull fractures were cut out and tumors were removed by incision, scraping, or drilling through the cranial vault. For burial the unattired corpse was first placed in a flexed or seated position and bound with cord to maintain the pose. Next the body was wrapped in textiles and seated upright in a large shallow basket containing elaborate garments and other offerings. Then the basket and body were wrapped together in many

63   Wool in this Paracas embroidered motif probably came from herd animals in the highlands.

layers of plain cotton cloth to form the final bundle. The bundle was then stationed in a subterranean crypt that held up to 40 other mummy bundles which were probably kindred of the deceased. If these were indeed family crypts, then the necropolis was very likely the resting place of élites who inherited their status, for these richly accompanied Paracas interments are suggestive of the later karaka class. However, comparable burials are rare or absent in other Early Horizon contexts and there is little to suggest inherited rule was widespread.

Owing to the dryness of its desert setting the Paracas necropolis has yielded more fine attire and elaborate fabrics then any other contemporary site. Furthermore, the technical characteristics of the textiles are more advanced than those occurring in coastal areas to the north. Among these advances is the *Plate 20* use of alpaca wool. Wool takes and holds a far greater range of dye colors than cotton, and exquisite polychrome embroidery is the hallmark of Paracas fabrics. Embroidered mantles, cloaks, tunics, and headgear depict mythical creatures, and ornately garbed humans wearing gold nose ornaments that look *Plate 21* like cat whiskers, and carrying trophy heads as well as staves that were probably emblems of status and office. Because alpaca fare poorly on the coast, the wool for such textile motifs certainly came from highland herd animals and provides evidence of mountain contacts. It is also noteworthy that burying the deceased in a seated position is characteristic of southern highlanders, whereas contemporary mortuary practices to the north favored extended burials. Links with the mountains and southern uplands probably developed because the Paracas Peninsula was a topographic fulcrum where coastal valleys to the south turn small as sierra and altiplano basins enlarge. The Peninsula and the nearby Ica and Nazca valleys maintain their own lowland cultural and artistic traditions, but strong and persistent connections with the sierra remain.

Chavín and the northern sphere

Chavín is associated with the northern sphere of Andean civilization. This magnificent highland center became influential after the fall of the U-shaped centers of the coast. Debate over Chavín revolves around whether Chavín de Huantar was the consequence or the origin of formative civilization.

Chavín de Huantar

At an elevation of 3,177 m, Chavín de Huantar is situated at the confluence of two small streams, the Mosna and Wacheksa, that feed into the Río Marañón. The site includes a substantial residential area. On the basis of stratified refuse and remains of unimposing dwellings investigated by Richard Burger the occupation is thought to have begun around 800 BC and closed six centuries later after passing through three phases. Set somewhat away from the residential zone, the famous monumental complex of masonry buildings, known as the Castillo, has long attracted great attention. Less than one-tenth the magnitude of the great platform at Sechín Alto, what the Castillo lacks in size is compensated for by remarkable engineering, fine masonry, and marvelous stone art.

Plate 43

Monumental construction is thought to have remained modest until a spate of building activity brought the complex into final form during the Janabarriu Phase (400–200 BC). At this time the Castillo was an amalgam of two contiguous U-shaped structures, called the Old and New Temples. The smaller, older structure was probably erected in one or a few construction stages, whereas the masonry of the larger New Temple attests to growth and remodeling over many stages. This situation is reminiscent of Caballo Muerto where a small U-shaped platform achieved sanctity and architectural immutability early in comparison to a larger companion structure that underwent ever greater elaboration. It may be that the smaller, unalterable structure was the more important, while the larger complex served as a more public venue in a hierarchy of rites and rituals. The Old Temple was highly symmetrical, with block-like wings framing a U-shaped plaza that opened to the east. Within the plaza there was a small, circular sunken court with a banded masonry frieze depicting a procession of anthropomorphic figures above a procession of jaguars.

The southern wing of the Old Temple was expanded laterally to the south in two phases of construction. This created a large block-like platform constituting the base of the New Temple. In front of this, to the east, two detached mounds were erected to create the wings of a U that framed a

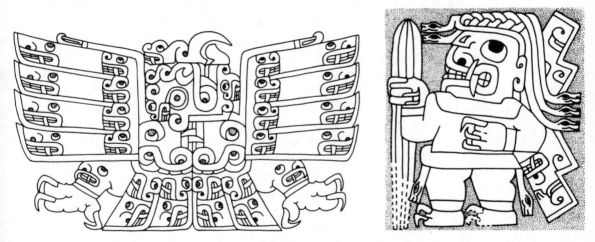

64 *A Chavín New Temple bas-relief of a raptorial bird with serpent motifs indicating feathers.*

65 *With exaggerated canine teeth denoting preternatural status, an anthropomorphic figure carries a hallucinogenic San Pedro cactus instead of a club.*

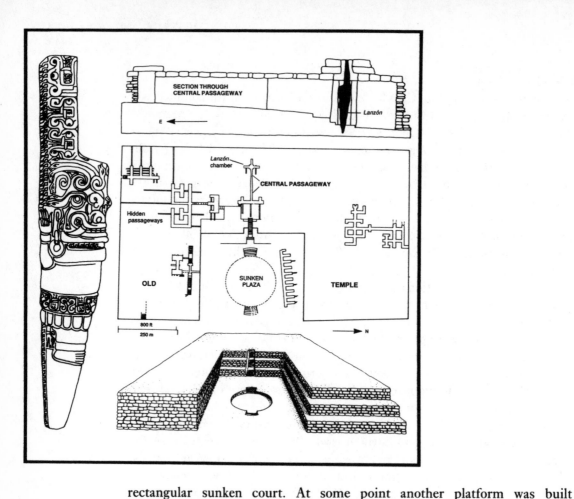

SECTION THROUGH CENTRAL PASSAGEWAY

E ←

Lanzón

Lanzón chamber

CENTRAL PASSAGEWAY

Hidden passageways

OLD

SUNKEN PLAZA

TEMPLE

800 ft
250 m

N →

rectangular sunken court. At some point another platform was built immediately in front of the north wing of the Old Temple. In final form the Castillo, which included all of the original temple and the base of the new one, measured about 80 × 160 m and stood 15 m high. Vertical changes in the masonry of the façade suggest that its elevation was increased over several stages of construction. Near the top of the façade there was a bas-relief cornice depicting spotted jaguars and raptorial birds with feline attributes. Below this *Plate 47* were one or more rows of large, round heads mounted on tenons so that carved heads projected out from the wall. These are the only three-dimensional sculptures at Chavín. They include stylized avian, canine, and anthropomorphic beings rendered with curved tusks, and hair in the form of serpents. Access to the New Temple was via a megalithic stairway, one side of which was black stone and the other white. This led to a black and white portico framed by *Plate 48* one black and one white pillar. Each depicted a ferocious being combining human, feline, avian, and serpentine characteristics. While the black and white entry bespeaks duality, its embellishing art was certainly other-worldly.

The engineering of the Castillo is fascinating because it is not a solid mound of rubble fill. Instead a quarter or more of the platform interior is occupied by a labyrinth of narrow galleries and masonry compartments roofed by great slabs of stone. Built at different levels the galleries are connected by stairways and by an elaborate maze of small vents and drains that pass beneath the exterior plazas

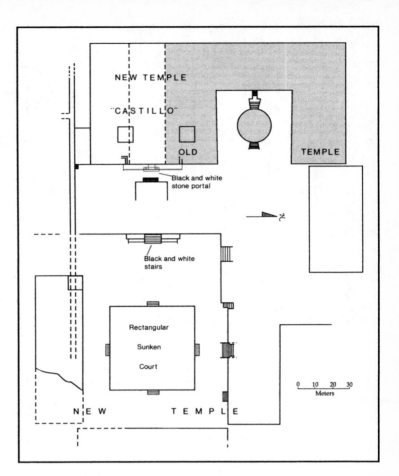

66, 67 *The 'Castillo' of Chavín de Huantar began as a U-shaped ceremonial center – the Old Temple (left) – with a circular sunken court. The Lanzón stela, or principal cult image (shown enlarged), stood in the central passageway. Then (right) the Old Temple, shaded, was expanded southward in two construction stages, and eastern platform mounds were erected to create the New Temple. The new complex held a rectangular sunken court that was aligned with a stairway and portal of black-and-white stone.*

and sunken courts. We have discussed early concerns with the ritual manipulation of water. Here Chavín is of interest because analysis of the hydrological and acoustical characteristics of its conduits and chambers by Lumbreras and colleagues in engineering suggests that by flushing water through the drains, then venting the sound into the chambers and out again the temples could, quite literally, be made to roar! If this were the case the ceremonial center would certainly have seemed other-worldly to the devoted multitudes assembling in front of it.

The galleries served more than acoustical purposes, however. Several contain slabs with traces of incised and painted figures, including a fish with feline attributes and four examples of what might be shrimp. Another, excavated by Lumbreras, was filled with votive offerings of fine ceramics. However, the most interesting galleries occur in the Old Temple. Here along the axes of the mound there are two groups of galleries one above the other in the form of a long cross. Built into the center of the lower gallery where the arms of the cross meet is an imposing stela, the Lanzón. Slender and 4.5 m tall, the *Plate 49* great stone is knife-shaped with the blade point embedded in the floor, and a narrow tang projecting into the ceiling, if not through the floor of the overhead, but unexplored, gallery. Carved in low relief, the stela depicts a being with a human body in simple attire and fingers and toes terminating in claws. Ears adorned with earspools are also human, but the face is markedly feline. Thick

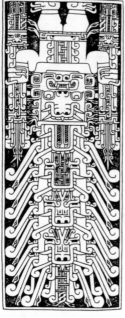

68 (left) The Staff God depicted on the Raimondi Stone could also be 'read' when inverted, as shown in the right-hand image.

69 (above) The Staff God painted on cotton cloth found at the coastal site of Karwa.

lips snarl up and back at their corners exposing two tusk-like canines, while eyebrows and hair are depicted as snakes. Variously called the 'Smiling' or 'Snarling God', the deity faces the eastward entry of the narrow chamber, forcefully confronting an arriving viewer. Above the Lanzón there is a small hole in the stone roof apparently connecting to the upper gallery. Presumably, by speaking into the hole from above, one could speak for the deity below. This has led to propositions that the Lanzón served as an oracle.

The Lanzón survives because it was securely built into the heart of the Old Temple, whereas hundreds of other stone artworks have been dislodged from their original position and carried off. The Tello Obelisk, discovered by Julio Tello outside the Castillo, is a long block of stone with complex, shallow carving representing two aspects of a great cayman, the South American alligator. Although rarely depicted, the reptile was probably a major Chavín deity. On the Tello Obelisk the cayman is depicted with manioc, gourd, pepper, and other cultigens in a manner suggesting that the beast was the mythical donor of these crops. Another important work, the Raimondi Stone, is a monolithic plaque discovered last century by the naturalist of the same name. It depicts an erect anthropomorphic being facing forward with an elaborate, rayed headdress larger than the creature itself, with serpents for hair, projecting canines, claws, and an elaborate vertical staff in each hand. Designated the 'Staff God', this was another central figure in the Chavín pantheon.

Changing conditions

The stonework at Chavín de Huantar was unquestionably the product of master craftspeople and the Castillo reflects not only substantial corporate labor, but professional engineering. How this marvelous center came to command such resources was no doubt related to the appeal of Chavín ideology and conditions that made it widely attractive during the Janabarriu Phase. This ideology seems to have filled a void left by the collapse of the coastal U-shaped ceremonial centers which were largely abandoned or in disarray by 500 BC. From the Jequetepeque to the Río Chillon many of the old centers exhibit dramatic damage from erosion. However, it is not clear if natural disaster, such as an El Niño event, contributed to their decline.

Economic conditions may also have contributed to change. During the latter part of the first millennium BC traces of ancient canals and other agrarian works begin to appear beyond the confines of modern cultivation. This reflects growing pressures on land, and competition for agricultural resources – conditions conducive to conflict. It has been suggested that the precocious Casma state at Sechín Alto was overrun by a military incursion of highlanders near the end of the Initial Period. Introducing maize and llamas, the intruders supposedly brought about many other cultural adjustments. Another source of change relates to propositions that social classes were pulling apart by the end of the Initial Period. Burger's excavations in the residential areas surrounding Chavín provide evidence that people who resided close to the monument enjoyed a better diet than those living on the margins of the settlement. Further afield the Paracas necropolis points to a gentry of privileged status. Thus, Chavín may have been a source of ideological and iconographic innovations that allowed an emerging class of élites to rationalize their superior status.

Chavín influence

Although elaborate stone art defines the corporate iconography of Chavín de Huantar, one thing this center did not do was produce megalithic art for export. When carved stone is occasionally found at contemporary centers in other regions it represents local production that may or may not include style attributes found at Chavín. Two problems are inherent in this situation. First, the ideas and material components of Chavín influence were but a veneer of elements that vibrant local cultures could reject, or accept and modify in whole or in part. Second, media other than stone, such as ceramics and fabrics, are the primary means of assessing the sphere of Chavín influence. Owing to their cultural value, display properties, and portability, textiles served as the major vehicle for disseminating iconography in the Andes, and the largest single body of undisputed Chavín-style art beyond the type site is a cache of several hundred fabric remains from a looted tomb at Karwa on the Paracas Peninsula. These were not garments, but large panels of cotton cloth with Chavín motifs and at least 25 Staff God representations painted in red-orange, tan, brown, green, and blue. The majority of these iconographically charged works were of substantial size well suited for public display as banners or wall hangings.

Plate 46

The Early Horizon was a time of far-reaching technological changes in many media, including textiles. Twining had persisted for the production of ornate, high-status cloth, but was now completely replaced by heddle weaving. Coastal cotton cloth saw the supplemental use of dyed camelid wool. Tapestry came into use along with supplemental, discontinuous warps. Painted, tie-dyed, and batik cloth appeared. These innovations revolutionized Andean textile

70 *A Chavín-style tapestry motif from the coastal Supe Valley.*

production. On the coast this new order of cloth included a widespread, but dispersed, corpus of specimens with Chavín-related motifs analyzed by William Conklin. He concludes that these fabrics do not exhibit regional distinctions in technology or style, as do ceramics, and thus constitute the purest expression of a horizon marker for Chavín times.

The broader distribution of Janabarriu elements reflects extensive communication networks for exchanging goods and ideas. For example, obsidian use at Chavín de Huantar increased five hundred-fold during Janabarriu times, with more than 90 per cent of the stone coming from the Huancavelica region 470 km to the south.

The Ayacucho region yielded Initial Period specimens of hammered sheet goldwork – the earliest in the Andes. Yet, precious metal only came into widespread use during the Early Horizon when metallurgy experienced a technological revolution comparable to the one in textile production. Innovations included soldering, sweat welding, repoussé decoration, and the creation of precious mixtures of gold alloyed with silver or copper. These inventions allowed three-dimensional gold and alloyed objects to be fashioned from preshaped metal sheets that were joined together by complex means to create magnificent artifacts. These bold works are a hallmark of the metallurgical tradition that came to characterize northern Peru and to distinguish it from traditions in the Titicaca Basin and in the northern highlands of Ecuador and Colombia.

There is scant evidence that artisans at Chavín de Huantar produced fine pottery for export. Thus, assemblages of pure Janabarriu pottery only occur in the vicinity of the type site. Less than 80 km away, the contemporary ceramic assemblage at Huaricoto is local. In such situations Chavín influence may be defined by the appearance of certain new vessel shapes such as stirrup-spout bottles, and of certain modes of plastic ornamentation, including surface texturing by combing or rocker-stamping, repetitive rows of incised or stamped circles, circles with central dots, concentric circles, and occasional motifs such as eyes and feline mouths that also appear in stonework.

The distribution of such elements indicates that the northern frontier of Chavín influence coincided with the Sechura Desert, while in the northern highlands recognizable Chavín traits occur at Pacopampa. On the eastern flanks of the Cordillera a strong veneer of Janabarriu-related elements appears at Kotosh and during the Kotosh Chavín Phase. On the coast evidence of Chavín attributes diminishes south of the Río Mala. However, limited influence does appear early in the Ocucaje sequence. In the sierra the southern limits of Janabarriu-like traits are manifested in ceramic assemblages from Atalla near Huancavelica and from Chupas near Ayacucho. In overview, the regional distribution of Chavín-related traits represents a counter-pole to the southern Pukara-Paracas culture sphere.

An ancient oracle

The means by which Chavín ideas and attributes were disseminated has long invoked religious propositions due to the supernatural nature of iconography at the type site. A cult spread by proselytizing missionaries has been suggested. More recently Burger has argued that Chavín was the center of an oracle or family of oracles. The marvelous Lanzón, with its presumed speaking hole, seems well designed to have served as a talking deity, similar to the oracle that *conquistadores* encountered at Pachacamac. Responding to inquiries ranging from Inca battle plans through future weather to the health, fortunes and well-being of individuals, the coastal oracle at Pachacamac drew devotees from far and wide. The cult of Pachacamac was promulgated by nodes of secondary oracles, portrayed as wives, sons and daughters of the prophesying patriarch. Promising appropriate tithes and tribute to the cult, people petitioned the priesthood at the Lurin Valley oracle centers to establish such 'sibling' shrines in their homelands, thereby adding a Pachacamac presence to their local pantheon and huacas.

If Chavín was the center of a cult that operated along similar lines, then the Karwa textile panels may have decorated the shrine of a satellite oracle located well within the territory of traditional Paracas orthodoxy. Karwa depictions of the Staff Deity are noteworthy because gender is frequently indicated and it is always female. Thus, the presumed satellite oracle could have been the wife or daughter of a Chavín patriarch.

Ultimately, Chavín de Huantar was both a center of innovation and a center of synthesis. In a fundamentalist vein older forms of ceremonial architecture were perpetuated, but integrated with new iconography and original ideology. The supernatural concerns of this ideology are curious because it stands on the evolutionary threshold of more mundane times when commoners would toil under karaka rule. How and why Chavín beliefs assumed regional influence is debatable. Nonetheless, they were accompanied by the spread of iconographic and technological innovations that mark the crystallization of the northern pole of Andean civilization both on the coast and in the mountains.

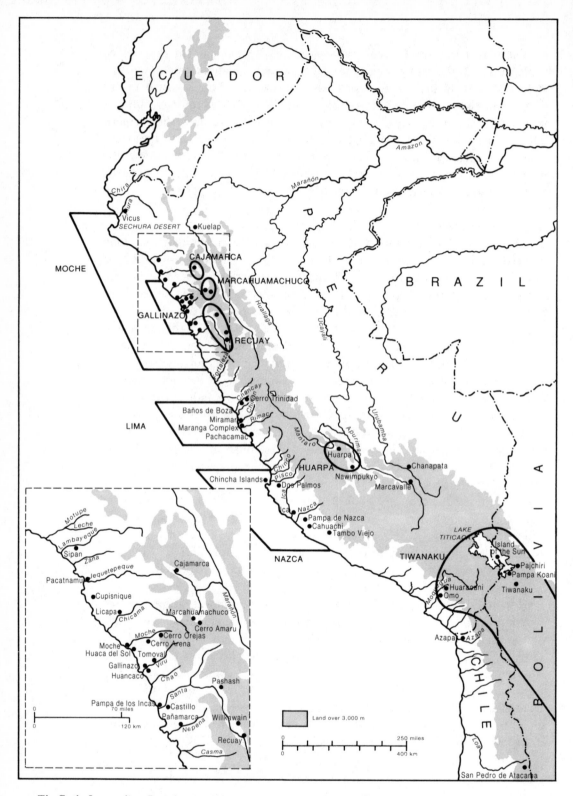

ECUADOR

BRAZIL

P E R U

BOLIVIA

CHILE

Chira
Piura
Vicus
SECHURA DESERT
Kuelap
Marañón
Amazon

MOCHE

CAJAMARCA
MARCAHUAMACHUCO

GALLINAZO

RECUAY

Huallaga

Ucayali

Chancay
Cerro Trinidad
Baños de Boza
Miramar
Maranga Complex
Pachacamac
Chillón
Rimac

LIMA

Mantaro

Apurimac

Urubamba

Huarpa

HUARPA

Chanapata

Nawimpukyo

Marcavalle

Chincha Islands

Chinco
Pisco
Ica
Dos Palmos
Nazca
Ica

Pampa de Nazca
Cahuachi
Tambo Viejo

NAZCA

LAKE
TITICACA

TIWANAKU

Island
of the Sun

Pajchiri
Pampa Koani

Moquegua
Huaracani
Omo
Tiwanaku

Azapa
Azapa

Loa

San Pedro de Atacama

Motupe
Leche
Lambayeque
Sipan
Zana
Pacatnamu
Jequetepeque
Cajamarca
Cupisnique
Licapa
Chicama
Marcahuamachuco
Marañón
Cerro Amaru
Moche
Cerro Orejas
Cerro Arena
Moche
Huaca del Sol
Tomoval
Gallinazo
Huancaco
Viru
Pashash
Chao
Pampa de los Incas
Santa
Castillo
Pañamarca
Nepeña
Willkawain
Recuay
Casma

0   70 miles
0   120 km

Land over 3,000 m

0   250 miles
0   400 km

71 *The Early Intermediate Period: principal sites and areas mentioned in Chapter Seven.*

CHAPTER SEVEN

The Early Intermediate Period

Initially, coastal irrigation and mountain agropastoralism supported economic boom times that saw people spread into under-exploited niches, prosper and increase their numbers. Yet, by the time of Christ most key elements of Maritime-Oasis and Arid Montane adaptations were well refined, and perfection of adaptations led to the filling-in of easily exploited habitats. Land that could be readily farmed was in production and further agrarian expansion required sizable investments. With nature no longer permissive of unbridled expansion the tenor of life changed. The metaphysical and 'other-worldly' emphasis of the early arts gave way to more earthly concerns. Ceremonial centers were dramatically outnumbered by residential communities, and fortified villages, redoubts, and bastions were not uncommon. Rule was no doubt in the name of the gods, but now governance was clearly in the hands of a karaka élite using wealth finance to distinguish their privileged status. The rise of well defined señorios and states with vibrant corporate styles has led some to call the Early Intermediate Period the 'Regional Developmental Period' or the 'Mastercraftsmen Period', and it was certainly both and more. Based on the Ica Valley ceramic sequence, the Early Intermediate Period is dated between *c.* 200 BC and AD 600. Reflecting both population growth and better archaeological preservation, it is not an easy period to summarize due to rich diversity and variation along highland–lowland and north–south axes. Because all remains cannot be reviewed in equal detail, this chapter will highlight economic and political transformations in the northern and southern poles of Andean civilization.

72 Art assumed a more worldly complexion during the Early Intermediate Period and conflict was portrayed in Moche ceramic painting.

North coast

Plates 37,38,50–53

The broad outline of developments in the northern desert were formulated by Rafael Larco Hoyle in the 1940s. Mortuary ceramics characterize a succession of early ceramic assemblages named Cupisnique, Transitory Cupisnique, Salinar, Viru or Gallinazo, and Mochica or Moche, which was subdivided into five phases. The first two assemblages were, in part, contemporary with the flowering of the Sechín Alto Complex. The collapse of U-shaped ceremonial centers and the breakdown of the widely shared ideology associated with them was followed by a period of fragmented readjustment, coeval with Salinar and dating to the end of Early Horizon. Gallinazo marks the emergence of a new cultural order that was politically centered in the Viru Valley. Growing out of this new order in a neighboring valley, Moche matured into a far-flung coastal state based on enduring institutions of Andean statecraft.

Moche was the first archaic state to establish hegemony over the northern demographic center of Andean civilization. The consolidation of a politically fragmented landscape with its multitudes of canal-based parcialidades was based on an ancient two-fold process of territorial expansion. Uniting the kin-based fiefdoms within a single valley was the critical first step. Then populations of smaller drainages could be overrun, or separate parcialidades of larger drainages picked off in piecemeal fashion. This process was played out a number of times. Valley size was important to the vital first act. The process was performed earliest in the small Casma drainages, as Sechín Alto testifies. Stepping up the coast to the somewhat bigger Río Viru, it was later replayed rather tentatively during Gallinazo times. The process then shifted to its final stage, the moderate-sized Moche drainage. Here it was performed twice, with Chimor providing the anchor of consolidating a minor drainage to conquer much larger ones. That the process did not march north into the biggest of all valleys and culminate in a vast coastal state based in Lambayeque suggests that great size tended to work against unification. In Lambayeque enormous irrigation works supported the largest of coastal populations, but the autonomous character of independent canal systems dissected the populace into multitudes of independent, powerful parcialidades. Lambayeque had several episodes of integration, but they reflect confederation more than centralization, and the powerful northern señorios never united to march south and overrun their smaller neighboring valleys.

Signs of change

If Initial Period canals supported the rise of autonomous kin groups that commemorated their identity by building ceremonial centers, then a shift from defining identity to defending it is indicated by the subsequent elaboration of fortifications. It is likely that hostilities increased as easily farmed land was filled in by growing populations, and usurping the property of others became a viable alternative to reclaiming difficult terrain. The distribution of defensive works exhibits potential correlations with the reclamation of arable land. Valley necks and pockets of canyon land were irrigated early because they could be reached by relatively short canals. Fortifications are often more numerous and earlier in these settings than in lower valley areas reclaimed later by larger canal systems. North of the Río Santa coastal valleys become progressively bigger, and it took longer to reclaim their agrarian potentials than it did to bring smaller southern drainages into production. From a regional perspective fortifications seem earliest in the smaller, southern Santa, Nepeña, and Casma valleys where defensive works appear during or before the Early Horizon. In the mountains behind the larger Viru, Moche, and Chicama valleys, surveys by John and Theresa Topic from Canada's Trent University indicate that fortified villages and hilltop bastions became conspicuous during the Early Intermediate Period.

Although the antiquity and elaboration of defensive architecture varies, works on the coast and in the sierra share certain similarities. Fortified villages generally occupy steep-sided ridges within an hour's walk of arable land and water. The route of easiest access to such settlements was along the ridge crest that was characteristically defended by ditches and walls. Bastions and redoubts typically occupy the summits of steep-sided hills, and comprise one or more encircling walls with narrow entrances. Ditches and dry moats often provided additional exterior protection. Interior buildings and rooms vary in number and arrangement, but piles of sling stones are a recurrent feature. The defenses were admirably designed to withstand armed assault, and attempts to storm the bulwarks would be costly. Yet, as the Inca discovered, the strongholds were poorly equipped to withstand long-term siege because most were far from water. Thus, we can conclude that the defensive works were primarily safeguards against armed assault in the form of raids and other short-term conflicts.

Chanquillo in the Casma valley is one of the most spectacular of ancient *Plate 50* keeps and has yielded dates of 342 and 120 BC. Oval in plan, it has three concentric walls of masonry enclosing two circular towers and a rectangular compound of rooms and courts. The Pozorskis attribute its construction to the descendants of sierra intruders who overran the old center of Sechín Alto about 900 BC and prompted the construction of Early Horizon fortifications in the nearby Nepeña Valley. With some 40 hilltop bastions, the Santa drainage has more ancient forts than any other valley. Providing a coast-sierra corridor, the great river carries more water than any other desert drainage. Yet, its arable land totals about half that in Viru, and occurs as discrete canyon or valley-flank pockets irrigated by independent canal systems. During Cupisnique times, the canyon and upper valley supported five separate site clusters. Each contained small habitation sites, several platform mounds (some with sunken courts), and from one to twelve nearby bastions. During Salinar times, most forts remained *Plate 52* in use and settlements clustered in the same areas, although one new pocket of canyon land was opened to occupation.

If defensive works are seen as symptoms of stress, then it is imperative to note that they are greatly outnumbered by undefended residential settlements, lest the rise of conflict be overemphasized. In the Viru Valley, Salinar sites include several fortified hilltops, numerous dispersed households on flatlands, frequent agglutinated villages of 20 to 30 residences, small rectangular compounds enclosing a dozen or so interior rooms, and low mounds of collapsed adobe buildings. Comprising spacious courts, corridors, and rooms, an example of the latter was excavated by Michael West who identified it as the residence and headquarters of local élites and their retainers, including metallurgists – indicated by the presence of copper slags and metalworking instruments in some compartments. This is noteworthy because the privilege of residing in adobe architecture and controlling metallurgical production became exclusive prerogatives of the coastal karaka class.

Salinar bastions are not evident in the Moche Valley, where foundations for later city life were laid at the nascent urban center of Cerro Arena. Occupied by a 2.5 square km sprawl of residential building, Cerro Arena is a rocky ridge that separates the southern middle, and lower valley. A small platform occupied the ridge top. The majority of other structures were made of stone and comprised simple households of several oval or rectangular rooms containing hearths, grinding stones, culinary ceramics, storage vessels, and food remains such as shellfish, guinea pigs, llamas, maize, and fruits. Where two roadways crossed the ridge on graded passes they were flanked by distinct concentrations of large, well-made masonry buildings that included the multi-room dwellings of the local élite. Élite ceramics included certain wares with striking resemblances to pottery from the Cajamarca region. There was certainly interaction with the sierra, but perhaps not of the bellicose nature postulated for the Nepeña and Casma region.

Gallinazo political constellations

The Moche or Mochica style of corporate art and architecture was associated with a well-defined kingdom or state. It is essential to recognize that distinct styles were only formulated after the corporate bodies they served had come into existence. The time lag between the formation of a state and the formation of its corporate style was understood in Inca lore, which portrayed Pachacuti as consolidating the Titicaca region long before he returned to Cuzco as an old man and rebuilt the city in an imperial style. The lore is correct as to the sequence of political formation preceding style formation, but compressing the two events into a single lifetime is suspicious. To understand the Moche state we must look for its political origins amongst the people employing Gallinazo arts and architecture.

Utilitarian ceramics, fired in an oxidizing environment, evolved out of Salinar antecedents, whereas Gallinazo élite wares employed a decorative *Plate 53* technique known as 'negative' or 'resist painting', in which vessels were ornamented with carbon smudge applied after undecorated surfaces were shielded with wax or a similar substance that burned off during firing. Gallinazo potters borrowed this technique from elsewhere to produce a relatively coherent style of élite ceramics. It reflects a high degree of consolidation within individual valleys. The broader distribution of the wares, from the Chicama to the Santa drainages, denotes shared aesthetic tastes, if not marriage or political alliances, among governing gentry.

By the first century BC, Gallinazo populations were undergoing dramatic growth sustained by the construction of large valley-neck canals, and large canals opening the lower valleys to farming and settlement. Indeed, agriculture expanded to its limits in smaller basins, and prehistoric population levels are thought to have peaked in the Viru and Santa drainages. All valleys included abundant, widespread, and varied types of sites. Settlement size was hierarchical. Numerous small farmsteads and hamlets gave way to progressively fewer but successively larger tertiary and secondary settlements which, in turn, were overshadowed by a single primary center of exceptional dimensions. This situation is thought to reflect valley-wide systems of organization based at local primary centers.

Social distinctions in architecture had crystallized. Commoners were relegated to simple quarters with cane walls on stone footings. Masonry and cane was not eschewed by the élite, particularly in canyon settings with few alternative building materials, but adobe – the subsistence of Pacha Mama – was reserved for quarters of the karaka class and for large buildings at corporate centers. Irrigation created soils suitable for producing mud bricks, and they became a hallmark of Gallinazo and later coastal monuments. Bricks were initially made by hand and varied in shape, but as corporate architecture regained the monumentality that had abated with the fall of the great U-shaped centers, construction of ever bigger works soon led to the mass production of mold-made adobes. Fashioned from sturdy cane, four-sided molds were employed to turn out millions of bricks during the later phases of Gallinazo building activity. Mit'a-like labor organization is reflected in what is called 'segmented' construction. When an adobe platform is viewed from the side it can be seen that the distribution of bricks is not homogeneous. Instead, the mound looks like a vast loaf of sliced sandwich bread with distinct vertical seams separating tall slabs of bricks. Slabs are four or more adobes in width, and the bricks in them are mortared together, but contiguous slabs simply rest against one another and are not bonded. With potential antecedents in the mesh-bag fill of preceramic platforms, segmentation is a means of subdividing construction projects into the same sort of repetitive modular units of work that characterized ancient canals and other corporate works on the coast right through to Inca times.

Gallinazo builders undertook enormous projects and the most dazzling reflect new notions about relations between huacas and mountains. Whereas old U-shaped centers were often aligned with and visually focused on a particular peak, now peaks were actually built upon in grand scale. These imposing works include vast terraced platforms perched high upon steep hillsides. One occurs at Licapa, a major center in Chicama. In the Moche drainage another flight of grand terraces was erected at Cerro Orejas, where settlement stretched for several km along a valley neck canal. Down-valley a second major

Gallinazo center existed near Cerro Blanco, but this was built over and largely obscured when the area was transformed into the capital of the later Moche state. To the south the most famous and spectacular of Gallinazo huacas were perched directly atop isolated valley peaks and include the majestic 'Castillos' *Plate 54*   of Santa and Tomoval. Surrounded by a 70 ha residential area accommodating more than 3,000 people, the Santa Castillo was the primary political center in the Santa drainage. In Viru similar numbers may have resided around the peak-top Huaca Tomoval, but the primary focus of élite residence was in the lower valley. Here the cultural type site is a concatenation of numerous mounds formed by collapsed adobe buildings scattered over a 4 to 5 square km area. Known as the 'Gallinazo Group' the poorly preserved standing structures are estimated to contain some 30,000 rooms and compartments, and modern farming has no doubt destroyed a multitude of ground level buildings between the mounds. No Gallinazo site of comparable size survives elsewhere, and many scholars have proposed that this was the nucleus of a multi-valley kingdom. This is reasonable if we envisage a confederated state loosely integrating a segmented power base split among valleys, each with its own hierarchy of monuments and kin-based corporations.

Moche

Political transformations leading to more centralized and consolidated rule arose during late Gallinazo times when the population at Cerro Blanco gained control over the Río Moche and then attained political integration with the much larger Chicama drainage. It is not known how the little valley forged links with the big one. They may have been made less by conquest than through marriage alliance and real or fictive kin alliances among the local karaka. Whatever the case, it was only after Moche and Chicama integrated that the nascent two-valley state adopted a new corporate style, Moche or Mochica, as its hallmark. Continuities in settlement patterns, monumental architecture, molded adobes, extended burials, and utilitarian ceramics point to uninterrupted cultural development. Within the imperial heartland late Gallinazo and early Moche remains are basically indistinguishable, except in the realm of corporate arts. Appearing after the fact, the Moche style tells us that political realities had changed.

The Moche capital. The capital at Cerro Blanco reflects consolidated, albeit potentially dual, power in the form of two enormous architectural complexes some 500 m apart. Built on the flanks of Cerro Blanco, Huaca de la Luna was the smaller and more southerly. Nearer to the river loomed the largest structure *Plate 56*   of solid adobe ever erected in the Andes, Huaca del Sol. The great huacas demarcated the imperial nexus and defined the apex of a regional hierarchy of administrative monuments erected by the state in its provincial coastal valleys. Magnificent buildings once sprawled around Huaca del Sol and Huaca de la Luna and included grand courts with niched walls, low platforms that served as mausoleums, multitudes of adobe residences for the aristocracy, workshops

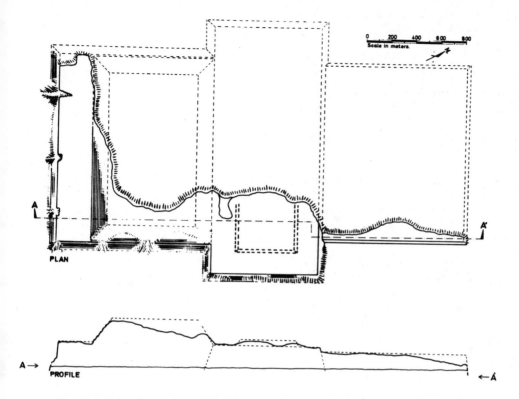

73 *Shown in solid line, the intact remnant of Huaca del Sol suggests that the vast platform was originally cross-shaped.*

producing élite ceramics and corporate arts, and extensive cemeteries of the karaka nobility. Yet, little of the once splendid metropolis survives, for during Moche Phase IV, shortly before AD 600, severe El Niño flooding struck the capital. The city was repaired only to be abandoned when enormous sand dunes swept inland, burying everything except the towering huacas. Although the area of former occupation reaches depths of 7 m, the site now covers only slightly more than 1 square km because the Spanish destroyed the entire western portion of the city when they diverted the Río Moche to hydraulically mine Huaca del Sol for its burial riches.

Today the Huaca del Sol platform measures 340 × 160 m and stands over 40 m high. It is one of the two or three biggest mounds ever erected in the continent, even though less than half of the original monument survives. To judge from the remaining eastern portion, the plan of Huaca del Sol once formed a giant cross with its front to the north. In profile there were four sections creating step-like changes in height. The first and lowest section was the northernmost, which probably had a ramp leading to the summit. The second section was higher and considerably wider, and gave Huaca del Sol its cross-shaped configuration. The third section was by far the highest, and no doubt the most important. The lower fourth and final section had the smallest surface area. Spanish looting focused on the third section, where gaping holes

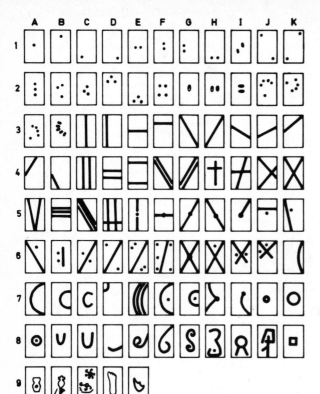

74 To account for their labor, different work forces impressed distinctive makers' marks on the millions of bricks produced to build the Moche capital.

were dug before the river was diverted to undercut the mound and wash out its content. There is scant but important colonial documentation indicating that treasure was discovered during one or more of the large looting operations. This and other lines of evidence suggest that Huaca del Sol was the imperial palace and mausoleum for the heads of state.

Hydraulic mining cut a high profile down the length of Huaca de Sol and reveals information about how the great monument was built and used. Construction was in segments, and more than 100 million bricks were used. To avoid confusion each work-force impressed a single distinctive symbol or 'maker's mark' on the bricks it produced and laid up for its assigned section. More than 100 maker's marks are known and we can assume that an equal or greater number of communities supplied workers. Section two was built in eight stages of construction separated by episodes of use when summit rooms, courts, and corridor complexes were seats of activity. Some activities were rather mundane because refuse was allowed to accumulate on the floors of out-of-the-way rooms. A Phase I burial near the base of Huaca del Sol, exhibiting the same north–south orientation as the mound, suggests early stages of construction were underway by this time. A Phase IV interment of a Moche couple was found atop the last construction stage, and significant building activity ceased after they were laid to rest. Thus, building and use of the colossal monument spanned many generations.

Huaca de la Luna differs from Huaca del Sol in important ways. It is a complex of three platforms that were once interconnected and enclosed by high adobe walls. The smallest mound and most of the largest mound were erected

50 (above) *Perched on a bedrock bluff above the Casma Valley, the Chanquillo fortress is surrounded by thousands of small quarry pits that supplied building stone.*

51 (right) *Gallinazo effigy vessel depicting a monkey.*

52 (below left) *A Salinar stirrup-spout vessel depicting a monkey.*

53 (below right) *Negative black painting decorates a Gallinazo vessel in the shape of a reed boat with a warrior at one end. The figure wears élite earspools and carries a distinctive club with a pike-like end and a pointed-disk mace head. This club form became a major Moche emblem.*

Mounds and pyramids of the Early Intermediate Period

54 (left above) The hilltop Gallinazo Castillo in the Santa Valley is flanked by poorly preserved residential buildings.

55 (left below) Erected in the Nepeña Valley, the Moche administrative center of Panamarca reflected many of the architectural and iconographic features of the imperial capital. An adobe pyramid with a switch-back ramp towered over spacious courts and buildings ornamented with polychrome murals.

56 (above) Only one terraced side of Huaca del Sol ('Pyramid of the Sun') remained intact after colonial looters diverted the Río Moche to hydraulically mine the vast platform. Originally cross-shaped, Huaca del Sol was once the seat of Moche imperial government, and probably the burial place of Moche emperors.

57, 58 *(opposite and above) Frequent in Phase IV of the Moche sequence, portrait heads realistically depicted specific Moche individuals, probably nobles and leaders. The portraiture suggests that while rule was in the name of the gods, governance was identified with real people.*

59 *(right) A late Phase IV libation vessel, decorated with fine-line painting, depicts richly attired 'runners' or chaskis. Each runner carries a small bag in one hand, thought to contain beans.*

60 *(below) A polychrome mural of spider-like motifs ornamented a summit court at the site of Huaca de la Luna, close neighbor of Huaca del Sol in the Moche Valley.*

Moche art

Moche ceramics

61 (left) Holding a typical Moche
mace-headed pike, this probably portrays
a human disguised as a deer.

62 (below) A Moche vessel depicting a
llama.

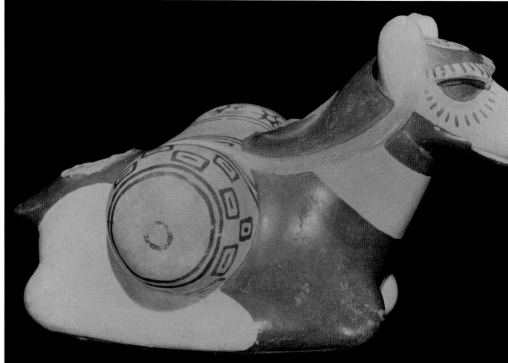

Sipan

63 (above) A head of embossed gold with inlaid eyes found at Huaca Sipan in the Lambayeque Valley, one of the richest unlooted burials to be discovered in the New World.

64 (right) Excavation of a Moche warrior priest tomb at the site.

Moche crafts

65 (left) *The emblem of Moche culture was a distinct mace-headed pike shown on the top of this vessel and carried by the painted warrior.*

66 (below) *Metal objects denoted status, and their manufacture was a highly sophisticated technique. Here, three metalworkers blow into tubes to sustain temperatures high enough for smelting in the dome-shaped kiln, while a fourth smith arranges the heated objects.*

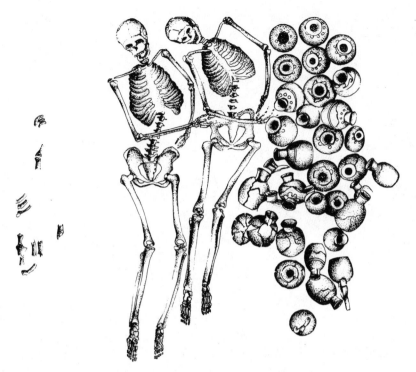

75 *A man with llama bones at his side and a woman with Phase IV vessels were jointly interred atop section two of Huaca del Sol.*

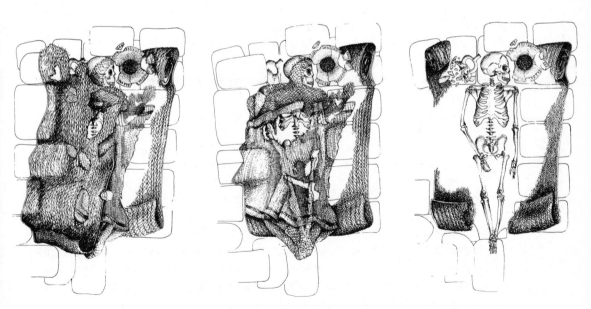

76–78 *Burial within the bricks of an upper construction stage preserved mats and textiles accompanying a Phase III adolescent grave in section two of Huaca del Sol.*

79 *A mural motif from
Huaca de la Luna.*

at about the same time that construction started on Huaca del Sol. The small platform must have had considerable sanctity because it was never altered, whereas after long use the large platform was partly reconstructed and its height increased. Building of the mid-sized mound began in Phase III, and it underwent many stages of construction interspersed with periods of use. The two larger mounds were heavily looted, but it is not clear if they yielded votive offerings or burials. Refuse was never allowed to accumulate on any floors in the Huaca de la Luna complex.

Even more telling of special status is the fact that the walls of the complex were ornamented with the largest and most varied corpus of Moche murals yet *Plate 60* discovered. They consist of rich polychrome depictions of anthropomorphic and zoomorphic beings, and of animated clubs, shields and other artifacts. Some share canons with the ceramic arts. Significantly, Huaca del Sol lacked a comparable array of murals although its façade was painted in red and other colors. If Huaca del Sol was a huaca sepultura where the heads of state reigned and were interred, then Huaca de la Luna seems to have been the imperial huaca adoratorio where the national pantheon was attended to. It is difficult to prove, but tempting to see the two great monuments as reflecting dual organization at the apex of rule, with a dominant imperial moiety operating from Huaca del Sol, and its counterpart from Huaca de la Luna.

As at other ancient capitals, Moche rulers invested substantial labor in opening new agricultural lands around their imperial metropolis. Where ancient planting surfaces survive, they reflect corporate land management, with fields laid out in a standardized manner and often divided into small rectangular plots of uniform size. Some field areas were replete with small adobe platforms that served as stations for supervisory personnel directing agricultural tasks. Working the fields was presumably an obligation or tax that the peasantry executed for the government, because there is little doubt that commoners and karakas had become distinct classes.

178

80 An anthropomorphic mural motif from Huaca de la Luna.

Art and iconography. Fine arts were fully in the service of the Moche state, which expressed its concerns in brilliant iconography that was marvelously realistic, yet highly symbolic. The corporate style was extremely standardized because it served centralized political concerns. Although the style was expressed in many media, the surviving sample of Moche art is dominated by ceramics and by stirrup-spout libation vessels in particular. Most libation vessels were made in multi-piece molds. Standardization was apparently achieved by producing molds in the imperial homelands of the Moche and Chicama Valleys and shipping them to workshops in the provinces. There were two different groups of libation vessels. The first comprised forms with bodies molded in highly naturalistic forms of people, such as warriors, animals that include felines and birds, and striking supernatural beings merging human and animal attributes. Some of the subject matter has Gallinazo antecedents, but the ceramic technology for producing realistic vessels was probably imported, and might have come from as far afield as Ecuador's Chorrera culture. The rise of three-dimensional realism, which marks the emergence of the corporate Moche style, coincides with the emergence of naturalistic painting on vessels, which comprised the second group of libation vessels. Negative or resist painting carried over from Gallinazo times, but there was a new focus on more durable pigments in the form of clay slips emphasizing figures in red rendered upon a white or cream background. Freed from the constraints of molds, painting was done with progressively narrower brushes and culminated in magnificent 'fine-line' depictions that invite comparison with Greek vase painting. Fine-line painting provides the fullest record we have of iconographic personages and their complex interactions.

Plates 61,62

Plate 59

Recent research by Christopher Donnan on Moche arts and their mortuary associations has revolutionized our knowledge of Moche iconography, showing that it was a means of symbolic communication based upon a limited number of themes. The entire corpus of Moche art may have revolved around fewer than

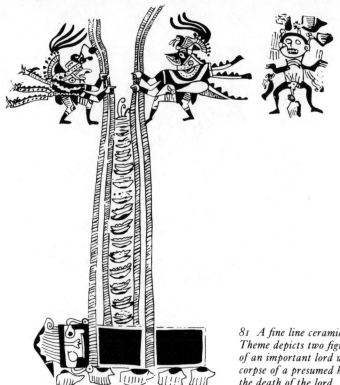

81 *A fine line ceramic motif from the Moche Burial Theme depicts two figures using ropes to lower the coffin of an important lord while vultures dismember the corpse of a presumed healer accused of malpractice in the death of the lord.*

two dozen themes, or stories. Similar to stories about the birth and resurrection of Christ or King Arthur's Camelot, Moche themes were recounted orally, depicted graphically, and acted out as pageants and rituals. Each theme entails a cast of characters that may include animals, humans, and fanciful beings. Similar to a scene from a play, the characters in a theme are depicted as interacting in a repetitive manner in recurrent settings. And, similar to an epoch play with multiple scenes, some characters reappear in more than one theme and interact with different casts in different settings.

We do not, as yet, understand the messages that these themes conveyed. Some may have been origin myths, while others pertained to heroic deeds of important figures. One is clearly a burial theme. It depicts the demise and interment of a kingly figure, while vultures consume a shaman apparently accused of malpractice. Different characters appearing in the iconography are set apart by distinct costumes and accoutrements, and it is significant that some burials contained individuals with the same costumes and accoutrements. The most noteworthy case is the 'warrior priest', who is the main character in the 'presentation theme'. Entailing a large cast, the iconographic action depicts the sacrifice of prisoners, collection of their blood in a special goblet, parading the goblet and then presenting it to the warrior priest, who is the central character, richly garbed with a distinctive uniform and headdress. This character is represented among major interments recently discovered by Walter Alva at *Plates 63,64* Huaca Sipan in the Lambayeque drainage. These are the richest unlooted tombs to be excavated in the hemisphere. Each individual was accompanied by much precious metal, a presentation goblet, and uniforms and headgear similar to those depicted iconographically. In the case of the warrior priest and other artistic figures, it seems that iconographic characters were identified with offices and roles that were held by living individuals. This raises the intriguing possibility that iconographic themes expressed corporate charters which defined political positions, official posts, and important vocations.

The Moche artistic world also admitted fanciful animals and strange beings. Incredible creatures fight against or assist important characters such as warrior priests. Weaponry, men in arms, and combat are frequently depicted. At the same time authentic people were depicted on portrait-head libation vessels, their facial features sculpted in intimate detail.

Plate 65
Plates 57,58

Moche iconography and burials leave no doubt that rule was in the hands of a karaka class and identified with real people. As in later times, élite status was probably justified by special creation myths that separated commoners from karaka and allowed the nobility to rule by divine right. Thus, lords who held the offices, such as that of warrior priest, were probably viewed as demigods. The dazzling funerary offerings of the Sipan tombs far outstrip the humble accompaniments that commoners took to their graves. Burials excavated at Huaca del Sol and elsewhere show marked differences in élite wealth, matching iconographic indications that the nobility was stratified by rank and role.

Imperial hinterlands. In the far north, Moche presence extended into the Vicus section of the central Piura drainage, which formerly lay within the sphere of Ecuadorian influence. In the south, frontiers reached into the Huarmey Valley, and Moche seafarers established a far-flung presence on more than 30 off-shore islands extending down the coast as far as the southern Chincha Islands. Thus, this ancient state extended its maritime hegemony far beyond its terrestrial

82 *Two Moche warriors fighting: painting from a vase. Both hold maces with pointed staves. The victor, who has knocked off his opponent's helmet, holds him by the hair. He wears a shirt and helmet decorated with a design like a medieval coat of arms. The device on the left is a trophy of arms, which includes two maces, two darts and a square shield. Hummingbirds hover above.*

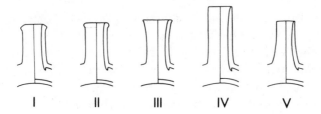

83 Larco Hoyle employed five different spout forms of libation vessels to define five phases of Moche ceramic arts.

frontiers. Dual organization seems to characterize the imperial hinterland. A pattern of direct, centralized rule typifies the small valleys south of Río Moche, while a pattern of multifaceted governance typifies large valleys to the north. The great northern valleys, with multitudes of powerful, but competitive, parcialidades, apparently called for more flexible political policies.

Corporate arts seem to have functioned rather differently in the north than in the south. Potters lavished exceptional care on the stirrup-spouts of libation vessels, and spouts were certainly of exceptional significance. There were five spout forms, each apparently demarcating a different phase in the development of Moche style arts. Phase I and II vessels appeared early in the Moche-Chicama imperial heartland but were largely absent elsewhere, with the striking exception of the Vicus region in the far north. Here the two spout forms made an early appearance and remained in use until AD 600. Thus, the northernmost stirrup-spouts became a conservative tradition that endured while later phase vessels were introduced in the south. Therefore, the Vicus spouts must demarcate kin, class, or social affiliation that did not change for centuries. The spout types were introduced more or less sequentially, with the Phase V form securely anchored by late radiocarbon dates, but the introduction of new shapes did not preclude continued production and use of prior forms, particularly in the north.

The occurrence of early, but persistent spout forms in Vicus may indicate that Moche colonists first reached the Piura drainage by sea. The intervening northern valleys may then have been incorporated on a piecemeal basis with some parcialidades entering the imperial fold generations before others. The imposition of centralized rule by means of a single state-built administrative center governing an entire valley does not characterize the northern provinces. Instead, each of the great northern drainages seems to have supported several Moche centers. Some, such as Sipan, were much larger and more important than others. Forging centralized organization among the largest of all coastal populations was seemingly avoided in favor of keeping the populace segmented among competing parcialidades, and revolts avoided by maintaining divisions between señorios. To this end the Moche administration apparently pursued a pattern of indirect rule in the north, based upon incorporating local lords and karakas within the imperial government and then ruling through them. Just such a policy was later used by both Chimor and Tahuantinsuyu in these northern regions. From this perspective the remarkable tombs at Sipan might represent the interments of regional governors or vice royalty.

84 *Defeated and stripped, vanquished warriors ascend the huaca of their noble victor in this drawing from a Moche vessel.*

South of the Río Moche, valleys grow progressively smaller, and this confronted the government with a different set of demographic and administrative realities. Once united, we may presume that Moche had the manpower to overrun southern valleys, irrespective of their degree of internal consolidation, and to assert direct rule. Expansion probably entailed conquest and coercion as well as voluntary conversion of local lords. In most valleys the state erected a monumental administrative center of grand design, using the architectural canons of the imperial capital, including Huancaco in Viru, Pampa de los Incas in Santa, and Pañamarca in Nepeña, the last ornamented with brilliant polychrome murals including a depiction of the presentation theme. *Plate 55*

A 'Pax Moche' prevailed, and local bastions ceased to be erected. People were moved from fortified villages into mid and lower valley agricultural lands. In some valleys, such as Santa, the total amount of land occupied by dwellings decreased. This could reflect the institution of either a mit'a-like tax requiring people to spend a great deal of time working elsewhere, or a mitamaq-like resettlement policy that moved people to new locations. It is significant that the heavy hand of the state ended in Nepeña, skipped over the Casma Valley, and reasserted its presence some 70 km further south in the Huarmey drainage. It is doubtful that the small Casma drainage was unconquerable, and more likely that the ancient nexus of Sechín Alto imbued the valley with special status and strong on-going traditions. Respecting such conditions, Casma was probably controlled indirectly from adjacent valleys. With imperial frontiers reaching from Huarmey to Vicus on the mainland, and from the southern Chincha Islands to islets in the far north offshore, Moche represents a remarkable achievement in statecraft. For the first time the largest of coastal populations were forged together as one nation. Yet, peace and prosperity were not enduring. Shortly before AD 600 nature turned pernicious, and in Phase V times the southern provinces were lost to internal and external pressures that will be examined in the next chapter.

The central and south coasts

In terms of frequency and size, early U-shaped monuments had their primary distribution in the Ríos Chancay to Lurin region. Conceptual unity disappeared when the centers collapsed. Corporate construction declined and became more variable as the complexion of life changed. After 400 BC people started producing red, oxidized pottery decorated with white pigment. White-on-red ceramics from the Chancay Valley are known as 'Baños de Boza', while 'Miramar' designates contemporary remains in the Chillon region. These are not corporate styles, but local mergers of folk and élite wares that drew upon a shared ceramic technology. Similar to Salinar in the north, they seem to reflect a time of transition.

Lima

By about AD 200 a stronger focus of settlement and monumental construction emerged in the central Rimac Valley. Called the Lima culture, it is now beneath the modern city. The primary center was probably the Maranga complex, which included numerous adobe buildings as well as three sizable platforms. The principal huaca measured about 270 × 100 m and stood 15 m high, and was constructed of hand-made bricks. A number of extended burials have been excavated nearby. The bodies were normally extended and laid out in the same north–south orientation as the large platform. Most contained few accompaniments, but one élite individual lay on a cane litter and was accompanied by two dismembered human sacrifices. Growing out of the earlier white-on-red pottery tradition, Lima decorative ceramics employed black pigments as well as occasional negative painting, and fish and serpents with triangular heads were common decorative motifs.

The pottery was fairly widespread, and may reflect loose political linkages. It occurs in the Chancay region at Cerro Trinidad, where a long adobe wall painted in four colors was found, depicting an interlaced fish design as on the ceramics. In the Lurin Valley the local population clustered along short canals irrigating pockets of land in the canyon drainage at the beginning of the Early Intermediate Period. Gradually, longer canal systems were opened in down-valley locations, and larger settlements arose nearby, as did élite residences on hilltops. Agricultural expansion into the lower valley facilitated the founding of Pachacamac which is not far from the shore. This became a notable Lima center and also included élite residential compounds. Built over in later times, the core of the large 'Sun' huaca was probably erected at this time, as was the flanking 'Pachacamac Temple', and another adobe platform exhibiting fish-motif murals. Numerous burials suggest that the center enjoyed sacrosanct status. Presumably the Pachacamac oracle came into existence at this time, and

85 *A Nazca ceramic depiction of a demonic creature holding a trophy head.*

86 *A Nazca ceramic painting of a richly attired demonic being.*

if so, the cult of the oracle and its priesthood endured for more than a millennium while petty kingdoms and great states rose and fell. Along with the Island of the Sun in Lake Titicaca, Pachacamac remained one of the most sacred places in the Inca realm until it was sacked by Pizarro's brother.

Nazca

Nazca is one of the most famous of Andean corporate styles because its polychrome ceramics exhibit both technological fineness and rich symbolism. Distributed along the coast from the Chincha to the Acari Valley, its core area comprised the Ica and Nazca drainages. In the Nazca drainage there were cemeteries with seated-flexed burials, whose grave goods provide the master stylistic sequence of periods and epochs. Resin painting characterized the earlier Paracas style, while polychrome slip painting, which defines the onset of the Early Intermediate Period, is estimated to have appeared around 200 BC.

Plates 68–70

The polychrome ceramic tradition has been divided into eight epochs or phases. Nazca 1 preserved the mythical content of Paracas art, but introduced realistic subject matter in the form of birds, fish, and many kinds of fruit. Realism increased in Phases 2, 3, and 4, collectively called 'Monumental' because of bold but simple renditions of plants, animals, people, and demons against white or red backgrounds. Nazca 5 witnessed many innovations, including bodiless human heads and demon heads, as well as new vessel forms, and is known as 'Proliferous' because backgrounds are cluttered and filled in. Phases 6 and 7 retained earlier motifs while adding militaristic motifs and élite portraits. At this time, some vessels exhibited design concepts similar to Moche ones, and cultural contacts may have come by way of the sea. Nazca 8 saw continuing break-up of design motifs with human and demonic figures rendered in disjointed manners. Over time the trends toward elaboration and complexity conveyed a rich iconography, which was intelligible to its users but eludes us today. Unfortunately, radiocarbon assays on the Nazca sequence are characterized as much by overlap as by sequential ordering. Although Phase 8 is estimated to end *c.* AD 600, there are seemingly associated dates of AD 755, or later. Thus, chronology remains a problem.

In addition to ceramics, Nazca is renowned for its textiles, and its core valleys have yielded more fine fabrics than any other region of Peru. Growing out of the sophisticated Paracas tradition, the technical characteristics of Nazca textiles were more precocious than those occurring in areas to the north. Textiles were the media of stylistic innovation and new motifs appeared on fabrics before ceramics. Although local use of camelid hair began early, massive quantities of alpaca wool now came into use. The north coast did not witness comparable expenditures of wool for almost a thousand years. Cultural esteem of wool, along with burials in a seated position, link Nazca with the south highland sphere of influence. The source of coastal wool must have been sierra herds, probably from the Ayacucho region which enjoyed close relationships with the coastal communities.

The corporate style was remarkably vibrant for a region characterized by small to moderate drainages and modest populations. The Río Nazca is formed by eight short drainages that cut across a wide, flat coastal pampa and then converge 35 km inland to form a single channel leading to the sea. In three cases, surface runoff disappears at a midpoint where drainages first leave the foothills. Moisture then flows under the stream beds as they begin to cross the pampa, but reappears as surface runoff down channel. Limited runoff restricted farming to the upper regions of individual drainages and resulted in a series of separate oases rather than an agriculturally unified valley. Habitation sites and small villages were frequently located on terraced hillsides adjacent to irrigated flood plains. The separate areas of surface flow were reclaimed early on and settlements clustered along the drainages above and below their dry midpoints during the first four Nazca Phases. Investigations by Katherine Schreiber and Jose Lancho Rojas indicate that Phase 5 settlement and agricultural patterns changed significantly. Dry drainage sections were reclaimed by a remarkable innovation: long tunnels, similar to Near Eastern *qanats*, were dug back into the aquifers. Intersecting subsurface runoff, the gently sloping tunnels channeled flow down their course to surface tanks that supplied canals. These subterranean conduits reached up to 540 m in length and were equipped with vertical ventilator shafts. The settlements in surface flow regions decreased in number during later phases, whereas tunnel-fed farmland remains densely inhabited, and it has been suggested that the new technology arose sometime after AD 500 in response to changing water conditions such as drought. Independent evidence shows that beginning about AD 560 the Andes experienced a very long drought.

The corporate style was, for a time, associated with a multi-valley state that incorporated four drainages during the early Nazca phases. Its northern incursion into the Pisco Valley is reflected in the Phase 2 site of Dos Palmos, a settlement composed of densely packed, contiguous rooms of rectangular form grouped around five scattered plazas. Southern expansion into the Acari Valley is expressed at Tambo Viejo, which was occupied during Phase 2 and abandoned at the end of Phase 3. The era of expansion coincides with the florescence of Cahuachi, the Nazca capital located on the south bank of the Río Nazca 50 km inland.

Studies by Helaine Silverman reveal that Cahuachi was markedly different from the Moche capital at Cerro Blanco. It was not so much a city as a congregation center. It covered some 150 ha, but less than half the area had structural remains. Occupation began as a dispersed agricultural village, and in Phase 2 a small-scale corporate construction was undertaken. In Phase 3, Cahuachi assumed regional importance with the building of 40 mounds, of varying size and form, with forecourts and attendant plazas. The platforms were not solid brick, but had adobe façades that enclosed natural hills and eminences. They reflect minimal labor investments to achieve visually impressive ends, and were clearly the focal points for special activities. Decorated pottery is found as much as 70 per cent more frequently on them than in other areas. Some platforms held elaborate textiles stored in large utilitarian vessels, while others housed élite burials. Beginning with multitudes of small mounds there was something of a hierarchy in platform size that culminated with the so-called Great Temple. Capping a natural rise, this was a stepped platform 20 m high with a façade of elongated, wedge-shaped adobes. Around the base, adobe rooms and courts were erected, including a spacious plaza measuring about 47 × 75 m.

If platforms reflect politics, then contrasts between the Moche and Nazca capitals speak of centralized versus confederated rule. Cahuachi gives the impression that every parcialidad or kin group participating in the confederation asserted its identity by erecting a separate mound complex. The paucity of domestic quarters and refuse leads Silverman to suggest that the center was built and used by people who, by and large, lived elsewhere. People residing along the separate Nazca drainages presumably came together at Cahuachi on a cyclical basis to conduct rituals and carry out common business. Cahuachi seems to have maintained a highly sacred and ceremonial character that overshadowed concerns of mundane rule. Corporate construction declined dramatically at the end of Nazca 3, and in the following phase, the center was transformed into a great mortuary ground and place of votive offerings. Its status as a special burial place persisted long after Nazca times and resulted in horrendous looting of the ancient capital.

Nazca is particularly famous for its desert markings and ground drawings that occupy the pampa flats between the river's tributaries. Called 'geoglyphs', *Plate 67* the markings were created by brushing away and removing the upper, dark, oxidized desert sediments to expose lower, lighter-colored surfaces. Experiments by Anthony Aveni and a small team of co-workers indicate that 16,000 square m of desert pavement can be cleared in about a week's time. Therefore, very large figures could have been created by relatively small crews. Created at many different times, geoglyphs are widely but sporadically distributed along

87 A Nazca geoglyph or ground drawing of a monkey.

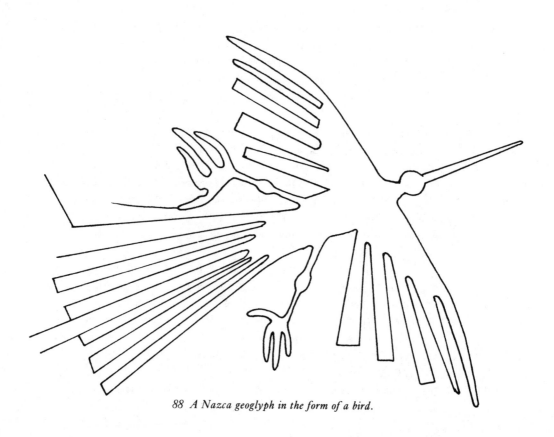

88 A Nazca geoglyph in the form of a bird.

89 *A killer whale depicted on a Nazca ceramic.*

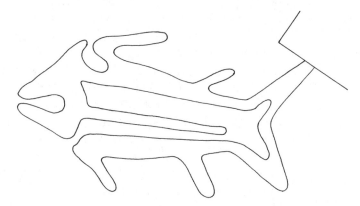

90 *A Nazca geoglyph in the form of a killer whale.*

the Andean coast, and occur from the Lambayeque region into northern Chile.

There are at least two broad categories of glyphs. One consists of figures rendered on hillsides so that they were readily visible to passers-by. Akin to billboards, these markings often depict humans, llamas, or other life forms as well as occasional geometric or abstract symbols. Occurring on flat, horizontal plains, the second category of compositions seems to have served as ritual pathways. In the Moche area I discovered a geometric line that issued directly out of the entrance of a small hut, and the figure was certainly intended to be walked on. Cleared sections of the desert are discernible at ground level, but very large compositions and long, flat lines cannot be seen in their entirety. It was only through the study of aerial photographs that Paul Kosok and Maria Reiche first discovered the exceptional concentration of glyphs on the 200 square km pampa flats of Nazca. There are some early hillside figures, but the dominant compositions are flat-land forms, including 1,300 km of straight lines of varying widths, and lengths reaching 20 km or more, and 300 geometrical figures consisting mostly of trapezoids, triangles, zigzags and spirals. Together, the linear and geometric figures cover a staggering 3.6 million square m, or about two per cent of the pampa surface.

Lines often radiate out from hills, called ray centers. Some 62 such nodes are interconnected by long lines that often lead to irrigated oases, and they were certainly trans-pampa pathways. Trapezoidal figures measure 40 × 400 m on average. Their axes are oriented along stream courses, the skinny ends pointing upstream about two-thirds of the time, suggesting symbolic connections with water. Compositions dating to Nazca times include three dozen animal drawings, comprising many birds, fish or killer-whales, a monkey, a spider, and a few plants. Most are relatively small and confined to one corner of the pampa. Unlike trapezoids these are not 'solid' compositions with cleared interior surfaces, but outlines. The line never crosses itself and has separate starting and end points, as if it was intended to be walked.

Geoglyphs at Nazca and elsewhere certainly served more than one function. Calendrical significance for the lines has been suspected, but not yet demonstrated. The great concentration of figures on the Nazca pampa represents by far the largest cultural artifacts of the region's ancient inhabitants. Similar to the many mounds at Cahuachi, they are numerous and impressive, but do not represent great expenditures of energy. Although the geoglyphs are technically similar, each seems to have been created separately, used for a time, and then forgotten. New figures cross old ones in amazing profusion, and the works were obviously not part of a larger, centralized conception planned by one mind at one time. As with mounds at the capital, one is left with the impression of confederated beliefs, and while everyone agreed that geoglyphs were important, each group erected its own. Thus, individuality – with cultural coherence, but without large-scale or integrated power – were Nazca hallmarks.

The sierra

Moche and Nazca had important and often powerful neighbors in the mountains. Much of the sierra was occupied by dispersed, rural inhabitants, but sizable populations clustered in the highland basins. Refinement of high montane adaptations facilitated a northward thrust into the Ecuadorian sphere of tropical-influenced sierra populations, known as Kuelap. These colonized mountain settings were in a sense more tropical than Andean. Kuelap is represented by mighty masonry ruins perched high atop hills shrouded with tropical vegetation in the modern Department of Amazonas. Many of the buildings were circular, and important corporate structures were ornamented with masonry reliefs of geometric and zoomorphic figures. The nature of Kuelap political organization has not been established, but the economy was based on the exploitation of vertically stratified ecological zones, with llamas herded in high pasturelands and crops ripened in the humid valley bottoms.

To the southeast in higher mountains, Cajamarca archaeological remains occur in the lush sierra basin of the same name. They are largely represented by a long, five-phase ceramic tradition characterized by the use of kaolin paste to produce fine white vessels painted in red, black, or orange. Phase 2 is broadly contemporary with Moche. Reflecting either verticality or trade, the pottery frequently occurs at Moche sites in the lower Jequetepeque Valley. Later in time, it reached the Ayacucho and Cuzco basins, indicating that the white ware was much esteemed. Although Cajamarca ceramics reflect a distinct corporate style, it has yet to be associated with sizable monuments indicative of political power as in the neighboring Crisnejas Basin.

Marcahuamachuco

In the Crisnejas Basin, a robust sierra state arose during the Early Intermediate Period. Its capital lay due east of the Río Moche headwaters at Marcahuamachuco, a hilltop site which is one of the greatest of highland monuments. These and other ruins in the region have been the focus of a Canadian archaeological mission headed by John and Theresa Topic. Their work indicates that the rise of this political center, around AD 300, was associated with regional economic and demographic changes. Local populations grew in size as new lands were brought under cultivation and as commerce increased along a sprawling network of roads, around which many settlements clustered. The capital was associated with a major north–south highway, while an outlying hierarchy of state-built administrative centers controlled roads along western slopes of the Cordillera. The western centers no doubt reflect state concerns with verticality. Although this was basically a folk adaptation, it was politicized by the rise of powerful coastal states governing sierra access to lowland resources. Furthermore, it is clear that Marcahuamachuco was not simply concerned with verticality, but with 'horizontality' as well. The capital's north–south highway asserts significant highland commerce moving along the mountain chain.

Long, narrow buildings, called galleries, are the hallmark of corporate architecture in the region. Construction of such edifices began before 200 BC. In some galleries interior floor space was left open, creating great halls, while in others internal cross walls formed rooms and compartments. Early one-story forms gave rise to very long, multi-storied galleries at the capital, where building began around AD 300.

Marcahuamachuco is perched atop a high, slim, steep-sided plateau 3.5 km long. Its many tall buildings created an imposing city visible from vast distances. Monumental masonry construction began at the northwest end of the plateau, then shifted to the central section, and to the elaborate southern 'Castillo' by AD 500, where building activity continued for another three centuries. Circular galleries, including the five-storied Castillo, are among the most striking buildings, enclosing a central area filled with other buildings and courts. Built on an elevated platform, the Castillo fronted a great stone-paved plaza enclosed by long rectangular galleries. Ornamented with niches, the massive walls of rectangular galleries framed great halls measuring up to 8×48 m and probably serving as gathering places for the governing élite. Long curvilinear galleries were often erected along the edge of the steep plateau. The ground floors of these buildings were residences, while the upper stories were often used for storage. Important people were interred above ground in mausoleums and chullpa-like towers scattered about the ruins.

Within a 10 km radius of Marcahuamachuco, there are more than half a dozen other monumental centers with similar large galleries and élite architecture. This concatenation of subsidiary sites reflects yet another imperial landscape different from Moche's where almost all monumental construction was concentrated at the Moche capital. Significantly, Cerro Amaru, the satellite center closest to the sierra capital, seems to have served religious purposes. Votive offerings found in three elaborate reservoirs suggest that observances included ritual manipulation of water. The Marcahuamachuco sierra state was long-lived, and we will return to its political fortunes in the next chapter.

Recuay

Plate 71

Recuay is a vibrant corporate style found in the Callejon de Huaylas and the headwaters of the Río Santa. It is known primarily from looted collections of fine ceramic vessels generally made of white kaolin paste. Decoration employed negative painting, positive painting, and three dimensional modeling. It is reminiscent of the Moche corporate style both in technical mastery and in portraying a standardized, repetitive iconography. There is a strong emphasis on men in arms, often bearing trophy heads. In some cases, a prominent male is accompanied by one or more female figures. Serpents, felines, and condors are common motifs and probably had supernatural connotations. Double-headed serpents, two-headed animals, and dragon-like creatures certainly had such significance.

Two types of stone sculptures were produced. One, a Chavín carry-over, comprised tenon heads for ornamenting important buildings. These are often realistic male heads presumed to be karaka warriors. None have been found in their original positions, nor have any free-standing sculptures of human form, which comprise the other category of stonework. Analysis of the statues by Richard Schaedel suggests that production began early and led to two phases of

Plates 72,73

Recuay works. Both are characterized by squat figures, about a meter tall, with oversized heads. About a third of the examples are women, while the males often carry clubs, shields, or trophy heads.

Looted long ago, important élite were interred in subterranean mausoleums, roofed with large slabs and covered with earth. At Willkawain they resemble subterranean houses with several rooms or crypts. One masonry chamber was about 1 m in height and width, and 7 m in length. Entered through the roof via a shaft, intruders had rifled the crypt leaving but a few fragmentary offerings. At the hilltop site of Pashash, Terence Grieder and Alberto Bueno excavated a much less elaborate tomb that contained 277 fine items distributed among three offering deposits. The deceased was a poorly preserved adult who must have been flexed because the body was placed in a masonry niche built beneath the southernmost chamber of a small, three-room shrine. A large offering of magnificent vessels, figurines, jewelry, ear spools, and other objects was placed on a cloth in front of the niche. A second offering of 66 ceramic and stone vessels was placed on a cloth at the doorway to the interment chamber. The chamber floors were then filled in, covering both deposits, and during the filling another offering was made. Although this included an axe head and some jewelry, it contained many vessels ritually smashed and scattered about. More fill was added and then capped with a flagstone floor. Finally, an elevated, rectangular altar was erected in the chamber above the tomb. One must wonder if the edifice was not an ancestral shrine, containing the entombed founding figure.

67 *Seen from the air, Nazca ground drawings are linear. They are thought to have served as ritual walkways.*

Nazca: a culture of the south coast

68 (left) A Nazca vessel depicting a trophy head whose lips are pinned shut with thorns.

69, 70 (below) A grave excavated in the Nazca capital, Cahuachi, yielded these vessels. One depicts hummingbirds, and the other, decorated with painted peppers, held peanuts.

Recuay

71 (right) A polychrome Recuay vessel of a feline clutching a man. The man's earspools denote high status.

72, 73 (below left and right) Stone Recuay statues.

74 (above) A gateway lintel shows a jaguar with a collar and leash. Tiwanaku depictions of collared felines indicate that the animals were kept as pets.

75 (right) A classic Tiwanaku polychrome vessel with feline and geometric motifs.

76 (below) A monolithic model of a Tiwanaku sunken court with three flights of steps, and sockets for gateways.

Tiwanaku: south highland capital

77 (top) A tenon head ornamenting the sunken court at Tiwanaku.

78 (above) A wooden spoon handle depicting a winged figure carrying a staff. Possibly carved by artisans at Tiwanaku, it was found in the Moquegua Valley.

79 (right) This half of the Thunderbolt Stela, with a central frog motif, was found at Tiwanaku. The other half was discovered at the opposite end of Lake Titicaca.

Tiwanaku: south highland capital

*80 (above) Monolithic stairs lead up to the
Kalasasaya gateway, beyond which stands the
Ponce Monolith.*

*81 (below) The Ponce Monolith depicts a richly
attired figure holding a beaker and short scepter.*

*82 (opposite above) Carved from a single block of
stone, the Gateway of the Sun is no longer in its
original architectural context.*

83 (opposite below) Detail of the Gateway God.

84 (above) Found in the Moquegua Valley, this Tiwanaku vessel portrays a mustached individual.

85 (below) Depicting an elderly man, this is an unusually realistic ceramic portrait for imperial-style Tiwanaku.

The shrine was but one aspect of a much larger complex of monumental architecture at Pashash, for many masonry buildings occupied the hill, including the impressive 'Caseron' which stood 15 m high and created a great platform terrace 30 m in width. The modern town of Cabana now surrounds the hill and there are indications that the settlement covers extensive ruins. There is no question that Pashash was a major Recuay center, but it is not clear yet if it constituted a capital, or one of a series of more or less equally important centers.

Recuay ceramics frequently appear at Moche settlements in the lower Santa and adjacent valleys, and it is clear that Recuay and Moche élites were exchanging corporate arts because Moche tombs have been found with Recuay vessels. This points to a higher order of interaction than folk-level verticality alone.

Huarpa

The most important archaeological manifestations in the Ayacucho Basin during the period are called Huarpa, named for the local river with which these sites are associated. The Huarpa evidence indicates a señorio associated with a rather loosely integrated corporate style beginning c. AD 200 and ending four centuries later. The principal decorative technique consisted of red and black painting on a white-slipped surface. Motifs began with simple forms and became more complex through time. They reflect marked Nazca influence, and a strong symbiotic relationship apparently linked the two populations. Huarpa people probably supplied wool, if not copper and other minerals, to their coastal counterparts, who reciprocated with salt, marine products, and other lowland produce.

The Huarpa homeland is arid and characterized by deep ravines and broken surfaces with little flatland. Where rainfall alone sustains agriculture Andean folk farm remarkably steep terrain, but it is difficult to irrigate steep terrain because water and erosion become unruly. As a consequence, sloping surfaces are terraced. Both terracing for residential purposes and canal-based farming were preceramic in origin, and could have arisen independently in different settings. But their combination is expensive because both require substantial labor investments. Thus, steep slopes requiring terraced irrigation were the last agrarian niche that people sought to reclaim.

Huarpa people were among the first to reclaim steep slopes and they employed terraces for both irrigated and dry farming. Their hillside reclamation works were corporate undertakings. Contour terraces were laid out and erected as integrated flights of farmland, each narrow but long step being of equal length, and some flights had as many as 100 terraces from the top of a hill to the valley below. Some terraces may have been irrigated from cisterns that caught runoff from rainfall. In other cases springs fed chains of small reservoirs situated at different levels supplying different terraces. Surviving examples of Huarpa canals are several kilometers long, have widths of up to 1.6 m and show evidence of impermeable clay linings.

Terraced agriculture supported a large, but scattered population represented by some 300 sites, most of which were small communities and dispersed
farmsteads. There was a preference for residing on hilltops near arable land.
Rural houses were built of irregular stonework and tended to be one or two-
room affairs of circular or elliptical form. They differ from much of the
architecture at Nawimpukyo, the presumed capital of the Huarpa people. This
was an urban center that occupied a hilltop overlooking the modern town of
Ayacucho. Buildings in the urban core are characterized by 'H-type' masonry,
which comprised large, narrow rocks set vertically apart in rows with courses of
smaller stone filling the intervening spaces. The center of the settlement was
occupied by several platforms, on both sides of which were groups of aligned
administrative buildings, spacious courts and patios, and élite residences. Fed
by springs, a canal system ran through the center and supplied residents with
water. Nawimpukyo is not an imposing governmental center, but it laid
important political and agrarian foundations for empire-building during the
Middle Horizon.

Southern basins

Further south in the sierra there is little evidence of hillside terracing during
the Early Intermediate Period, and large political centers have not been found.
A dispersed occupation characterizes the Andahuaylas Basin. Here ridge tops
were the preferred sites for small villages and hamlets. The settlements lack
defensive walls, and warfare is not in evidence. Reflecting the exploitation of
dispersed habitats, sites were strategically situated at intermediate altitudes
below the tuber-growing zone, but above deep valley floors where maize is
grown. Herding is indicated by both camelid burials and clay models of
camelids. Thus, the occupation is thought to reflect verticality. Operating at a
folk level, this apparently entailed relatively localized movement within the
Andahuaylas region because exotic goods from distant lowlands are not in
evidence.

A similar Early Intermediate Period adaptation seems to characterize the
Cuzco basin in the upper Urubamba drainage. Whereas earlier Marcavalle
Phase sites were on the valley floor, Chanapata Phase settlements occupy
somewhat higher altitudes. This suggests that they were intermediate
residential bases for the exploitation of higher and lower ecological zones.

The altiplano

Representing the southern demographic pole of Andean civilization, the vast
altiplano surrounding Lake Titicaca saw early stirrings of conceptual
integration in the stone artwork of the Yaya–Mama tradition. The flowering of
Pukara laid foundations for political integration at the north end of the lake. To
the south, a contemporary settlement arose and then gradually matured into
the great center that would unite the cradle of high altitude civilization. Ever
since *conquistador* Cieza de León visited Tiwanaku in 1549 the imposing ruins

91 Bas-relief motifs comprising the border of the Gateway of the Sun design panel.

and sensational stonework of this extraordinary city have fascinated explorers and tourists. The colossal monument looms out of the annals of antiquity as the highest capital of an ancient empire that the world has ever known. It reflects the fact that for the entire first millennium AD the cultural and political history of the Titicaca Basin and adjacent altiplano was shaped by the fortunes of a single people and their singular metropolis.

Tiwanaku

Located 15 km southeast of the lake on a small river, the site is dominated by an urban core of monumental edifices, monolithic gateways and great stelae, surrounded by 8 to 10 km of house foundations, refuse and surface artifacts. Radiocarbon dates reaching back to 400 BC indicate unpretentious beginnings for a long, five-phase occupation. The first two phases witnessed a gradual rise to southern prominence. Prodigious construction projects, both architectural and agrarian, were underway during Phase 3 (*c.* AD 100–375), and were expanded in the succeeding Classic Tiwanaku of Phase 4 (AD 375–600 or 700). During Phase 4 the metropolis attained truly imperial standing, establishing a hierarchy of administrative centers, as well as far-flung colonies and caravanserai throughout the altiplano, the dry puna, and the lowlands of southern Peru and northern Chile. The Titicaca empire declined through Phase 5 and the metropolis finally collapsed about AD 1000 or shortly thereafter.

Plates 74–85

The urban core

Cieza de León recounted that the ruined megalopolis was dominated by a man-made hill of enormous size, erected upon massive stone foundations. This is our earliest account of the 'Akapana', the largest structure at the capital and the southernmost of great Andean platforms. It measures some 200 m and stands over 15 m high. The flat summit, surmounted by stone buildings, probably held a sunken court similar to that at Chiripa. Excavations have revealed that the platform was formerly terraced with more than three mammoth stone-faced retaining walls. The two basal walls were built of cyclopean sandstone blocks measuring several meters on a side, whereas higher retaining walls were of smaller and finely finished andesite blocks. At the bottom of one of these walls lay a large cache of elegant keros beakers. The libation vessels had been

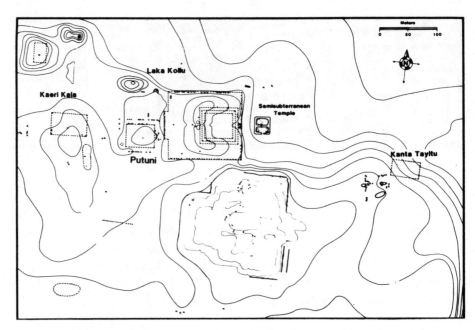

92 A plan of the main platform mound at Tiwanaku, the Akapana, indicates that a sunken court occupied the summit.

deliberately smashed and then covered. Near the basal terrace dozens of dismembered male bodies were interred, apparently the victims of sacrifice.

Surrounding the great mound the eroded topography is characterized by low rises and shallow depressions of unexcavated courts and other buildings. To the east the partially explored 'Kantatayita' is a minor rise with a jumble of big slabs. It has a majestically carved stone lintel of a regal gateway and a great *Plate 76* stone maquette of a rectangular sunken court, replete with staircases and sockets for miniature stone portals. A sunken court, measuring about 30 m square, flanks the Akapana 200 m to the west. The court walls were ornamented *Plate 77* with numerous tenoned heads depicting males or human skulls. A large collection of stelae were once set in the court floor, including the 'Bennett' monolith, the largest known Andean stela. Rendered in Classic Tiwanaku style it depicts an elegantly garbed human figure, probably a potentate or a god, holding a keros in one hand and baton-like object in the other. Other stelae in the court and elsewhere at the site are not always Tiwanaku-style carvings. *Plate 79* Indeed, half of one monolith, known as the Thunderbolt Stela, was found at the city and the other half at the north end of Lake Titicaca. We can reasonably conclude that imperial policies included holding subject peoples' sacred or ancestral objects hostage at the capital.

Due west of the sunken court, and aligned with it, monolithic stairs surmounted by a prominent gateway provided access to the spacious summit of *Plates 80,81* the 'Kalasasaya' platform. Here a central court holding the Classic 'Ponce' monolith was framed by a northern and southern row of small, one-room buildings. Measuring more than 100 m square, and standing about two stories high, the exterior Kalasasaya walls exhibit massive H-type masonry with finely cut small blocks filling the spaces between gargantuan vertical slabs. Directly west, at ground level, the 'Putuni' rectangular building complex has been interpreted as a palace compound where the rulers of Tiwanaku resided. Sections of finely carved water conduits occur in this precinct and the others mentioned above. While they certainly served functional ends, the lavish amount of effort expended on them suggests that ritual manipulation of water was important.

About a kilometer away, the very finest andesite and sandstone block masonry, along with exquisitely carved gateway fragments, are found at the 'Pumapunku' platform. Standing 5 m high and measuring 150 m square, the front of the platform had a majestic megalithic façade with two or three separate stairways leading to an equal number of grand portals individually carved from single slabs of andesite weighing tons. Behind the gateways lay a sunken court that has yet to be excavated.

Tiwanaku exhibits many stunning architectural features, among them an unprecedented elaboration of gateways. Numerous stone lintels, both plain and decorated, have been found at the site. They reflect a long evolution that culminated with great portals rendered from single blocks of rock. The largest is the Gateway of the Sun, which is also the most complex statement of Tiwanaku iconography. The top of the portal is ornamented with an incised frieze, dominated by a large, central character called the 'Gateway God'. This is a forward-facing anthropomorphic figure that stands atop a triple-tiered platform centered above the monolithic doorway. Resembling a sun-burst, the deity wears an elaborate headdress with 19 ray-like projections ending in circles or puma heads. Garbed in a decorative necklace, tunic, and kilt, the god holds

Plate 74

Plates 82,83

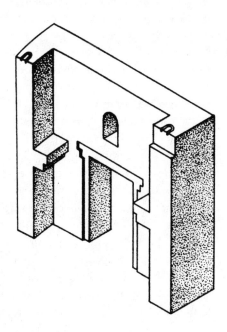

93 The Pumapunku platform was graced with monolithic gateways.

94 *Standing on a three-tiered platform the staff-bearing Gateway God was the central figure on the Gateway of the Sun at Tiwanaku.*

two vertical staffs terminating in condor heads. The Gateway God is thought to be a solar deity by some scholars, and invites comparison with the Chavín Staff God. Entitlement to two staffs may be an Andean means of calling out a paramount deity. Arranged in three horizontal rows one above the other, smaller, winged attendants converge upon the central figure from each side of the portal. Depicted in profile the attendants have either human or avian heads and each marches toward the center of the portal in rich attire carrying a vertical staff of office. The converging sets of profile staff-bearers is suggestive of dual organization in the pantheon. That this rich, but mysterious, iconography graces a great entrance implies that people were expected to change their attitudes and behavior upon converging and passing through gateways, and that portals divided mundane from sacrosanct space.

Agrarian hinterland

As at other ancient Andean capitals, the rulers of Tiwanaku invested great effort not only in corporate art and architecture, but also in agriculture. Opening new farmland and improving yields for terrain around a capital was a major means of banking labor taxes. Headed by Alan Kolata, a team of scientists from many disciplines investigated imperial farming practices near the city and on a large, lake-side plain called Pampa Koani. They found little evidence that Tiwanaku agronomists were interested in hillside terracing. Instead, befitting the altiplano, reclamation focused on flatlands and the construction of ridged fields. The discovery of deeply buried Chiripa pottery suggests that ridged field farming may have begun quite early. However, it was Tiwanaku corporate construction that created the fields which survive today. The agrarian enterprise was managed by a hierarchy of state-founded sites.

95 *On the Gateway of the Sun three rows of winged 'angels' carrying staffs converge upon the central depiction of the Gateway God.*

Two major centers occupied the apex of the Koani administration, Pajchiri to the north of the pampa and Luqurmata on the south. Both featured monumental masonry buildings, stone-faced platforms, sunken courts, gateways, and stelae. Scattered about the pampa there were smaller administrative centers, and multitudes of little mounds representing farm-steads dispersed among the fields.

Caravans, colonies, and outposts

Tiwanaku was truly an agropastoral state because its fortunes were tied both to agriculture and to camelid herding. Although herds supplied food and fiber, llamas were vital to the political economy. As pack animals for great caravans, they carried commodities over long treks up and down the mountain flanks and deep into the Chilean salt puna. The state procured goods by two means. In distant settings it used local élites as richly rewarded clients to promote exchange and procure desired resources. Reliance on local agents is evident at San Pedro de Atacama in the salt puna, 800 km from the altiplano capital or a month and a half's caravan travel time. It is also evident in the Azapa Valley of northern Chile, where reclamation of mid-valley lands was promoted. In both settings cemeteries are dominated by interments of local folk with traditional grave forms, corpse orientation, garments and goods. In these cemeteries a minority of burials – those considered Tiwanaku agents – interred in local form and orientation were accompanied by fine Tiwanaku textiles, keros beakers, snuff tubes and trays, ornate wood carvings, and occasional gold objects. These rare accompaniments are typically very well made, lavishly decorated, and small or lightweight – indicating long-distance transport.

Closer to home the state procured goods from outlying areas by means of

96, 97 Portrait head beakers excavated at Omo.

colonization. In the Moquegua drainage, above 1,500 m, mid-valley flatlands were first irrigated by Huaracani peoples who used fiber-tempered ceramics related to Chiripa wares in the altiplano. This long occupation persisted into Tiwanaku times when a modest number of Phase 4 settlers arrived from the altiplano, perhaps about AD 500. The majority took up residence on a spacious flat-topped bluff adjacent to land that could be irrigated. This is called the Omo Phase after the principal Tiwanaku settlement which had some 500 rectangular rooms. Built of cane, rows of several rooms formed households that were grouped into three separate plaza clusters. Imported Tiwanaku goods, and local imitations of goods with Tiwanaku iconography, dominate the artifact assemblage. Excavations revealed an interesting special-purpose structure where chicha beer was brewed and then consumed in magnificent portrait-head keros beakers originally made in the altiplano capital. The excavator, Paul Goldstein, argues that the undefended Omo Phase sites suggest a peaceful settling of altiplano people who gradually brought the original inhabitants into *Plate 78* the Tiwanaku cultural sphere. Although colonization seems to have been a folk affair, the quantity of Tiwanaku imports suggests it was state approved, if not instigated.

In overview, Tiwanaku reflects the evolution of complex economic and political adaptations. Moquegua indicates that verticality was assuming imperial importance. Farther afield llama caravans and local agents of the state allowed Tiwanaku to cast a vast economic net over the south-central Cordillera that served the political interests of the Titicaca capital. Uniting the southern demographic pole of Andean civilization proved to be remarkably long-lived. While Moche would fall, and a new state, Huari, would arise in Peru, the Bolivian capital at Tiwanaku perpetuated its longevity far beyond that of any other ancient Andean empire.

CHAPTER EIGHT

The Middle Horizon

The Middle Horizon was an era of profound cultural change that was triggered, in part, by a great drought. Evolution did not proceed gradually. Rather, it was punctuated by a stressful down-turn in environmental conditions and by wide-ranging cultural responses. Old empires fell and new ones arose. This chapter will examine the changing fortunes of three: Moche, Huari, and Tiwanaku. Major change began in AD 560, but technically the Middle Horizon dates between AD 600 and 1000 in the Ica Valley. Uhle first distinguished the horizon on the basis of coastal graves at Pachacamac, Ica, and elsewhere that he thought were related to Tiwanaku. Using the Inca as a model, he postulated that the altiplano metropolis of Tiwanaku gave rise to a great wave of empire building that swept over the Cordillera. In 1948 Larco Hoyle came to the conclusion that there were two Middle Horizon states: a southern one based at Tiwanaku and a northern counterpart at Huari in the Ayacucho sierra. Larco proposed that the coastal materials which Uhle found were derived from Ayacucho. He called these remains 'Northern Huari' because they occurred sporadically over much of northern Peru. The rise of Huari was a dynamic time. People were on the move, and linguists have identified great flux in the distribution of languages and dialects.

Nature contributed to this movement and change. Evidence comes from two ice cores drilled in the Quelccaya glacier, situated between Cuzco and the Titicaca Basin, showing climatic conditions during the last 1,500 years. The varve-like cores measure annual precipitation, dust accumulation, tempera-ture, and atmospheric chemistry. There are many frozen signatures of El Niño episodes, which struck in AD 511–12, 546, 576, 600, 610, 612, 650, 681, and at similar frequencies in later centuries. The greatest long-term fluctuation was the Little Ice Age that began in 1500, shortly before Pizarro's arrival, and lasted more than three centuries.

The second most dramatic event that the ice core measurements show is a great drought that began abruptly in AD 562 and continued until 594. Precipitation was about 30 per cent below normal during the 32 years, and there was a marked increase in atmospheric dust, attributable to decreased plant cover. The soil was blown away from fields laying fallow, thereby reducing food production, perhaps by as much as one-third for an entire generation. With agrarian systems in many settings stretched well beyond their modern limits, famine must have exerted selective pressure. Ethnic movement, strife, conflict, and militarism would ensue. Yet, the need for more to eat also encouraged agricultural innovations.

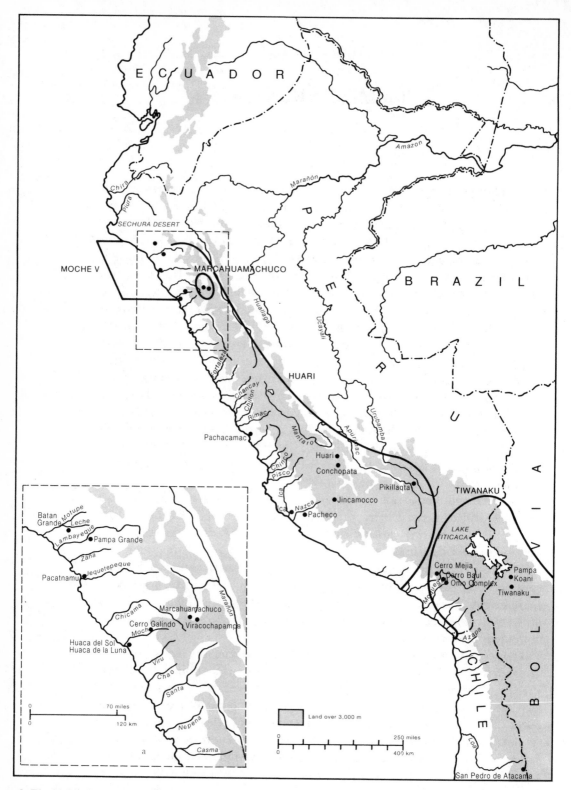

ECUADOR

Chira

Piura

SECHURA DESERT

MOCHE V

MARCAHUAMACHUCO

Fortaleza

Chancay
Chillón
Rimac

Pachacamac

HUARI

Huallaga

Marañón

Amazon

Ucayali

B R A Z I L

P
E
R
U

Urubamba

Apurimac

Mantaro

Chincha
Pisco

Ica
Ica

Nazca

Huari
Conchopata

Jincamocco

Pacheco

Pikillaqta

TIWANAKU

LAKE
TITICACA

B O L I V I A

Cerro Mejía
Cerro Baúl
Omo Complex

Moquegua

Pampa
Koani

Tiwanaku

Azapa

Loa

C H I L E

San Pedro de Atacama

Batan
Grande

Motupe
Leche

Lambayeque

Pampa Grande

Zaña

Jequetepeque

Pacatnamú

Chicama

Cerro Galindo
Moche

Marcahuamachuco

Viracochapampa

Marañón

Huaca del Sol
Huaca de la Luna

Viru

Chao

Santa

Nepeña

Casma

a

0   70 miles

0   120 km

Land over 3,000 m

0   250 miles

0   400 km

98 The Middle Horizon: principal sites and areas mentioned in Chapter Eight.

Moche demise

The last chapter described the rise of Moche statecraft to its height. Political consolidation of the north coast had been achieved by about AD 500 and Phase IV ceramics had come into production. Unbeknown to its leaders, the desert nation was soon to confront the wrath of nature.

Shortly before or during the ten-year drought the imperial heartland was ravaged by severe El Niño flooding that washed massive loads of sediment into the sea. The sea deposited it as sand along the beach, which strong daily winds off the ocean blew inland as massive dunes that buried fields and cities. These disasters were played out gradually over the course of several decades to change the fortunes of the Moche state.

The capital at Huaca del Sol and Huaca de la Luna had matured into a splendid city when it was suddenly devastated by one of the early El Niño events recorded in the Quelccaya glacial cores. Flood waters inundated the city with such power and force that sections of the urban landscape were completely stripped away removing several meters of deposit. Surrounding fields and irrigation systems were similarly stripped and damaged. The Jequetepeque Valley was also affected. Erosion may have been exacerbated by drought or by an earthquake that loosened the landscape and made it easier to wash away. For up to 18 months there would have been drought in the southern mountains and rain on the desert, with flooding most intense in the north where the largest irrigation systems supported the most densely settled regions. Houses of cane and adobe would have collapsed, and flood water inundated the valley bottom settlements. Potable water and sanitation systems would have broken down, disease and pestilence broken out, and infant mortality soared. Famine would have been acute as irrigation systems were washed out, taking years to repair.

The Moche landscape was so deeply scarred and stripped that entirely new irrigation systems must have been built to adjust to the altered topography. We may reasonably infer that the nation confronted severe food shortages for many years. El Niños disrupt nearshore fishery, but fishermen do not starve because there is an influx of marine life from warm equatorial waters. Yet the sea would not have been able to support all the people who depended on farming while they rebuilt their irrigation systems. Significantly, a new strain of maize with large cobs and more kernels came into use after the flooding, apparently introduced from the mountains to the east, and suggesting that Moche sought aid from their highland neighbors.

The capital weathered the flood, and survivors repaired the Huaca del Sol and Huaca de la Luna, heightened their platforms and gave them new façades to mask erosional damage. During this short, final occupation, one of the Huaca de la Luna courts was ornamented with a distinctive polychrome mural showing a large front-facing anthropomorphic being. Although the upper body and head were not preserved, the figure held a vertical staff in each hand reminiscent of the central figure on the Gateway of the Sun at Tiwanaku. The *Plate 83* mural was executed in Moche artistic canons and was later painted over by another mural, but the brief appearance of the staff figure indicates foreign influence and perhaps changes in the imperial pantheon, probably brought on by diminished confidence in the old order and its perceived inability to control the environment.

After the flooding, as the sand dunes encroached on inland fields, people removed the important contents of houses and buildings. Roof beams were carried off to be reused elsewhere. The capital was abandoned by the close of Phase IV, completely buried by sand. Farmland was also lost on the south side of the valley, and dunes probably also struck other desert drainages. It is not clear exactly when this disaster occurred in relation to the great drought, but it is clear that a dramatically different social and political order emerged in the wake of disaster.

Reorganization

The beginning of Moche Phase V is thought to coincide with the opening of the Middle Horizon. Lasting until about AD 700, this short phase reflects revolutionary changes in life ways on the north coast. Some of these, but by no means all, were responses to environmental stress. The construction of forts and fortified settlements seems to have increased both on the coast and in the sierra, and conflict no doubt accompanied the rise of new economic and political realities. For the Moche state these included northward relocation of the capital, loss of valleys from Huarmey through Viru, contraction of the southern frontier back to Moche, and loss of the upper canyon lands. Why and how the southern territories escaped the old dominion is not clear, but it seems reasonable to suppose that they broke away when the state was not in a position to do anything about it.

Plate 86   Transformation of the Moche Valley from imperial heartland to frontier hinterland is reflected in the Phase V occupation centered at Cerro Galindo. The site was strategically situated on the north side of the valley neck, beyond the reach of blowing sand and near the intakes of the largest operable canals. The occupation began as a fortified hillside settlement surrounded by a great wall with parapets and piles of sling stones. However, the élite soon moved out onto the lower flats, and scattered residences and other buildings eventually sprawled out over some 4 to 5 sq. km, according to studies carried out by Garth Bawden. Significantly, one entire section of the city, representing a fifth of the total occupied area, was set aside for small one-room structures filled with food storage vessels. This is by no means the first evidence of such facilities; they had also existed at the old Moche political center of Huancaco in Viru. But, the quantity of storage structures at Galindo point to heightened concern with centralized administration of staples.

The Phase V settlement had a large population and a great deal of masonry and cane architecture, but very few corporate structures of adobe. The largest adobe structure, reflecting a sharp break with the previous Moche tradition of erecting towering mounds, was a large, rectangular, thick-walled enclosure, measuring about 240 × 130 m. Most of the structure was occupied by a complex

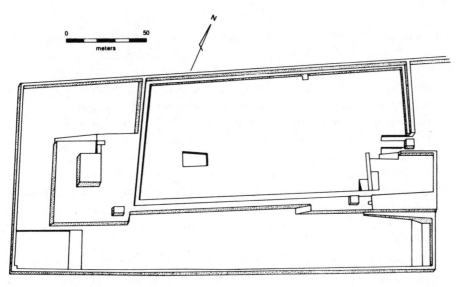

99 *A reconstruction of the Galindo enclosure. The entry court housed a small rectangular sunken court behind which lay a burial platform.*

of spacious courts. Double doorways through the east wall led to an expansive entry plaza ornamented with murals. A small depressed rectangular court, about one meter deep, was centered in the rear of the plaza and represents one of the last coastal vestiges of the ancient sunken court tradition. A rectangular adobe platform two-stories high lay behind the plaza and separated from it by a high wall. Although looted, the mound was once a mausoleum for élite burial. The Galindo enclosure can be interpreted as a huaca sepultura serving as the residence and burial place of local rulers. The second largest monument, a nearby adobe platform, was probably the city's huaca adoratorio and principal shrine.

Beyond the southern frontier, Phase V ceramics have been reported up the coast and into the Vicus region of the Piura drainage, making the new reorganized Moche state essentially a northern north-coast phenomenon. With the exception of the coastal site of Pacatnamu, the larger settlements tend to be strategically situated well inland near the intakes of major canals.

The Moche capital was relocated at Pampa Grande in the Lambayeque valley neck, 50 km from the sea. Spread over six square km, this well-preserved ceremonial city was investigated by Izumi Shimada and co-workers. The new center preserved some earlier Moche traditions, such as building gigantic pyramids, but if it were not for the corporate arts, few relationships with the old capital at Cerro Blanco would be evident. The differences are striking and invite analogy with those arising when the capital of Christendom shifted from Rome to Constantinople. A few leaders may have moved, but basically power was transferred to new hands that shaped things in different ways. Agglutinated housing of commoners, workshops of artisans and coppersmiths, and rectangular walled enclosures of the élite were concentrically distributed around the urban core. One formal enclosure combined large-scale cotton processing with ceremonies in a niched court with an elevated bench where ceramic frames for drums were found along with racks of deer antlers that may have been ritual headgear. The urban core was completely dominated by a gargantuan mound, Huaca Fortaleza, at the rear of an enormous enclosure measuring 600 × 400 m. Associated adobe architecture included rows of contiguous, one-room storage facilities set in walled courts. Access was strictly controlled by check points in adjacent courts and halls. Although the original contents had been systematically removed, it is likely that the banks of storerooms stockpiled élite goods integral to wealth finance. Near the base of the pyramid, a spacious walled enclosure was used for the production of sumptuary artifacts made of Ecuadorian *Spondylus* shell. The coveted shells may have been imported by sea or by caravans of llamas that were bred and herded on the coast.

The adobe architecture at Pampa Grande is quite different from that of the Huaca del Sol and Huaca de la Luna. Bricks often bear makers' marks, but these are mixed together, indicating that brick makers and masons, if not labor taxes in general, were organized differently than they had been at the old capital. Measuring 275 × 180 m, and standing 55 m high, the Fortaleza platform ranks as one of the largest mounds ever erected in the Andes. Yet, unlike Huaca del Sol, which was solid brick, Fortaleza achieved its great magnitude with a less labor intensive construction technique, known as 'chamber-and-fill', in which loose earth was dumped into walled cribs that

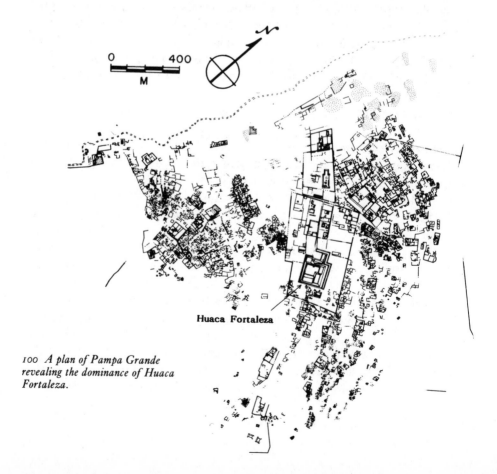

100 A plan of Pampa Grande revealing the dominance of Huaca Fortaleza.

Huaca Fortaleza

101 Moche concerns with the sea persisted at Chan Chan with friezes depicting maritime motifs.

stabilized the deposit while allowing a rapid build up of bulk. Nonetheless, at least two separate stages of major construction were needed to bring the Fortaleza structure to its final dimensions, as a four-tiered huaca. A broad basal platform, 20 m high, was surmounted by three terraces rising from the front to the towering rear of the mound. Summit buildings included courts and rooms ornamented with polychrome murals. A great perpendicular ramp almost 50 m long provided access to the first terrace. The ramp itself was probably a stage for ritual display, and it marks the beginning of a far northern architectural tradition emphasizing prominent perpendicular ramps.

The new capital was rapidly established at a time of ideological change. Scrutiny of Moche and later Chimu arts indicates that profound iconographic changes occurred at the beginning of Phase V, and the new ideology that emerged was subsequently adopted by Chimor. Much of the old Moche pantheon was dropped, but figures associated with the sea were elevated to new status and maritime themes assumed great importance. Significant figures included an elderly individual, known as wrinkle face, and an anthropomorphized iguana. These companions, depicted traveling on reed boats and shown with Strombus shells from Ecuador, were major actors in a new Phase V theme. Called the burial theme, wrinkle face and iguana are shown interring a potentate who died at the hands of a malpracticing female curer, who is fed to vultures. Concern with the sea and a maritime iconography persisted at Chan *Plates 101,102* Chan. Why it replaced more terrestrial oriented iconography is a speculative matter. One proposition holds that the maritime economy was less disrupted and recovered far faster than agriculture did from the natural cataclysms that brought down the Moche state at the end of Phase IV.

Phase V was by no means calamity free. Evidence of El Niño flooding has been found at Galindo, Pacatnamu, and at Pampa Grande. Perhaps renewed environmental stress finally broke the back of the imperial camel, or the demise of the Moche may have been for entirely cultural reasons. Whatever the case,

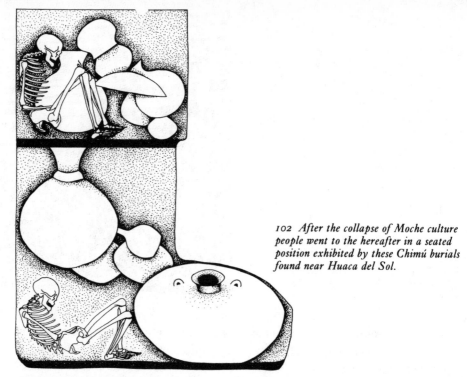

102 *After the collapse of Moche culture people went to the hereafter in a seated position exhibited by these Chimú burials found near Huaca del Sol.*

Pampa Grande was literally abandoned in a blaze, as its inhabitants torched the city and moved elsewhere. After the final fall of Moche, people changed their concepts about the hereafter and went to their graves in a seated position rather than lying down. Subsequently, a new iconography and corporate style, called Sican, emerged in the Lambayeque region, as did a new political center, Batan Grande, as we shall see in the next chapter.

Huari adaptive dispersal

By the Middle Horizon two types of Andean state had emerged called *intensive* and *extensive*, whose organizational fabrics were quite different, particularly in the provinces. Intensive states, such as coastal Moche, submerged local populations under their administrative and cultural presence. Alternatively, extensive regimes, such as highland Huari, established administrative nodes dispersed among local populations. But the two types were not mutually exclusive. With dense settlement around the shores of Lake Titicaca and small communities scattered over the altiplano and dry puna, Tiwanaku had an intensive heartland and extensive hinterland. The evolutionary origins of extensive states lie with highland folk adaptations and the practice of sending out satellite communities to create economic archipelagos. When states took up this adaptation, economic islands were transformed into political nodes. Taxes and clientage obligations replaced kin commitments as the motivation for production, and satellite territories were strung together by roads, caravans, and formal channels of communication. Nodes were in turn tied to a capital by various combinations of force, ideology, and wealth finance with sumptuary goods. The adaptive advantage of extensive political nets lay in capturing scattered, far-flung resources with minimal investment in intervening areas of little economic or strategic benefit.

Huari's political dominion was anchored by its capital of the same name, whose urban core comprised a 3–4 square km sprawl of multi-story walls and masonry buildings, accommodating an estimated 20,000–30,000 inhabitants, and situated on a hilly plateau 25 km north of the modern city of Ayacucho. The *Plate 87* Ayacucho region had long-standing ties with the coast and the Ica Valley, where Huari corporate arts first appeared *c.* AD 600. This marks the beginning of the Middle Horizon which is divided into four epochs. Epochs 1 and 2 saw political expansion and imperial consolidation, while Epoch 3 saw imperial collapse; therefore the capital did not have great longevity.

Investigations by Luis Lumbreras, his Peruvian colleagues, and William Isbell indicate that the metropolis grew gradually with complex changes in architectural canons, organization, and orientation. The settlement was originally surrounded by extensive irrigation, and a sophisticated system of underground conduits transported water through the city. Much of the urban core was terraced to create broad habitation surfaces, and massive walls of substantial length compartmentalized Huari into separate, irregular sections. Indeed the city was so heavily partitioned by towering sections and compound walls that it is difficult to imagine how traffic flowed through it. The architectural emphasis was on segregation rather than integration, and presumably based on kin, class, rank, and occupation. Different urban sections were occupied by numerous building compounds separated from one another by high-walled enclosures of rectilinear and irregular form measuring 40 to 100 m on a side. Within walled enclosures, buildings were two to three stories high. Early on the structures may have been arranged around oval courtyards, but the dominant pattern was one of dividing enclosures into a number of rectangular patios. Each large patio was formed by elongated, rectangular buildings reminiscent of the great halls and galleries at Marcahuamachuco. Some ground-floor rooms contain hearths, food refuse, and other domestic remains indicating that they were residences, while others were kept clean.

Some compounds were associated with specialized crafts such as ceramic, jewelry, and projectile point production. One exhibited a high frequency of serving-bowls and elaborate libation cups, suggesting ritual feasting and drinking. Another enclosure, called Cheqo Wasi, contained the remains of looted subterranean megalithic chambers, made of finely cut and carefully dressed stone slabs. The disturbed human remains in them were accompanied by abundant luxury goods, including gold and many exquisite artifacts. These may well be the tombs of Huari potentates, who once occupied the compound. Sumptuary goods from Cheqo Wasi, and elsewhere, show that Huari imported raw materials and finished products from great distances, including *Spondylus* ornaments from Ecuador, cowrie and other types of shell from different coastal locations, pottery from Cajamarca, and minerals such as chrysacola, lapis, and greenstone from distant sources. Copper, silver, and gold were also imported.

103 Staff-bearing 'angels' on Tiwanaku's Gateway of the Sun (left) were transformed by Huari weavers who conceptually subdivided the winged figures into a series of vertical panels that could be expanded, contracted, or transposed at will.

Adaptation

How is it that Huari arose and prospered at a time when Moche was brought to its knees by environmental stress? To probe for answers, we must recall that during the Early Intermediate Period most sierra farming took place at high elevations where rainfall supported potato and tuber cultivation. Complementary irrigation agriculture also took place in the bottoms of the sierra basins, but steep mountain slopes were not farmed to a significant degree. Huarpa people in the Ayacucho area were among the first to terrace and irrigate inclined terrain. However, most canals were relatively short and low, limiting the amount of land they could water. Huarpa people lived at Huari long before it assumed political stature, and William Isbell has shown that they constructed an exceptionally large and innovative agricultural system. Their system combined a high altitude water source situated far above the city; a long primary canal routed across high elevation contours to feed lower secondary canals; and extensive terraces that facilitated the irrigation of steep slopes. Building such a reclamation system required substantially more labor than other communities were investing in agricultural works at the time. Nonetheless, such investment gave Huari distinct economic advantages over its neighbors, and in a sense preadapted it to weather the great drought. Irrigation drawn from elevated streams or springs can escape many vicissitudes of irregular rainfall, and rights to it can be claimed before it reaches lower terrain.

Thus the people of Huari had developed reclamation technology that could bring into production the vast quichua zone, which had previously been underexploited in the Ayacucho region and seemingly unexploited in other sierra settings because of the costs of building irrigated terrace systems. Bringing steep terrain into agrarian production was obviously critical during the great drought, and was one of the few ways to compensate for decreased yields in traditional farming areas. Initially, concerns with food shortages must have overriden concerns about labor costs, and once the process of reclaiming mountain slopes began, it remained the major means for expanding highland

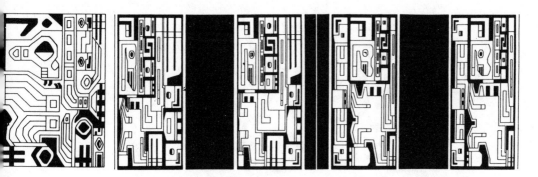

agricultural economies long after rainfall returned to normal levels. Maize was found to grow in the quichua, and by borrowing and experimenting the Huari people added new, high-yield varieties of this crop to their farming, gaining both relief from drought and economic expansion into the last of the Andean agrarian habitats.

The residents of Huari built their own terraced irrigation system, but the political fortunes of the city were furthered by having other populations build similar systems elsewhere. In a process similar to patenting and marketing a major invention, the new technology was packaged with innovative organizational, ideological, and iconographic wrappings, and the conceptual package may have emphasized hierarchical organization and reciprocity. These changes were associated with what is called the Okros style, which saw early political expansion and consolidation. Many Huarpa settlements, including Nawimpukyo, were abandoned and people relocated at Huari and Conchopata (a site on the outskirts of modern Ayacucho). The Okros style preserved local traditions, but also showed a significant increase in decorative concerns, with strong borrowings of Nazca design elements, suggesting that symbols were *Plate 89* being sought for the newly emerging political and economic order.

During Okros times, elements of Tiwanaku corporate art and architecture also appeared at Huari and Conchopata. How these elements reached Ayacucho is a matter of speculation and debate. Some investigators propose

104 Huari spread the iconography of staff bearers far and wide. In this ceramic painting of an 'angel' the staff base ends in a maize cob motif.

105 A Huari ceramic depiction of a fallen 'angel'.

that Ayacucho people made pilgrimages to Tiwanaku and returned with altiplano ideology and icons. Others suggest that missionaries or ambassadors from the Titicaca capital introduced such elements. There is also a possibility that the introductions were transferred from a fortified colony that Huari established in the Moquegua Valley, which lay within Tiwanaku territory. Among the interesting elements to appear at Huari was a magnificent rectangular sunken court, built of beautifully cut and finished stone, discovered ceremonially entombed deep beneath a later building complex. Carbon associated with initial construction has yielded a date of AD 580 ± 60. The court may have been a temple, for it was kept scrupulously clean during long use, and saw a series of renewed floors, of plain clay, white plaster, red plaster, and polygonal cut stones. One of the middle floors produced a radiocarbon date of AD 720 ± 60. Thus, the court, as well as the special activities it housed, remained important for more than a century before the structure was carefully buried. It is probable that this distinctive form of ceremonial architecture was borrowed from Tiwanaku along with much of the ritual and ideology that made sunken courts critical symbols and seats of corporate activities.

It also seems that the leaders of the blossoming Ayacucho state were consciously seeking appropriate symbols of power because they adopted the most potent of Tiwanaku icons: the emblems embellishing the Portal of the Sun, and most particularly the Gateway God. If the Gateway God was derived from the old Chavín Staff God, Huari's resurrection of the figure may reflect religious fundamentalism and revival. At Tiwanaku the Gateway God was probably a solar deity, but in Huari hands it seems to have been reinterpreted and transformed into a deity of agrarian fertility. The sun rays of the headdress were sometimes replaced with ears of corn, and the god's staffs, costume, and baton-carrying winged attendants were all changed and given new meanings.

The transformed Gateway iconography provided central themes in Huari corporate arts, but the corporate style was otherwise rich in original symbolism. Detailed portrayals of the Huari rayed deity figured prominently on ceremonial vessels that were ritually broken and carefully interred: Tiwanaku rites were concluded with the smashing and burial of magnificent keros beakers, but Huari rites often involved large urns with ornate iconography, a dozen or more *Plate 89* of which were first used to dispense chicha for ritual intoxication, before being destroyed and buried. Two caches of such vessels have been discovered at Conchopata, one at Huari, and still others in the imperial provinces, including the site of Pacheco in Nazca. The vessels in each hoard are similar, but the *Plate 90* different caches vary in terms of urn shape and decoration, suggesting that each group of vessels was produced for a single ceremony. And variation in the ceremonies is evident at Conchopata where young women were sacrificed and interred adjacent to the vessel deposit.

A fortified colony

Both during and after the long drought, I would argue that Huari's innovative agrarian technology placed it in an unusually favorable position to promote economic betterment, with overtones of appealing state ideology and iconography. Proposing that the imperial realm was based more on adaptive dispersal than on militarism differs from traditional interpretations, which stress conquest.

Within the sierra, two types of imperial policies are suggested by two contrasting categories of Huari architecture. A bellicose policy is vividly evident at Cerro Baul (2,300 m), a grand mesa 600 m high with steep sides *Plate 88* grading to vertical cliffs. Cerro Baul and the hill behind it, Cerro Mejia, are strategically situated above the confluence of the Río Moquegua's major steep-sided sierra tributaries, and both were fortified by Huari. (The defences were later used by the Moquegua population in retreat from Inca invasion. The impregnable bulwark could not be taken by storm, but a long siege denying water and supplies to the defenders finally forced their capitulation.)

At the time the fortified colony was founded Tiwanaku people lived only 20 km away, downstream at the Omo Complex and at adjacent sites where flatlands in the valley bottom were irrigated. The adjacent sierra slopes were unfarmed and unoccupied and Huari people moved into the open niche. Drawing on a high altitude water source, they built an extremely long contour canal, crossing the lofty divide between Cerros Mejia and Baul, to irrigate terraces constructed along the mountainsides. Where the canal crossed the divide a single, narrow trail led to the mesa summit over an hours' climb away. It was guarded by Cerro Mejia, which had two sets of enclosing ramparts. The steep route up Baul was fortified with walls and parapeted terraces. A heavily defended switchback path, which was limited to single-file traffic, led up the final cliff face.

A large complex of Huari monumental multi-storey buildings was erected atop Cerro Baul, including long, hall-like buildings framing spacious patios. Deposits of ritually broken vessels were found, and other ceramic remains include Okros pottery, and a high frequency of imported wares from Ayacucho.

The colony at Baul was apparently established to extract onyx and other

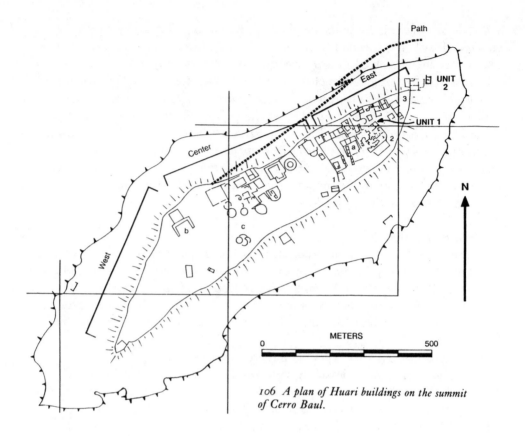

106 A plan of Huari buildings on the summit of Cerro Baul.

minerals, and the defensive character of the complex leaves no doubt that Huari was concerned about its deep plunge into Tiwanaku territory. A competitive relationship was certainly anticipated, and hostilities may have developed. Tiwanaku's Omo Phase settlements were abandoned, and later Chen Chen Phase settlements (see below) were systematically razed. Either of these changes might reflect a military encounter with the Ayacucho. The Baul colony was pulled out of Moquegua in Epoch 2, leaving a wide buffer zone between the Titicaca and Ayacucho dominions and suggesting that hostilities had led to avoidance. Concomitantly, Huari pulled its political frontiers back to the Sihuas drainage in the north.

Sierra dispersal

Cerro Baul tells us what a Huari military presence looked like. It contrasts sharply with Huari administrative centers, built on easily accessible open flatlands, and neither defended, nor associated with adjacent Huari-built forts. Administrative centers consisted of one, or occasionally several, large rectangular enclosures, measuring from 25 to 800 m on a side. Open courts occupied much of the interior floor space, and excavations have revealed high frequencies of serving vessels and cups suggesting corporate feasting and drinking. Some buildings are thought to have been food preparation areas for such ceremonies, and many rooms may have been produce storage areas. Others were apparently élite quarters. Some very long buildings, divided into repetitious cell-like rooms may have been barrack-like quarters for people rendering mit'a labor. No two enclosure complexes are the same, but similarities in style and layout suggest that their construction was supervised by Huari architects. The complexes are associated with élite ceramics from Huari and copies or regional variants of such wares. However, utilitarian ceramics were locally produced and exhibit local attributes. The overall impression is that these complexes were built and used by local folk and their nobles working with a small contingent of Huari overlords.

Located near Cuzco, Pikillaqta is the largest and southernmost of the highland Huari centers. Northward for more than 1,000 km all major sierra basins, including Cajamarca, were strung together by such widely scattered, state-built administrative centers. Many were apparently instrumental in transforming local settlement and subsistence patterns, as in the Carahuarazo basin on the route between Huari and Nazca. In Epoch 1B, Jincamocco, a 27 ha Huari complex, was founded on flat bottomlands adjacent to major roads that were also paved at the time. Much of the steep-sided valley was terraced and irrigated for the first time. With the opening of large tracts of new land local people abandoned high altitude hamlets near the juncture of the herding and tuber growing zones, and moved downslope to reside in villages and farmsteads near the terraces to grow maize and other crops.

As in Moquegua, Huari opened a vital agrarian niche in the Carahuarazo Valley, but here there is no evidence of fortified colonization or militarism. Rather, Huari policy in Carahuarazo was apparently one of promoting cooperative innovation that motivated local ethnic groups to build and benefit from irrigated terraces, as well as the state buildings, roads, and facilities that integrated the region within the national economy.

Farther north, Huari interacted with the powerful, well-established highland state at Marcahuamachuco. At the very doorstep of the thriving northern capital, less than three km away, lies the second largest of all Huari compounds, Viracochapampa. Measuring more than half a km on a side, the compound enclosed vast courts, and a core of systematically aligned patios, halls, and other structures arranged around a central plaza flanked by halls. As at Jincamocco there are no indications of fortification, or of conflict with Marcahuamachuco.

Coastal influence

Huari expressions are fundamentally different on the coast. Centers such as Jincamocco or Viracochapampa are rarely found in the desert oases, nor are there great forts similar to Cerro Baul, and evidence of Huari presence is more ideological than architectural. This is probably because Ayacucho innovations in canal-fed terracing could reclaim little additional desert terrain whereas it had far-reaching potentials for steep sierra land. Some authorities argue that the coast was invaded and conquered by Huari, and perhaps this happened in some southern oases. Alternatively long-standing verticality ties between the Ica and Nazca valleys and the Ayacucho region may have simply been politically strengthened and formalized without recourse to force of arms.

Nor is conquest evident on the north coast within the Moche realm, where as we have seen late murals at Huaca de la Luna depict a front-facing figure holding two staffs, that was very likely the Huari rayed deity.

Plate 92

Plate 90

Huari influence is clearly evident in coastal grave goods, but imports from the highland capital were not particularly common. Items produced on the coast in accord with Huari canons, such as the Pacheco cache of urns, are much more frequent. The most common coastal productions involve Huari-derived attributes of a rather generic and long-lasting nature. At Pachacamac, a substantial number of Middle Horizon tombs exhibited Huari influence, and studies of Pachacamac mortuary wares suggest that the oracle center incorporated many elements of the Ayacucho corporate style, but reinterpreted these in very basic ways. There is little evidence that Huari people erected residential buildings or monuments at the oracle center or elsewhere on the coast, yet, elements of the Ayacucho corporate art style are found as far north as Batan Grande in the Leche Valley.

After the fall of Pampa Grande and the end of the Moche state, coastal people adopted many Huari ideas. Analysis of the skeletons from Moche graves which contain Northern Huari ceramic elements shows them to be desert folk who had adopted Huari concepts.

Huari contributions to Andean civilization were far-reaching and lasted long after Huari collapsed. Ultimately they changed the nature of coast–highland relationships. Once underway, quichua reclamation continued into Inca times and fostered significant population growth that ensured demographic dominance of the highlands over the coastlands.

Tiwanaku

Tiwanaku's political integration of the southern, highland pole of Andean civilization occurred more or less concurrently with Moche's consolidation of the northern, coastland pole. The Titicaca capital, its corporate architecture, and fine arts were in their classic stage when the state was confronted by the

Plate 93

long drought. There is dramatic evidence that the prolonged crisis caused progressively greater state involvement in agricultural reclamation and management in both Tiwanaku's heartland and hinterland, but the dating of cause and effect needs refinement. The final epoch of Tiwanaku, Phase 5, is variously estimated as beginning between AD 500 and 750, but by its end, *c.* AD 1000 or 1100, the altiplano empire had collapsed.

The Moquegua hinterland

Tiwanaku Phase 4 occupation of the Moquegua drainage began modestly when several communities of altiplano farmers settled in the lower sierra adjacent to the valley bottom. There was no apparent resistance from the local Huaracani

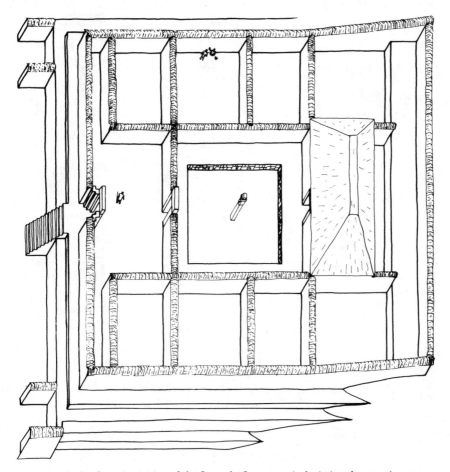

107 An idealized reconstruction of the Omo platform summit depicting the summit court.

population, and the new arrivals founded their largest community at the Omo Complex, an area with five sites spanning three sequential Tiwanaku occupations. Excavations by Paul Goldstein suggest that after a century or so the Omo community was deserted, and altiplano colonists abandoned the sierra for some time. Colonial settlement was resumed on an imperial scale early in Phase 5 – the Chen Chen Phase, named after a looted cemetery near modern Moquegua. Transformation of the region from a former folk colony into an *Plate 91* imperial province was marked by a large influx of settlers and by agricultural expansion. The focus of reclamation was on flatlands, irrigated by long canals built with corporate labor. Chen Chen agrarian works expanded mid-valley farming far beyond the confines of contemporary cultivation, growing maize, tubers, beans, peanuts, squash, pumpkin, fruit, and other crops for local consumption and presumably for export to Tiwanaku 300 km away.

Tiwanaku's colonies were organized hierarchically by size differences and by elaboration of corporate construction. A new settlement at the Omo Complex sat at the apex, covering 7.7 ha with dense housing remains and deposits of

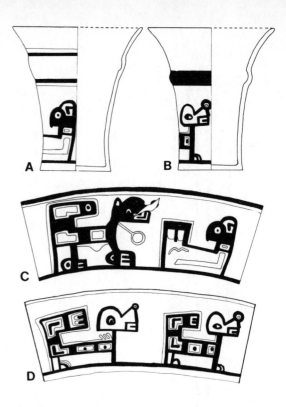

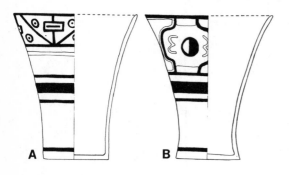

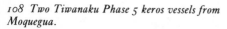

108 Two Tiwanaku Phase 5 keros vessels from Moquegua.

109 Two Chen Chen Phase keros beakers (A, B) and their painted motifs (C and D respectively).

cultural debris. The exceptional status of Omo was demarcated by monumental architecture and the only Tiwanaku platform mound to be erected outside the Titicaca Basin. Built of adobe, with cut stone blocks, the platform was banked against a hill and measured 120 m in length. It rose in three tiers, each forming a spacious plaza, the highest of which had rectangular compartments arranged symmetrically around a sunken court. Free of domestic refuse, excavations produced two finds: an offering of a llama fetus accompanied by a starfish, and an elaborate tapestry fragment depicting a staff-bearing figure. The monument may have housed statuary, for the head of a stela, carved in Classic Tiwanaku style, was discovered on the surface of a nearby area. It depicted an anthropomorphic face with round eyes and a wide headband of the type represented on monoliths at the capital. It was apparently made of stone from the Moquegua region and represents the first truly Tiwanaku monolith fragment found outside the altiplano. Another stone sculpture, of the same material and found at the site years ago, is different, depicting an oval human face, with a protruding nose, round eyes, and a grinning mouth. This work is vaguely reminiscent of the tenon heads ornamenting the rectangular sunken court at Tiwanaku. Yet another surface find of the same type of stone is a maquette of the Omo platform.

Surrounding the terraced platform, but separated from it, a large residential area comprised densely packed cane dwellings arranged round a series of spacious plazas. The settlement was in turn ringed by a series of separate cemeteries where different kin groups were buried. Tiwanaku people considered cranial deformation a mark of beauty and bound the heads of babies to shape their skull growth. Individuals in a cemetery shared the same deformation pattern, and patterns varied from one Omo graveyard to another. Mortuary populations at other settlements have yet to be studied, but the Omo sample is large.

After several centuries this prosperous Chen Chen occupation came to a violent end. The canals were destroyed, and virtually all the houses and other buildings were systematically razed. Cemeteries were violated when tomb lids were pried open exposing the deceased to the elements. The destruction and desecration were truly extensive and intensive, but what prompted this ferocity and who was involved remains unsolved. What motivated the rulers of Tiwanaku to take over administration of the Moquegua region during the Chen Chen Phase, and why the area was abandoned at the end of the Omo Phase, are also uncertain. Improved archaeological dating may show that the great drought, or the Huari colonization of Cerro Baul contributed to some of these changes, and internal revolt after AD 800 has also been suggested.

The ensuing Tumilaca Phase shows occupation of a different tenor – one that was folk rather than state oriented. It started very late in Tiwanaku Phase 5 times and seems to have lasted a century or more after the collapse of the altiplano imperium. Ceramics lack their former standardization, as altiplano imports disappeared and local communities each produced their own wares. Mid-valley canal systems contracted back to their present confines, and there were relatively few settlements. A new Tumilaca settlement was erected at Omo, occupying a defensible hill spur fortified with an enclosing wall and a dry moat. Although houses were of cane construction as they had been earlier, there was no public architecture here or elsewhere. Most other settlements were also enclosed by ramparts and walls. The political fabric of the region seems to have dissolved into one of independent, competitive communities.

The Tumilaca Phase saw a gradual change to irrigated terrace farming. Settlements shifted up-valley, first to the base of Cerro Baul where relatively short canals could irrigate steep terrain. The Tumilaca works were low, small, and often attempted to cultivate the tops of flat ridges. Their modest size indicates that reclamation was in the hands of individual communities. By the close of the phase a few farmsteads had appeared in the high sierra. Here the emphasis was still on irrigating flat ridges rather than investing labor in terraces, but this marks the opening of the high sierra, where vast terrace systems were later erected by Aymara-speaking colonists from the altiplano.

110 Tumilaca Phase ceramic motifs.

Huari's brief intrusion seems to have left an agrarian legacy that would restructure Moquegua sierra farming centuries later.

On the Moquegua coast Tiwanaku presence was different again. Occasional grave goods with Phase 4 affiliations suggest that the state worked initially through local clients. Later, a few Tiwanaku people settled at Loreto Viejo, Algodonal, and several localities in the lower valley dated to the later centuries of Phase 5 and more or less contemporary with the Tumilaca occupation. Unlike the sierra settlements the coastal sites were not fortified, and the colonists may have instigated the opening of new lands by construction of the largest of the lower valley canals. They also introduced polychrome painting, a tradition that was later elaborated upon by local populations in creating the brilliant Chiribaya style. Chiribaya people reversed the direction of colonization when they founded enclaves in the upper drainage not far from the ruins of Omo. Thus, some aspects of Tiwanaku's legacy seem more enduring on the coast than in the sierra.

The Titicaca heartland

Tiwanaku was the political quintessence of high montane adaptation and a true agropastoral state. The capital was sustained by high altitude crops from intensive farming around the shores of Lake Titicaca, and the metropolis was linked to distant provinces by huge llama caravans. The prolonged drought that began in AD 562 must have affected all aspects of the imperial economy. The 1982–3 drought impoverished mountain pastureland with devastating effects. Undernourished llamas and alpacas lost resistance to infection, parasites, and pests, and great numbers died of disease as well as starvation. Tiwanaku must have suffered even greater herd losses, disrupting caravan communications, and llamas may have been moved to lower elevations along the eastern forested flanks of the mountains. During the recent drought and famine, large numbers of folk also fled the altiplano, and it seems likely that Tiwanaku's distant colonies would have provided places of relief in the past.

More than half the potato harvest was lost in 1982–3, and the consequences of the great prehistoric drought may have been similar. But Tiwanaku relied upon ridged field farming that was more productive than present practices. Enormous tracts of flat lowlands along the shores of Lake Titicaca are characterized by high water table conditions, and the lake has fluctuated as much as 4 m a decade within historic times, alternatively submerging or exposing land.

This situation characterized the ridged fields at Pampa Koani. Maintaining adequate, but not excessive, moisture for crops was a major agricultural concern because the pampa experienced seasonal inundation from both flooding streams and from lake level fluctuations, and Tiwanaku engineers controlled runoff by channeling rivers, stream beds and springs. Canals, some atop massive aqueducts, removed excessive water and redistributed it in better-drained areas. Many kilometers of Pampa Koani were farmed by now abandoned raised and ridged fields. As the name implies, these were long, narrow, artificially elevated planting surfaces, with maximum dimensions reaching 15 × 200 m. Occurring in parallel sets, ridges can be simply made by excavating earth from either side of a projected field and piling soil in the center to create a flat-topped mound bounded by low ditches with standing water. Excavated examples of Tiwanaku Phase 3 and 4 structures on the Pampa Koani, however, reveal far more complex construction. Boulders and cobbles were first hauled in to create a solid, but permeable footing, then covered by one or more meters of good soil quarried from distant hills.

If the pampa's 75 square km of ridged fields were all created in a similar manner labor expenditures were truly prodigious. Why expend so much effort? A decade ago Clark Erickson rebuilt and reactivated ridged fields at the north end of the lake, as Alan Kolata's team has recently done on the Pampa Koani. In both cases the yields were double or more those from plowed fields in the same region. Ridged fields have traditionally been considered a response to drainage problems. In part this is true, but exceptional yields point to other positive qualities as well. High altitude farming benefits from the thermal qualities of the ridged fields: daylight warms the water in the furrows, and at night releases heat to mitigate frost damage. The combination of water and thermal qualities permits two or more crops per year, which would be impossible with rainfall farming. It also seems that nitrogen-fixing plants thrive in the ditch waters which is rich in other nutrients as well. Each year when the furrows are cleaned the muck is dumped on the planting surfaces and naturally fertilizes them. The technology may also have a mitigating effect upon nematodes and other pests. Science has yet to figure out exactly how ridged fields worked or why they were permanently abandoned, but there is no question that Tiwanaku's agrarian economy was far more productive than contemporary farming.

The capacity to sustain crop growth during dry periods was certainly understood by ancient agronomists. (The old fields that archaeologists revitalized on Pampa Koani remained productive during the 1982–3 drought because nearby springs watered their deep furrows.) During the great drought, the lake levels must have dropped precipitously. Springs could sustain some field systems, but others would have been stranded without moisture. New ridged fields were probably built along the freshly exposed lake margins as higher inland systems were fallowed. This would have been a costly response, but would nonetheless have allowed Tiwanaku to endure the drought and thrive for centuries.

The focus of imperial cultivation was clearly upon flatlands. A great canal ran from the capital to the lake region, and farming extended well beyond the thousands of hectares of ridged fields that now lie abandoned. Farmers do not readily forsake productive land, and the collapse of Tiwanaku's reclamation works from natural or political causes may well relate to the downfall of the capital and its altiplano empire. With the loss of ridged field land later populations brought other types of terrain into production. During the Inca occupation this was done by terracing lakeside hill slopes, much of it still farmed, and by building magnificent flights of andenes on the sacred Islands of the Sun and Moon. However, none of this compensated for the estimated loss of 100,000 ha of ridged fields. The shore region of Lake Titicaca traditionally supported the largest and most compact of high altitude populations, but when Tiwanaku's vast reclamation works collapsed population levels certainly declined.

The Tiwanaku capital

As with other ancient capitals, little is known about the circumstances surrounding the demise of Tiwanaku. It is not clear how the agrarian and political collapses were related, or even if abandonment of ridged field farming was concurrent with the fall of the metropolis. The region was never fully deserted, and rainfall has long supported farming within former urban areas of adobe architecture. The stone buildings and marvelous stelae certainly commanded the interest of later peoples, including the Aymara kingdoms, the Inca, and the *conquistadores*. Many things were moved or destroyed, and it is difficult to tell who was responsible.

Plates 80,82 The city reveals very late architectural modifications that could pertain either to its final occupation or to activities after its fall. The Gateway of the Sun, for example, is certainly out of context, for it now stands incongruously in the northwest corner of the Kalasasaya platform and leads neither to nor from an important building. But on stylistic and architectural grounds, William Conklin argues that the solar gateway originally graced the magnificent Pumapunku platform, which was richly embellished with similar stonework and other monolithic portals. Thus, the greatest hallmark of Tiwanaku was moved by unknown parties more than a kilometer and placed in a conspicuous, but isolated position. Much the same may be said for the nearby Gateway of the Moon, which now stands prominently atop an otherwise formless mound.

At a late date, the upper terrace walls of the Akapana keeled over, other buildings failed, and monolithic gateways toppled. Walls were later repaired, but in a markedly haphazard manner, mixing blocks from different contexts. Megalithic gates at the Pumapunku were also righted, but their faces were marred by large holes for reinforcing rods needed to anchor the works in a vertical position. Obviously somebody believed in the sanctity of the city, but lacked the finance, technology, or the knowledge to restore it to its original condition. Several explanations have been suggested: destruction by earthquake in the waning days of Tiwanaku's fortunes when skilled labor wasn't available to repair the city; poor restoration following a destructive revolt at the capital; or, instead of a single event, architectural collapse might have been a matter of gradual deterioration following abandonment. In this case the presence of numerous Inca artifacts at the site might indicate that the masters of Tahuantinsuyu resurrected the ruins. Imposing stelae provided fossil proof for the contention that giants once ruled the world, and royal mythology held that Viracocha came to Tiwanaku to fashion the primordial human race from sacred lake clay. What better place for an Inca park validating imperial lore?

CHAPTER NINE

The Late Intermediate Period

The Late Intermediate Period is a particularly fascinating era because Spanish documents and colonial records enrich the archaeological record with an ethnohistorical perspective on Andean societies. Castilian administrators wrote voluminously about the Inca and about Tahuantinsuyu. However, the Spanish crown did not recognize pre-Inca conditions as a judicial basis for legal claims by indigenous peoples, and this practice limited inquiry into earlier times. Nonetheless, some documents do contain native accounts about events predating the conquest of Cuzco, and in other cases, what is recorded about life under Inca rule provides insights about prior conditions. Thus the Late Intermediate is sometimes called the 'Protohistoric' period. The period ended with the Inca incorporation of the Ica valley in 1476, and technically it began in AD 1000, but many developments first emerged several centuries earlier in the wake of the Huari collapse. In this chapter we will start our review in the Titicaca Basin and work north so that we can conclude with Chimor, the great rival state of Tahuantinsuyu.

The Titicaca region

There are extensive sixteenth-century accounts about the Titicaca Basin and the so-called 'Aymara kingdoms', particularly of the powerful Colla and Lupaqa nations on the northwest and southwest borders of the lake. Other Aymara groups, about which much less is known, included Cana, Canchi, Charca, Umasuyo and Pacaje. Whether the Aymara were descendants of the Tiwanaku empire, or new arrivals who followed its fall, is a much-debated question. Some scholars see the altiplano as the primordial homeland of the Aymara. They believe its speakers pioneered high-altitude tuber cultivation and agropastoralism, whereas Quechua speakers exploited lower mountain habitats. Other authorities argue that Tiwanaku people spoke a local language, such as Pukina, and that the Aymara homeland was in the mountains inland from the Cañete valley. They believe the Aymara began to disperse into new settings during the Middle Horizon and swept into the Titicaca Basin after the demise of Tiwanaku. The archaeological record does not resolve the issue because it exhibits both change and continuity to support either interpretation. Inca accounts portray the altiplano as a feudal landscape of petty, warring states that the lords of Cuzco played off against one another and conquered in piecemeal fashion. This interpretation is compatible with the evidence of both fortifications and stylistic heterogeneity. 'Collao' style pottery is associated with habitation sites in the Colla territory, fancier 'Allita Amaya' pottery accompanies graves in the Lupaqa area, and in the southern lake region of Bolivia, pre-Inca ceramics are called 'Mollo'. Although many vessel shapes are shared, altiplano pottery assemblages vary from area to area, and there is nothing akin to Tiwanaku's standardized corporate style.

The collapse of the old capital was associated with the collapse of ridged field agriculture and changed where people lived and how they made a living. Inca rule saw the introduction of extensive terrace agriculture, and most earlier sites are in hilly terrain, where rainfall supported cultivation of steep slopes. Yet, it is not clear to what degree, if any, the Aymara kingdoms built terraced irrigation systems in their homelands, although they did build extensive irrigated terrace systems in their colonial hinterlands, such as the Moquegua sierra. A survey of sites in the Lupaqa region by John Hyslop revealed that after the demise of Tiwanaku there was a pronounced shift in settlement away from low-lying land near the lakeshore to distant hilltop localities at elevations above 4,000 m. The number of sites doubled, but all major settlements were ringed by defensive walls. Most were associated with corrals for llama and alpaca, and facilities for herding were much more in evidence than they had been earlier. Thus, intensification of pastoralism was one response to the loss of ridged field farmland.

Within fortified settlements, dwellings tended to be circular or oval, but rectangular forms were used elsewhere in the region. Dwellings were often arranged in two discrete clusters, suggesting dual organization. Settlements conformed to a size hierarchy: the largest covers 150 ha; four were about 30 ha; followed by numerous smaller villages and hamlets. There is no evidence of older ceremonial traditions persisting in the form of platform mounds, sunken courts, or carved gateways. Seated burials in circular cists did persist, and a new mortuary practice arose in the form of large burial towers called *chullpas*. Some stately towers, one to three stories tall, were erected adjacent to settlements; *Plate 94* others in separated groups. Located west of Puno, Sillustani is one of the most famous tower groups. It includes round and square chullpas of magnificent masonry, and although looted long ago, some towers are known to have contained 20 or more bodies of adults and children. There is no doubt that chullpas were the mausoleums of ruling families and represent huacas sepulturas. Chullpas continued in use after the Inca conquest and many contain Inca-style remains, indicating that local rulers were incorporated into the provincial administration and received substantial rewards for their service to Cuzco.

In addition to opening terraced farmland, the state removed people from fortified hilltops and resettled them at low-lying sites near the lake and along the imperial highway system. For the Colla, for example, resettlement included building a new capital at Hatunqolla, near modern Puno.

John Murra's original exposition of Andean verticality drew heavily on Spanish accounts of distant Lupaqa colonies in low-altitude habitats. Along the

86 *A large rectangular enclosure and élite buildings (bottom right) occupy the flatlands of Cerro Galindo in the Moche Valley. Above a dry moat and high wall, residential terraces cover the hillside.*

87 (above) Huari seen from a hillside cave overlooking the ruins.

88 (below) Deep within Tiwanaku territory, Huari established a fortified colony atop the natural bastion of Cerro Baúl.

Huari

89 (above)   A classic Huari-style polychrome vessel.

90 (above right)   A Huari-style urn from a ceremonial cache at the site of Pacheco.

91 (right)   A Tiwanaku-style four-cornered hat from Chen Chen in the Moquegua Valley.

92 (below left)   A vessel from the coastal Huacho Valley exhibiting Huari stylistic influence.

93 (below right)   A Tiwanaku portrait head vessel found in the Moquegua Valley.

94 (left) *Ruins of a chullpa burial tower at Sillustani near Puno.*

95 (right) *Depicting a human figure holding a libation beaker, this is a typical Chancay black-on-white funerary vessel.*

96 (below) *A Chiribaya-style polychrome vessel.*

97 (right) With wings on his shoulders, the Sican Lord is depicted on the handle of a gold tumi or ceremonial knife.

98 (far right) A Chimú wooden figure discovered at Huaca Tacanaymo.

99 (below) Air view of the city of Chan Chan, capital of Chimor, with its vast rectangular compounds reserved for members of the élite.

Chan Chan

100 (above) Typical of late U-shaped offices of the ruling nobility, this Tschudi audiencia *had two large niches in each interior wall.*

101 (right) An adobe frieze in the Uhle Compound at Chan Chan depicts fish, sea fowl, mythical creatures and wave motifs, reflecting an interest in the sea.

102 (below right) Detail of a Chan Chan adobe frieze showing fish.

103 (overleaf) Guardian figures lined the entry to Ciudadela Rivero at Chan Chan; each wooden sentry once held a staff or spear.

eastern forested slopes of the mountains, sites with Mollo ceramics have been found at elevations down to 1,500 m. Many are associated with irrigated terraces, such as Iskanwaya, a superb Mollo complex of barrack-like quarters that may have served for both farming and mining the local gold deposits.

Lupaqa colonies were established along the desert watershed, in the Moquegua sierra. Here the post-Tiwanaku occupation is called the Estuquina Phase, and is associated with both flatland canal systems in mid-valley, and with extensive irrigated terrace systems in the steep upper drainage. People in each settlement built their own agricultural system, independent of their neighbors, and initially communities were small and open. Over time they increased in size and number, and all were defended by walls and dry moats. The fortified sites were associated with small chullpas for the élite, while commoners were interred, seated, in circular pits.

The Estuquina Phase exhibited strong cultural links with the altiplano. Some similarities may have been due to acculturation brought about by local communities acting as economic clients of the Aymara. However, some sierra communities were certainly composed of altiplano colonists. This is particularly the case with the later fortified settlements, where a number of different groups seem to have been vying with one another for agrarian resources; and it is interesting that those settlements identified as colonies exhibit greater ceramic and architectural affiliations with the Colla than with the Lupaqa, suggesting that the Inca probably realigned the vertical archipelagos of Aymara satellites in favor of the Lupaqa. When the Inca subdued the Moquegua region after laying siege to Cerro Baul, they found that many of the terrace systems had long been abandoned, and they pursued a policy of resettling people in lower, undefended settlements.

The Inca also found that highlanders were not the only people occupying the middle valley. During the Late Intermediate Period, Chiribaya coastal folk established upland enclaves in the region.

From the Vitor Valley well into northern Chile, cultural evolution along the coast followed a totally different pattern from that in the adjacent sierra and altiplano. The region was never conquered by Huari or Tiwanaku, and although the latter did maintain desert valley colonies, littoral populations pursued their own maritime-oasis lifeways. The small size and limited agricultural resources of most southern drainages fostered independent populations that developed in parallel, with little or no evidence of empire building. Instead, during the Late Intermediate Period the lower valleys and adjacent littoral were occupied by a series of petty states. Several were associated with ornate corporate styles expressed in ceramics and textiles, including the San Miguel and Gentilar styles of the Arica drainage, and the Chiribaya style of the Moquegua coast.

Chiribaya ceramics employ geometric motifs painted in vibrant poly-   *Plate 96*
chromes, and in a sense preserve some of the colorful aspects of earlier Tiwanaku arts, which the Aymara rejected. The potential capital, Chiribaya Alta, was located inland on a high bluff overlooking the valley. Covering about

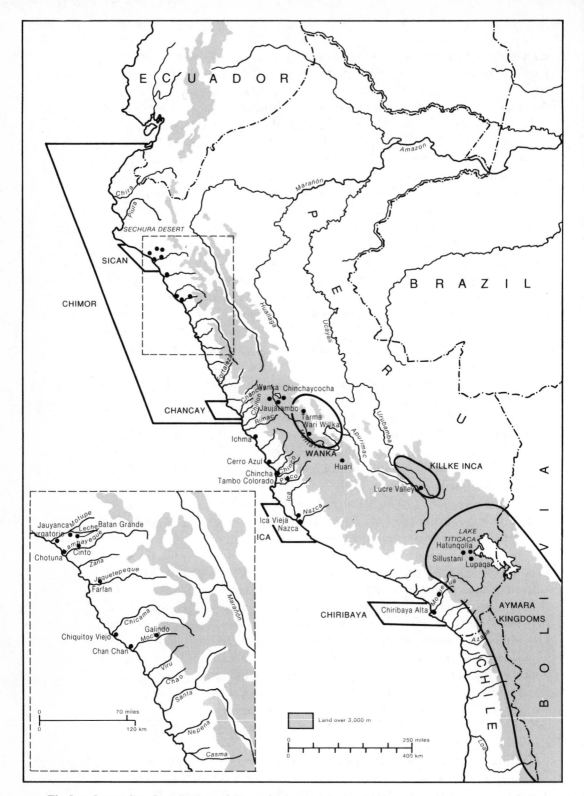

Map labels:

ECUADOR

BRAZIL

PERU

BOLIVIA

CHILE

Amazon

Marañón

Huallaga

Ucayali

Urubamba

Apurímac

Chira

Piura

SECHURA DESERT

SICAN

CHIMOR

CHANCAY

Fortaleza

Chancay

Chillón

Rímac

Wanka Chinchaycocha

Jauja Tarma

Ichma

Cerro Azul

Chincha
Tambo Colorado

WANKA

Huari

Wari Willka

KILLKE INCA

Lucre Valley

Chinco
Pisco
Ica

Ica Vieja
Nazca

ICA

Nazca

LAKE
TITICACA
Hatunqolla
Sillustani
Lupaqa

CHIRIBAYA

Chiribaya Alta

Moquegua
Azapa
Loa

AYMARA
KINGDOMS

Inset map labels:

Jauyanca
Purgatorio
Chotuna

Motupe
Leche
Lambayeque
Cinto

Batan Grande

Zaña

Jequetepeque

Farfán

Chicama

Chiquitoy Viejo

Chan Chan

Galindo
Moche

Virú

Chao

Santa

Nepeña

Casma

Marañón

0 ___ 70 miles
0 ___ 120 km

Land over 3,000 m

0 ___ 250 miles
0 ___ 400 km

111 The Late Intermediate Period: principal sites and areas mentioned in Chapter Nine.

one square kilometer it was made up of rectangular dwellings with masonry footings that supported walls of cane. Long occupation of the site included a late phase of corporate construction when a thick rampart of loose earth was mounded up to encircle the community. This is a unique example of monumental construction, albeit humble by north coast standards. It may have been undertaken in response to competitive colonization of the upper drainage by Chiribaya people and folk from the altiplano.

Chiribaya settlements are associated with burials in dwellings and in separate cemeteries. Corpses were seated in rectangular, stone-lined tombs and common accompaniments included pottery and textiles. At Chiribaya Alto graves are distinguished by frequent llama accompaniments. At another site near the valley mouth, the deceased were buried on crudely fashioned litters left on top of the tombs. Cemeteries near coastal springs, away from the valley, yield burials accompanied by miniature log rafts with reed sails.

Coastal springs supported small canal systems, which reached their maximum agrarian expanse around AD 1000 and then began to contract. Half the agricultural land had dropped out of production by 1570 when the Spanish introduced olive cultivation. The olive groves in turn shrank to a quarter or less of their original size by 1950. Ongoing loss of agricultural land was due to declining spring flow and a 20 m drop in water table over the last 1,500 years.

The southern sierra

The imperial capital of Cuzco has long drawn archaeological attention to the upper Urubamba drainage and the marvelous landscape that the Inca crafted for themselves by studding the vista with masonry buildings and covering the quichua slopes with great flights of agricultural terraces. Terracing was among *Plate 2* the many Huari contributions to the region, and scholars have long looked to the Middle Horizon for Tahuantinsuyu's antecedents. This is because the old Ayacucho empire transformed the Urubamba sierra into its most strategic of highland frontiers and a great provincial buffer against Tiwanaku's nearby altiplano dominion.

Huari's concern with the region is represented at Pikillaqta, the largest provincial complex erected by the ancient state. Pikillaqta, located in the Lucre Valley not far from Cuzco, is a formally planned administrative center with lines of symmetrical, contiguous buildings grouped into sectors by enclosing walls up to 10 m high. The core of the complex covers more than one square kilometer, and excavations by Gordon McEwan indicate that it served residential, storage, and administrative ends.

After the collapse of Huari, inhabitants of the area continued to enjoy relative prestige, if not power. They retained aspects of Huari's architectural and artistic traditions, and no doubt passed them on to the emerging Inca. Known as Killke, Late Intermediate Period ceramics of the region developed out of much earlier local antecedents, to which Huari influences and later innovations were added. Killke pottery is a regional folk tradition with some fine wares decorated with black and red geometric motifs on cream or buff surfaces. Studies have revealed considerable variability in ceramic assemblages from one valley to another within the broader Urubamba region, but as a whole Killke ceramics were directly ancestral to later corporate style ceramics of the Inca. A similar relationship between Inca corporate architecture and local antecedents has been demonstrated by Ann Kendall working in the lower Urubamba drainage, 80 km from Cuzco.

The political foundations of Cuzco rest in Killke times. Defensive hilltop residence characterized most Killke settlements within the greater Urubamba region, with one glaring exception – the Cuzco Valley. This suggests that the valley was politically consolidated early on, and strong enough not to require defenses. Cuzco may even have had sufficient early power to threaten its neighbors.

Because corporate styles only emerge after the states they represent are well formed, conquest is difficult to recognize, particularly among peoples sharing the same folk traditions. Therefore, Cuzco's expansion during Killke times is not well-understood. One later Inca policy was to move subject populations out of defended hilltop sites and resettling them in lower, undefended communities. In the lower Urubamba Valley such a shift in settlement began in the latter part of the Late Intermediate, suggesting that Cuzco's territorial expansion began in an incremental manner much earlier than imperial lore would have us believe. Indeed, ethnohistorians debate the historical validity of what the Inca said about their origins. One group argues that the story of ten successive monarchs each founding a royal clan in upper or lower Cuzco is simply a myth rationalizing a state that began as a federation of local, independent kin groups occupying the imperial heartland. Others argue that the oral traditions possess varying degrees of historical authenticity. Some accept the chronicler Cabello Balboa's description of a chronological succession of monarchs, but the problem with this chronology is that Cuzco's dual organization into hanan and hurin moieties suggests rule by a king, and a kingly counterpart. Thus, while Balboa names ten potentates, only two may have been in office at a time. It is also clear that some rulers, such as Pachacuti's brother, were purged by the Inca from their imperial rosters, thereby truncating official history. Similarly, if consolidation of the Cuzco Valley and initial territorial expansion by its residents began in Killke times, then Inca lore consolidated real time and events.

Historically, the homeland must have been consolidated first, and then adjacent lands conquered. These events were set in motion by Pachacuti's ancestors, but claimed by him for his own aggrandizement. Thus, there is certainly a great deal of truth in what the Inca said about their exploits and conquests, but their rendering of events assumed heroic proportions when it was compressed into only three generations.

The central sierra

Inca expansion into the central sierra met stiff resistance from a powerful ethnic group known as the Wanka or Huanca. They occupied the region where Lake Junin feeds the upper Mantaro River and highlands to the east in the Río Tarma headwaters of the Chinchamayo River, where other groups known as the Tarma and Chinchaycocha also lived. Here herding had long been emphasized over farming. The adoption of large-kerneled varieties of maize and intensification of farming did not begin until *c*. AD 1000, much later than in other regions. The intensification process was associated with dramatic settlement changes in the verdant Yanamarca Valley, if not in other Mantaro tributaries. Reflecting a shift from low to high population densities, small, low-lying sites were replaced by larger, more numerous walled communities defensively situated atop hills. With Huari less than 200 km away, the complex of corporate buildings at Wari Willka, the Wanka capital, was influenced by Ayacucho style. But elsewhere in the Mantaro area there was surprisingly little Huari influence. The later residence patterns fit Inca descriptions of the Wanka as a people fraught with internal hostilities. Nonetheless, there was a pronounced size hierarchy, grading from many hamlets of 5–10 ha, through a few between 15 and 40 ha, to one of more than 100 ha. Most sites had fewer than 50 buildings per ha, but numbers more than twice as high characterized several of the larger Wanka sites in the rich Yanamarca area.

Dwellings were predominantly round, and clusters of up to half a dozen structures around open patios formed household groups. As with contemporary sierra settlements there was little formal planning, but dual organization is suggested by villages split into two spatially distinct subdivisions, or by pairs of adjacent settlements. Following the Inca conquest, an imperial administrative center was erected at Jaujatambo in the Yanamarca area and inhabitants of the region were encouraged to resettle in lower zones. Agriculture was reorganized to emphasize production for the state and vast numbers of qollqa warehouse facilities were erected.

In the headwaters of the Tarma region and the lower Río Chinchamayo Valley, the Campa or Amuesha peoples pursued Amazonian adaptations in the montaña zone of the lower valley up to about 1,800 m, above which manioc staples did not grow. Concentrated on alluvial terraces near the river, their houses were primarily of wood and thatch, and stone architecture was generally absent or poorly executed. Their pottery was entirely different from that of the sierra, and very limited interchange is indicated by negligible amounts of sierra wares in Campa sites and vice versa.

With a vertical range of almost 3,000 m, the highlanders traversed an extraordinary gradient of environmental zones from the montaña at *c*. 2,000 m, through the sierra valleys, to the high, wet puna. It appears that the Wanka, and more particularly, their Tarma and Chinchaycocha neighbors each maintained a contiguous vertical swath of territory spanning these altitudinal extremes, rather than discrete satellite holdings in each zone. Given the politically fragmented nature of these populations it seems likely that each community worked for itself rather than for the ethnic group as a whole. Thus, verticality adaptations here were rather different than among the Aymara kingdoms of the altiplano.

The central and south coasts

Prior to Inca subjugation, the desert lowlands of central and southern Peru formed a feudal landscape occupied by numerous independent states. The Ichma were among the more powerful and important of these because their territory in the Rimac and Lurin valleys was home to the great oracle at Pachacamac. An architectural florescence transpired at the sacred city during the Late Intermediate Period, and many of its splendid sanctuaries and élite architectural compounds were erected at this time. The temple of Pachacamac, where the oracle resided, was the supreme huaca adoratorio, but the numerous other temples and shrines at the center reflect a rich and cosmopolitan pantheon. It is likely that some sanctuaries were commissioned and built to serve deities foreign to the Ichma. This was certainly the case in Inca times when Topa Inca had a shrine erected dedicated to the cult of the Sun. In part this reflects a particularly close relationship between the Inca and the Ichma who formed a military alliance for purposes of attacking and defeating their great northern adversary of Chimor.

Shortly before the Inca–Ichma alliance was struck, ethnohistorical sources indicate that Chimor expanded its frontiers south through the Chancay Valley and perhaps into the Chillon drainage. A vibrant corporate style, known as Chancay, occurs in these two valleys and suggests that they achieved a degree of political integration prior to Chimor's late intrusion. Chancay ceramics are *Plate 95* characterized by black and occasionally red painting on a whitish slip. Vessels exhibit a matt finish. Motifs are usually geometric, but plants, animals, and people were occasionally depicted, and many vessels have modeled and painted human faces. Some were molded in the form of birds and llamas, and large human figures, generally females, were common. Mold-made ceramics are common and reflect mass production of corporate wares.

Chancay tombs contained seated figures, and are notable for their textiles, which include elaborate gauzes, brocades, openwork fabrics, and a great deal of painted cloth. Corporate architecture is noteworthy for its use of *tapia* construction, in which sections of walls, foundations, or floors were framed in wooden molds. Moist adobe was then poured and pounded into the forms and allowed to dry. Relative to more arduous brickwork, tapia is a means of mass production, and it was used to create many impressive monuments on the central coast. In a sense Chancay reflects an industrialization of corporate art and architecture that permeated many Andean polities to varying degrees during the Late Intermediate Period. More people had access to mass produced ceramics and textiles, but the nobility still guarded its symbols of privilege by monopolizing the production and use of precious metals.

To the south of the Chancay and Ichma states, the señorio of Huarco controlled the lower Cañete Valley. Here, on a high rocky promontory jutting into the sea, Cieza de León described '. . . the most adorned and handsome fort that there was in the kingdom of Peru, built upon great square slabs, with very well-made facades, reception rooms, and large patios.' This monument, Cerro Azul, still retains marvelous Cuzco-style masonry, and its beautiful stonework is unique among Inca coastal works, which elsewhere were of adobe.

Cerro Azul rose to prominence during the Late Intermediate Period as a prosperous maritime center. There were at least ten monumental complexes of large multi-room tapia constructions, surrounded by numerous smaller buildings and dwellings. Excavations did not reveal evidence of subsistence farming, but of an economy based on net fishing. Emphasizing surplus production, anchovies and sardines were dried and then packed by the thousand into storage rooms and filled over with dry sand to ensure the conservation of the catch. From the warehouses the fish were presumably exported to farmers in the rest of the señorio, if not beyond. Cerro Azul was probably founded by the Huarco nobility when this small state initially organized economic production, and fishing would have been formally organized through the social hierarchy.

Parallel developments seem to have transpired in the neighboring valley to the south. Here the Chincha señorio reportedly had 30,000 male tribute-payers, including 12,000 farmers, 10,000 fishermen, and 6,000 merchants. Chincha merchants are of particular interest, but what is known about them comes primarily from ethnohistorical sources. Their exchange network handled many commodities, but they were particularly noted for travels to Ecuador to procure *Spondylus* shell. The sacred shell was shipped back to Chincha to supply the Inca and the nobility of their conquered realms. It is not unlikely that Chimor had previously monopolized the *Spondylus* trade, and following Inca conquest it was turned over to the Chincha.

112 Painted decoration on a Chancay textile.

Still farther south people residing in the Ica and Nazca drainages continued their long tradition of producing fine textiles and distinctive polychrome ceramics, known as Ica. This artistic tradition witnessed a particularly strong influx of Huari iconographic and ideological influence that gradually faded and underwent local reinterpretation over time. Burying the deceased in a flexed and seated position persisted, accompanied by cloth, pottery, and other offerings. Unifying ceramic characteristics are polychrome wares with white and black painting on red surfaces. Motifs are predominantly geometric, but fish and sea birds are also depicted. The Ica style is corporate in nature, but its broader distribution reflects prestige more than political power.

Old cultural links with the Ayacucho region persisted as indicated by the occasional occurrence of Ica ceramics in highland sites in the Río Pampas area. On the coast the pottery has also been found with tombs in the Chincha señorio. Yet, within its heartland there is little to suggest that the style was associated with a powerful state. Large urban settlements are not evident in the Nazca drainage at this time, and the only noteworthy center is Ica Vieja, 10 km south of the modern city of Ica. This complex of structures, built on mounds, was probably the node of local government because it was taken over by the Inca to serve as a bureaucratic center.

Although the Inca may have preferred working through established centers, they also erected new ones, of which Tambo Colorado in the Pisco Valley is the most noteworthy and best preserved in the desert lowlands. Here adobe buildings, ornamented with trapezoidal niches, fronted a great plaza with an *usnu* platform.

Chimor and the north

Encompassing 1,000 km of Pacific coastland, Chimor is the second largest native state in South America that can be documented by both ancient remains and ethnohistorical accounts. At its height, the empire encompassed two-thirds of all irrigated land along the desert and, by inference, two-thirds of the coastal population. In evolutionary perspective, Chimor synthesized maritime–oasis development and integrated the northern demographic pole of the Andes *Plate 99* within a single nation. Residing at the metropolis of Chan Chan, the governing royalty bitterly contested Inca territorial ambitions until the coastal nation was defeated by Cuzco *c*. 1470. Ensuing generations witnessed Chimor's brutal dismemberment as the Inca exiled them to distant colonies, and divided their state into independent parcialidades and señorios loyal to Cuzco. Smallpox and the first New World pandemics further ravaged what survived of the old kingdom.

Thus the *conquistadores* encountered only a few, fragmentary accounts of the royal dynasties that had forged Chimor into the continent's penultimate empire. Four Spanish writers briefly mention native oral accounts about the founders and governing lords of the two coastal empires. The first was the Taycanamu dynasty, based at Chan Chan and comprising the rulers of Chimor.

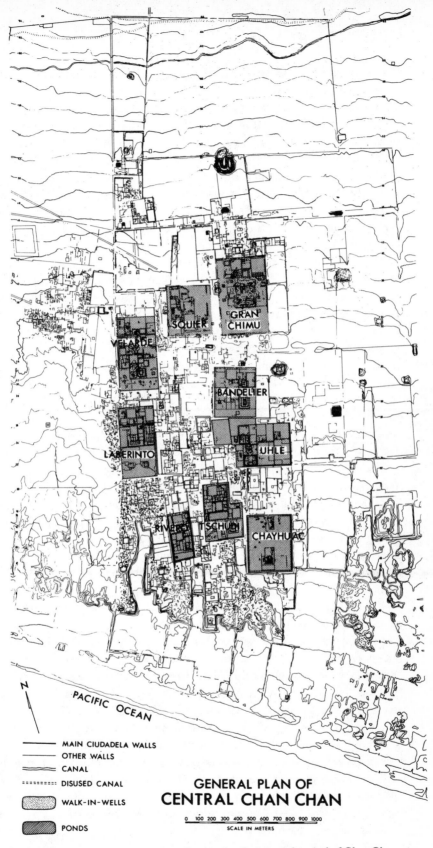

GRAN
CHIMU

SQUIER

VELARDE

BANDELIER

LABERINTO

UHLE

RIVERO
TSCHUDI
CHAYHUAC

N

PACIFIC OCEAN

MAIN CIUDADELA WALLS
OTHER WALLS
CANAL
DISUSED CANAL
WALK-IN-WELLS
PONDS

GENERAL PLAN OF
CENTRAL CHAN CHAN

0 100 200 300 400 500 600 700 800 900 1000
SCALE IN METERS

113 *At the height of Chimor's political prosperity the imperial capital of Chan Chan was
dominated by palatial compounds.*

The second was the Naymlap dynasty of the Lambayeque region, which Chimor came to incorporate.

The term dynasty is somewhat misleading because these were probably dual rulerships rather than monarchies. Furthermore, Naymlap lore describes a political confederacy, whereas Taycanamu lore describes centralized rule. Unfortunately, neither royal succession is described in detail. The lore clearly contains myth and allegory, but also mentions places and events identifiable in the archaeological record. To judge from radiocarbon dates on associated sites the deeds and events are related in correct chronological order; transpired over the course of many centuries; but were compressed by native accounts into a short span of ten or twelve generations.

Naymlap lore describes developments in the Lambayeque Valley after the abandonment of the Moche capital at Pampa Grande. Correlated with the archaeological record, the dynastic story probably begins in the early Sican Phase between AD 700 and 900. Landing at the valley mouth with a flotilla of balsa boats, a lord called Naymlap arrives with his wife, a greenstone idol, and a large entourage, including a retinue of 40 officials. Saying he was sent from afar to govern, Naymlap builds a palatial court at a place called Chot, thought to be Chotuna, a complex of platforms and ruins 4 km from the sea. In prosperous old age, as death approaches, the patriarch has himself entombed, but commands his offspring and followers to spread the tale that Naymlap sprouted wings and flew away to the hereafter. A senior son, Zolzdoni, has 12 sons who with other followers go off to found a dozen new Lambayeque settlements.

Beginning with the dynastic founder, there are 12 named rulers in the dynasty. It ends with Fempellec, who is tempted by a sorceress to move Naymlap's stone idol, a sin which occasions '30 days' of disastrous rains and devastating floods, followed by famine and pestilence, and causes the potentate's vassals to rise up and cast him into the sea. Following an interregnum of unknown duration, Chimor conquers the region and holds it through a brief succession of three governors before the Inca subdue the region.

The number 12 is a recurrent motif in the story and its limitation to the number of months in a year leads some ethnohistorians to argue that the story had calendrical significance. Arrival by sea may be a fanciful embellishment meant to confer special status on ancestral founders and Naymlap's large entourage bespeaks a new élite. (The Taycanamu story begins similarly but the leader arrives alone.) Many nobles in this retinue bear official titles that reflect specialized tasks, such as Lord of the Feathered Cloth Makers, suggesting the guild-like economic specialization prevalent when the Spanish arrived.

As yet, there is no archaeological evidence of an incursion of seafaring foreigners at Chotuna or in the valley, although commerce with Ecuador is later evident. The region did, however, experience profound upheaval following the collapse of the Moche polity at Pampa Grande. When centralized rule disappeared and coastal communities were on their own, highlanders from Cajamarca seem to have pushed into lower elevations along the mountain

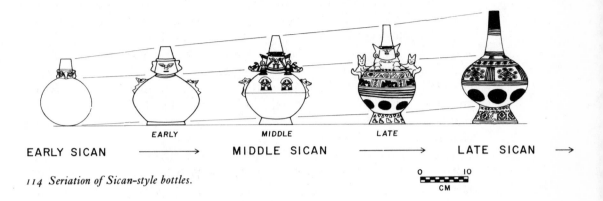

EARLY

MIDDLE

LATE

EARLY SICAN ⟶ MIDDLE SICAN ⟶ LATE SICAN ⟶

114 Seriation of Sican-style bottles.

0   10
CM

slopes, introducing new artistic elements. Noteworthy aspects of Huari iconography were also adopted. Combined with older Moche traditions, there was also a synthesizing surge in local innovations and this brought forth a new regional style, called Sican. This saw the introduction of ceramic ornamentation by stamping moist clay surfaces with decorated paddles that leave design imprints. Decoration by modeling and painting persisted, but black ware vessels and double-spouted libation vessels became increasingly common.

There is but scattered evidence of monumental construction at this time, but construction activity increased dramatically during the Middle Phase (AD 900–1100), when Sican crystallized as a sharply defined corporate style. The central design element is a male figure called the Sican Lord. The richly attired image *Plate 97* is often depicted with small wings on each shoulder, a beak-like nose, and occasionally with talons instead of feet. On libation vessels he is often shown in a flight-like attitude atop a serpent with a head at each end of its body. On double-spouted vessels the serpent forms a handle bridging the two spouts. On single-spouted vessels, the head of the Sican Lord was often modeled on the spout and flanked by two serpent heads, as well as by smaller human attendants shown in ritual flight. The double-headed serpent is an old Moche motif often associated with the sky, and the Sican Lord is a very strong iconographic candidate for Naymlap.

Reflecting the vast size of the greater Lambayeque irrigation complex, this region contains more large cities and settlements than other Andean regions. Many centers, including Chotuna, arose during Sican times but precisely when is not clear in most cases. Including the imposing ruins at Cinto, Tucume and Juayanca, at least five of these cities may be sites reputedly established by Naymlap's grandsons. Large Sican centers are sufficiently numerous to accommodate the claim that all 12 heirs founded important settlements. Yet, here the dynastic lore is best understood in an allegorical sense and seen as rationalizing the emergence of a confederation of local city-states. (On the basis of archaeological site clusters and ethnohistorical information, it has been suggested that there were ten.) Several others no doubt occupied the nearby Zana drainage to the south.

These ethnic centers probably arose independently at different times and only later put forward claims of descent from Naymlap as a means of forging alliances. Alliances were critical for building and maintaining the great inter-valley canal systems that carried abundant water from the Lambayeque River to dryer northern and southern drainages. Here for example, the Lambayeque city of Cinto sat at the beginning of the Taymi Canal supplying water to the area around the city of Tucume in the Leche Valley. Therefore, lore purporting that both urban centers were founded by Naymlap's heirs provided a kinship charter for mutual cooperation. Inter-valley canals involved not only great labor and engineering skills, but sensitive claims to water and land. An inter-valley system extending south from the Zana and north from Jequetepeque was fully completed except for its narrow, mid-point linkup. Here each great canal simply turned down slope and did not bond with its counterpart. Thus, what was technologically feasible was not always politically attainable.

Chotuna was occupied from early Sican times into the Late Horizon to judge from excavations by Christopher Donnan. The civic core of important buildings grew over time, but early construction was largely removed by catastrophic flooding *c.* 1100, and the remnants covered by later reconstruction. Building apparently began with a modest, but ornate set of rooms and courts attached to a small platform, Huaca Gloria, two stories high. Later, this architectural nucleus was isolated and enclosed by tall brick walls built and remodeled several times. Two high platforms overlooking Huaca Gloria were erected against opposite, exterior sides of the spacious court, and adjacent to the long ramp leading to the top of the larger mound, there was an enclosure housing buildings used for metalworking, particularly small copper items. Huaca Gloria was ornamented with distinctive friezes depicting double-headed serpents and other figures, but the Sican Lord is absent, and looters did not leave behind sufficient evidence to tell who or what was buried in the small platform. Nevertheless, it is tempting to see Huaca Gloria as Naymlap's shrine.

Chotuna was neither the biggest settlement nor the largest monumental center in the region. Its special status was as an ancestral center bonding a confederation rather than as a political capital dominating the region. Batan Grande, in the Leche Valley, was the region's pre-eminent center up to the end of the middle Sican Phase. Covering an enormous area, this complex of domestic and monumental buildings probably contains more mounds of exceptional size than any other Andean center of comparable antiquity. Called the Sican Precinct, the civic core covers 4 square km and includes more than a dozen truncated pyramids. Huaca Corte is among the largest and measures 250 m square. Many architectural elements were carried over from Pampa Grande, including an emphasis on large platforms with prominent perpendicular ramps, summit colonnades, chamber and fill construction, and the use of marked adobes.

The pyramids of Batan Grande tower over a landscape that resembles the pitted surface of the moon because grave robbing has been practiced here for centuries, and even include gaping holes carved by bulldozers. People were

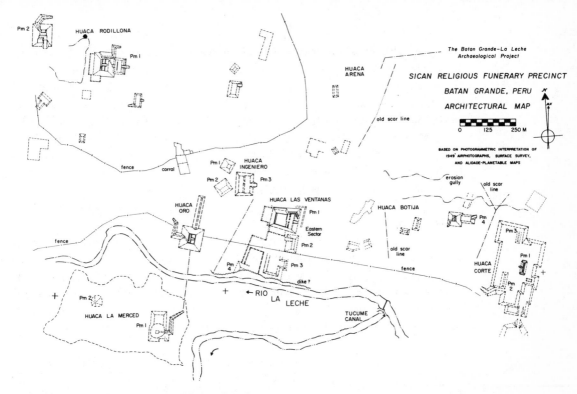

115 A plan of the Sican Precinct of Batan Grande.

buried in a flexed and seated position, reflecting new beliefs after the collapse of
Moche, and were often richly accompanied. Izumi Shimada's detailed studies
indicate that the graves number in the tens of thousands, reminiscent of
Pachacamac's vast cemeteries, and one must wonder if more people were not
buried at Batan Grande than resided in the center. The center may have been a
religious capital similar to today's Vatican. Much of the plundered Peruvian
goldwork now in private collections and museums reputedly came from élite
burials at Batan Grande. A single tomb in the central precinct yielded some 200
gold and silver necklaces, mummy masks, repoussé vases, *tumi* knives, and
other artifacts, in addition to quantities of shell, turquoise, lapis lazuli, emerald
inlays, and other adornments. Another tomb held 17 human sacrifices,
quantities of Ecuadorian *Spondylus* shells, lapis lazuli and precious metal items,
as well as some 500 kg of copper artifacts including orderly stacks of *naipes*
arranged 500 to a stack.

Naipes were common grave accompaniments at Batan Grande, but rare
elsewhere. They are small, flat I-shaped objects of hammered and cut sheet
copper, ranging from 5 to 7 cm long and from 3 to 5 cm wide. When found
stacked together the specimens are often of similar size. Similar objects found
in western Mexico and coastal Ecuador are called 'copper axe money' and are
thought to have served as money. Copper deposits are rare in coastal Ecuador,
and the metal for axe money, if not the objects themselves, must have been
imported. The 6,000 seafaring Chincha merchants traveling to Ecuador are

reported to have used copper as a medium of exchange, and it seems likely that Batan Grande was a mint for the production and distribution of naipes. Copper arsenical cores were locally mined and there is abundant evidence of smelting and crafting of metal artifacts from about AD 850. Combined with seafaring trade, metallurgical production was clearly a key contributor to the Middle Sican florescence of Batan Grande. During this florescence much of the Chira and Tumbes regions of northern Peru first entered the Andean cultural fold, a transformation undoubtedly fostered by lively coastal commerce.

In the midst of great prosperity Batan Grande came to an abrupt end about 1100, when massive floodwaters swept through the metropolis. Unlike Chotuna, it was not rebuilt. Instead, piles of wood and brush were heaped up against the towering pyramids, and the entire city was burned and abandoned in a conflagration strikingly similar to that accompanying the abandonment of Pampa Grande. It certainly symbolized a dramatic rejection of the political and cosmological order of the universe. If the karaka class and nobility claimed divine status and were self-purported intermediaries between the cosmos and humankind, then unmitigated natural disasters could well bring about their rejection.

In addition to Chotuna, monuments to the south, including Pacatnamu in the Jequetepeque Valley and Chan Chan, show evidence of concurrent torrential rainfall and catastrophic flooding. Irrigation systems in the Moche Valley, and elsewhere, experienced calamitous destruction. Deprived of the means of making a living, the famine and pestilence of lore ring true, and glacial ice cores in the high mountains register a strong El Niño event at AD 1100.

For the north coast, if not farther afield, these times must have occasioned major cultural changes. The after-effects seem less dramatic than those following the thirty-year drought of AD 562, but the El Niño disaster was both shorter lived and of a different nature. The ensuing Late Sican Phase ushered in new beliefs and new realities. The Sican Lord was conspicuously excised from the iconographic tradition. The city of Purgatorio in the Leche Valley replaced Batan Grande as the region's pre-eminent metropolis. Here, the tradition of erecting colossal mounds culminated in the construction of a gargantuan platform. However, the new order was short lived and the region was conquered by Chimor c. 1370.

The dynastic lore of Chimor is meagre and vague, listing only nine to eleven pre-Inca rulers. Arriving alone by boat, a man called Taycanamu says he was sent from afar to govern, and settles in the Moche Valley, presumably at Chan Chan. A son subjugates the lower drainage, and his son, Nancenpinco, consolidates the upstream portion of the valley, then carries out the first stage of external expansion, extending the imperial frontiers from the Río Santa to the Río Jequetepeque. Five to seven unnamed rulers supposedly follow, leading up to the reign of Minchancamon. Initiating a second stage of expansion, he reputedly conquers the coast from the Río Chillon through the Río Tumbes, but is defeated by the Inca and taken off to Cuzco. An heir is installed as a puppet, and his heirs lasted into the Spanish colonial period.

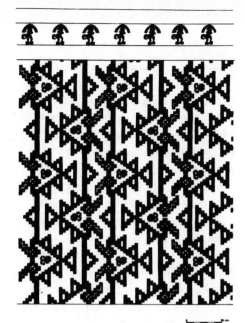

116 *Adobe friezes were reserved for royal palaces and exceptionally important buildings. This Gran Chimú example depicts interlocking birds with a border of monkeys wearing hats.*

A different Spanish account says that the Jequetepeque valley was subdued by a general from Chimor called Pacatnamu, who became the first provincial governor and who built an administrative center that came to bear his name. Pacatnamu's exploits pertain to the first episode of expansion, and the center he built is Farfan. Dates from Farfan and fortified sites closer to the Moche Valley indicate that the first stage of expansion was actually a composite episode of incremental conquests that spanned many generations. The same can be said for the second stage because Lambayeque was incorporated several generations before Minchancamon's reign. Other Spanish sources indicate that the imperial artisans at Chan Chan were moved to Cuzco and that there was at least one violent coastal revolt against the Inca.

Ethnohistorical sources describe how coastal lords resided in walled compounds with spacious, open courts and other facilities for receiving their subjects and entertaining the karaka élite. Vast rectangular enclosures with high adobe walls and an interior mortuary mound, are the dominant monuments of Chimor's imperial heartland. Associated with centralized, secular administration, the mighty structures bespeak of rule by divine right that included the privilege of being buried in a platform mound – a structure once exclusively associated with the gods. Built more or less sequentially over the course of a millennium, 12 such palatial monuments still stand to commemorate graphically the political fortunes of the desert valley. The earliest was built in the valley-neck at the Moche V city of Galindo. Later the majority, including the largest and most elaborate, were erected at Chan Chan near the sea. Finally, with the demise and dismemberment of Chimor, the last great enclosure, Chiquitoy Viejo, was built under Inca aegis on the south side of the Chicama Valley to control the main road leading to the former capital.

With the abandonment of Galindo the valley reverted to the petty city-states encountered by Taycanamu. This was a time when Huari influences melded with local customs to bring forth the new artistic and iconographic tradition

Plates 101,102 called Chimu, and best represented at Chan Chan. Maritime themes and sea creatures are prominent and dominate the adobe friezes gracing the most prestigious buildings. The imperial marine motifs first arose in Moche V times, when ideological and cultural adjustments were triggered by the fall of the Huaca del Sol and Huaca de la Luna. Noteworthy among the many *Plate 100* architectural continuities with the past are small U-shaped buildings called audiencias. These are usually set in a small court and raised slightly above the court floor. About 4 m square, they have interior wall niches and gabled roofs. Standing in the center of the building, iconographic depictions show a richly garbed figure holding audience with people assembled outside the front of the structure. The architectural form recalls the great U-shaped ceremonial centers of the Initial Period, but at Chan Chan, instead of housing gods, these special buildings were offices of the god-kings of Chimor and its ruling nobility.

The Taycanamu narrative lists nine to eleven pre-Inca rulers, and, depending on how certain of the earliest edifices are categorized there are nine to eleven monumental enclosures at Chan Chan. There is also evidence of at least two large enclosures that were razed and buried. This situation suggests that the heads of state not only manipulated imperial lore by compressing events and eliminating rulers from the dynastic rosters, but that they also selectively retained and eliminated the monuments of previous rulers.

Nonetheless, in final form Chan Chan was a vast metropolis. Its northern city wall bracketed some 20 square km of the valley mouth, much of which was open, seemingly set aside for further urban expansion. The densely packed civic center of great enclosures and other buildings covered 6 square km. Different types of architecture and construction material distinguish class and occupation. The lower class metropolitan majority lived and worked in quarters comprising small patios and irregular rooms of cane construction. Evidence excavated in these structures indicates that they were occupied by technicians and craftsmen. There was wood and lapidary work, but the dominant concern was large-scale metallurgical production, complemented by weaving. These people enjoyed the social privilege of wearing ear tubes, married among themselves – metalsmiths taking weavers as wives – and were buried in their own cemeteries. It is estimated that some 26,000 craftsmen and women resided in densely packed neighborhoods along the southern and western margins of the civic center when the city was at its height. Another 3,000 lived immediately adjacent to different royal enclosures, which they served directly. By this time neither farmers nor fishermen were allowed to live in the city, which was exclusively concerned with rule and governance.

At its height the urban minority of rulers, lords and karaka may have numbered 6,000 or less. They lived and worked in two classes of detached brick enclosures. The lesser nobility lived in 30 small compounds with low walls, while paramount rulers held court in the palatial enclosures described above. Monumental construction began about AD 850 with initial political consolidation of the valley, starting with three or four early phase enclosures of variable form, then shifting toward standardization with two middle-phase compounds

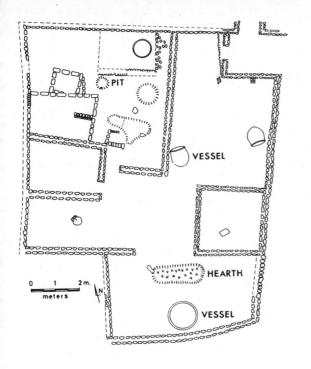

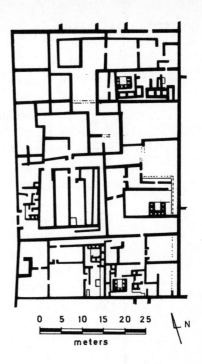

117 (above left) Living and working in cramped quarters made of cane, thousands of artisans and technical personnel resided at the Chimú imperial capital of Chan Chan.

118 (above right) The lesser nobility at Chan Chan resided in irregularly organized adobe compounds that had U-shaped offices but lacked friezes and burial mounds.

119 (right) To serve a ruler and his family in life, as well as death, Ciudadela Rivero at Chan Chan was equipped with U-shaped audiencias for offices, store rooms for wealth finance, and a burial platform for a mausoleum.

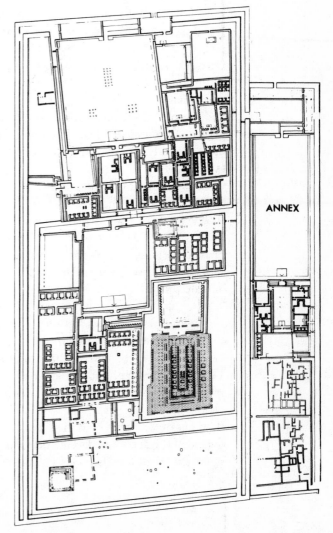

ANNEX

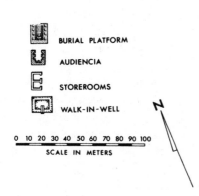

BURIAL PLATFORM

AUDIENCIA

STOREROOMS

WALK-IN-WELL

0 10 20 30 40 50 60 70 80 90 100
SCALE IN METERS

(*c.* 1125–1350) and four late-phase (*c.* 1350–1470) palaces of highly repetitive form, called *ciudadelas* (little cities). The palatial complexes are named after early explorers and archaeologists. Within a particular architectural phase two enclosures often exhibit close chronological pairing, and interpretations differ as to which was built first, not surprising if propositions that the ordering of the great enclosures and their spatial distribution were governed by principles of dual rural and moiety organization which split the metropolis into eastern and western sections.

Plate 100

Plate 103

Plates 101, 102

The final pair of enclosures, 'Rivero' and 'Tschudi', are classic ciudadelas, built shortly before the conquest of Chimor. Tschudi yielded otherwise rare specimens of Chimu-Inca ceramics and is a potential candidate for Minchanca-mon's court. Both complexes were enclosed by thick walls towering three stories high. Erected in segments by mit'a labor, the lofty walls seclude the royalty and graphically distinguish their grandiose quarters from the lesser nobility and the rest of humanity. Other than a royal family and servants few people lived in the stately compounds, even though the smallest, Rivero, is six times the size of a football field. Entry was through a narrow northern gateway and limited to single-file traffic. High curtain walls partitioned the interiors into northern, central and southern sectors and sometimes a fourth, eastern sector. Residing in humble cane quarters, retainers lived in the southern sector, which lacked brick buildings. The northern and central sectors each held a large centrally positioned entry court, often ornamented with carved friezes. A ramp at the southern end of the reception court led up to an elevated complex of maze-like corridors connecting smaller courts housing U-shaped audiencias and warehouses comprising rows of cell-like rooms for the storage of élite goods. Often embellished with maritime friezes, the audiencias were hierarchically arranged and controlled access to one another and to the storage facilities.

In late ciudadelas the northern sectors contained many more audiencia offices than the central sectors, which sometimes had only one – possibly a throne room. Alternatively, more warehouses occupied central than northern sectors, and these facilities were probably imperial coffers serving wealth finance. It is likely that the paramount royalty held court and resided in the central sector, while attendant nobles worked in the northern offices, but lived outside the palaces either in annexes or in small enclosures of their own.

The largest construction associated with almost all of the imperial compounds was a huaca sepultura. This was secluded within a high-walled court and generally set within the central sector. Platforms were one, two, or more stories high, and all had multiple interior chambers and cells. The Tschudi huaca and other late mounds, were built with rectangular cells symmetrically arranged around a central chamber. This compartment was distinguished by great size and a T-shaped ground plan. The T-shaped chamber presumably held the corpse for which the platform was built, and the richest of the accompaniments placed in the cells at the time of interment. It is significant that in many cases a smaller platform, itself containing a number of

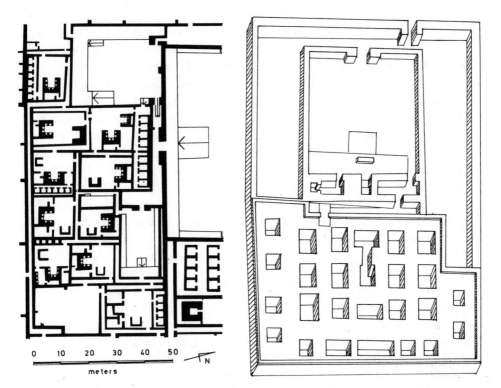

0 10 20 30 40 50

meters

120 A plan of the hierarchical organization of U-shaped audiencia offices in Ciudadela Tschudi at Chan Chan.

121 Chimú heads of state were interred in sepulturas huacas. The smallest and best-preserved, Huaca Avispas, had a central T-shaped chamber and ancillary cells that once contained great wealth and the bodies of young women.

smaller T-shaped cells, was later annexed to the principal huaca. These cells were apparently put into service over a span of time to accommodate a number of important, yet less richly accompanied, élite. Excavations of looters' dregs in cells, chambers and votive deposits around the platforms reveals a 'shrine complex' of rich and distinctive remains, including abundant *Spondylus* and *Conus* shells, llama bones, bones of numerous human juveniles (largely young women) and phenomenal concentrations of fine textiles, pottery, and other élite goods. Spanish documents record that the Chan Chan huacas sepulturas also contained inordinate quantities of precious metal.

Among later ciudadelas each burial platform is thought to be the mausoleum of the ruler who built the associated compound to serve as his imperial court. This lord was the founding ancestor of a kingly lineage and important heirs were subsequently buried in T-shaped chambers of platform annexes. If this interpretation is generally correct, then rule was in the hands of multiple royal kin-groups associated with different palaces in the eastern or western moieties. The ruling lineages seemingly proliferated over time and new enclosures and ciudadelas were built. However, each palatial compound witnessed an initial era of use when substantial architectural remodeling went on, followed by a critical turning point when all interior construction ceased and the monument was simply maintained, 'frozen' in immutable form. It is not clear if the associated lineage turned dormant or simply shifted its activities elsewhere when the monument was frozen, but it *is* clear that the four late-phase ciudadelas spanned a very short period of perhaps only four generations, whereas construction and use of each early-phase enclosure spanned more than a century. 'Tello' and 'Uhle', the last pair of early enclosures, were actually composite complexes of three and four separate imperial compounds. Built at different times, the primordial compounds witnessed prolonged use before they were joined together in final form.

Growth of Chan Chan was tied to both political and agrarian expansion. For potable water the city depended upon large wells with walk-down ramps. The earliest monuments were erected near the sea, where relatively shallow wells could tap the aquifer. To the east low ground and an elevated water table allowed farming in sunken gardens to extend up to 5 km inland. The focus of canal reclamation was upon higher flatlands to the north and west. Because this terrain lay up-slope from Chan Chan irrigation charged the urban aquifer. Therefore agrarian expansion elevated the water table and allowed the well-dependent metropolis to grow inland onto higher ground. By 1100 tremendous labor, directed from rural administrative buildings within audiencias, had been invested in erecting a vast canal system above the city. The form of audiencias changed over time, and the rural ones were similar to those in the Uhle enclosure. Early sections of this enclosure were severely damaged by the El Niño event of 1100, which devastated the entire irrigation system. Great time and energy were spent on canal repairs, but little of the reconstructed system ever worked because flooding had altered the river course, making the canal intakes inoperative.

Chan Chan continued to grow inland during its middle phase, but this required excavation of very deep wells. To recharge the urban aquifer, the Lords of Chimor initiated construction of an enormous inter-valley canal, more than 70 km long, designed to irrigate the land above the city with water from the Río Chicama. The entire course was trenched, but only the first portion of the channel was lined and completed. Where this section ends, the canal now runs uphill, suggesting that the builders unsuccessfully tried to cross an active fault. When the inter-valley canal failed the metropolis was forced to contract toward the sea where wells could reach the depressed water table.

Incremental conquest and territorial expansion beyond the Moche Valley were underway during the city's early phase, when great labor was also being invested in land reclamation around the city. When the El Niño floods of 1100 rendered such investments inoperative and curtailed further reclamation, the lords of Chimor turned their attentions to obtaining agricultural land by force. By about 1200, General Pacatnamu had won the Jequetepeque region and erected Farfan as an imperial administrative center there. This center and a similar state-built facility in the Viru Valley have audiencias similar in style and date to the final section of the Uhle enclosure at Chan Chan. Both sites also have a burial platform, suggesting Pacatnamu and his southern counterpart governed as vice royalty.

But this pattern of rural rule changed by the time the Lambayeque region was incorporated, when administrative centers were erected with audiencias, but not burial platforms. Governors ruled indirectly through local karaka, while the kings of Chimor monopolized the privilege of platform burial. Subjugation of Naymlap's former dominion fostered dramatic changes at Chan Chan as its last architectural phase opened. The victory was attributed to the western moiety, previously the junior family of royal kin groups. Formerly, western palaces were not built with burial platforms, but they were now erected with great mausoleums, and mortuary mounds were even added to earlier ciudadelas which originally lacked them. The urban population also changed, and it is estimated that almost 10,000 skilled metallurgists and craftsmen and women from the north were brought into the city to serve their new masters.

From the perspective of multi-linear evolution, the long trajectory of maritime-oasis lowland development culminated in Chan Chan and Chimor; while the Inca carried mountain and highland evolution to fruition. From a geopolitical perspective, the rise of these competitive nations pitted the two great demographic centers of the Andes against one another in a protracted struggle for suzerainty over the Cordillera. Ultimately, the greater forces of the southern highlands prevailed over those of the northern lowlands. This brought about the final political synthesis of the Andes that was known as Tahuantinsuyu, and the Late Horizon of unity was the last.

Epilog

In reviewing the evolution of Andean civilization, we have shared thoughts about world class monuments and fabulous antiquities. Unfortunately, it is no longer safe to visit many of the greatest ruins, and others are being destroyed at an alarming rate. If the present learned from the past, then things might be different, but this is not the case in the Cordillera. The quincentenary of Columbus' landfall frames a new era in social evolution. The forces of this era, which drove species to extinction and destroyed habitats, were impacted first upon native populations, and now affect their archaeological remains. The era opened when Tahuantinsuyu was potentially the largest nation on earth, and certainly one of the greatest of Native American nations. The Land of Four Quarters has dissolved among half a dozen modern countries. Within the heartland of this former civilization, one country has witnessed more coups and changes of government than years of statehood, and another sees the majority of its national territory beyond control. Maintaining rule has never been easy in the Cordillera, but some forms of government are certainly more appropriate than others. Tahuantinsuyu rested upon institutions of statecraft that grew out of folk adaptations to global extremes in environmental conditions. Therefore, government was structured by symbiotic relationships that complemented the well-being of its host populations. This changed in the wake of European pestilence, people, and their policies, plants and animals. This alien order has never reproduced itself well in hypoxic mountain habitats where indigenous populations survive. Seats of government moved to lower, warmer settings where Old World forms of life could successfully replace New World ones. Spatially segregated, the native mountain people became an ethnic underclass governed indirectly from capitals of Spanish establishment, and ruled remotely from abroad by the Castilian Crown and more recently by international financial institutions. Because European institutions of statecraft are foreign to mountain life they have worked against Andean adaptations. No government has ever recognized the existence of verticality. However, its foundations in scattered land holding patterns has been an anathema to Old World notions about how territory should be organized.

Beginning with Spanish land ownership practices and continuing through recent agrarian reform policies, vertical adaptations have been systematically undercut for 500 years. Thus, there is a basis for popular unrest and political instability, and the reasons we can no longer travel to great ruins in the mountains may be understood in evolutionary perspective.

In developing an evolutionary perspective we have seen that agricultural systems are by far the very largest of human works in the Cordillera. Remains of ancient systems cover millions of hectares, and in many regions people farmed 35 to 85 per cent more land before Columbus arrived than is in production upon his quincentenary. Investigating these remains I have encountered ancient canals that now run uphill, others washed away by enormous floods, and still others where water no longer flows. My suspicion is that the loss of farmland in the Cordillera is an ongoing process driven by environmental forces that contemporary agrarian planners are neither aware of nor immune to. With international financing and western technology, Andean countries are constructing very sizable reclamation projects. Many of the very biggest are erected within the ruins of ancient agricultural works, and all proceed with no study or knowledge of why the earlier, larger systems collapsed in the first place. This reflects an unstated premise that western technology and institutions are divorced from the Andean past. The scale of destruction of archaeological remains by reclamation projects far exceeds that of Egypt's Aswan dam. Yet, there is no international hue and cry to save the great monuments, nor measurable assistance to salvage ruins and antiquities. This may also be understood in evolutionary perspective. Governments that raise their national debt to build yet another dam in the Cordillera, trace their origins to Spain and the Old World. For those in power salvaging prehistory is not a priority because it is associated with the ethnic underclass in the mountains. With few to claim it as their own, Andean civilization is the orphan of the ancient world. Thus, the adage that the present learns from the past seems not to apply to the past of other people, whom we do not understand.

Bibliography

GENERAL WORKS

Bankes, George. *Peru before Pizarro*. Oxford, 1977.
Coe, Michael, Dean Snow and Elizabeth Benson, *Atlas of Ancient America*, New York, 1986.
Hidalgo L., Jorge, Virgilio Schiappacasse F., Hans Niemeyer F., Carlos Aldunate Del S. and Ivan Solimano R. *Culturas De Chile, Prehistoria: Desde Sus Origenes Hasta Los Albores De La Conquista*. Chile, 1989.
Ibarra Grasso, Dick and R. Querejazu Lewis. *30,000 años de prehistoria en Bolivia*. La Paz, 1982.
Kauffman Doig, F. *Manual de Arqueologia Peruana*. Lima, 1978.
Keatinge, Richard W. (ed.). *Peruvian Prehistory*. Cambridge, 1988.
Lanning, Edward P. *Peru before the Incas*. Englewood Cliffs, NJ, 1967.
Lathrap, Donald W. *The Upper Amazon*. London and New York, 1970.
Lumbreras, Luis G. *The Peoples and Cultures of Ancient Peru*. Washington, DC, 1974.
—, *Arqueologia De La America Andina*. Lima, 1981.
Masuda, Shozo, Izumi Shimada and Craig Morris (eds.). *Andean Ecology and Civilization: An Interdisciplinary Perspective on Andean Ecological Complementarity*. Tokyo, 1985.
Murra, John V. *Formaciones economicas y politicas del mundo andino*. Lima, 1975.
Murra, John V., Nathan Wachtel and Jacques Revel (eds.). *Anthropological History of Andean Polities*. Cambridge, 1986.
Pease G. Y., Franklin. *Del Tawantinsuyu a la Historia del Peru*. Lima, 1978.
Ravines, Rogger. *Panorama de la Arqueologia Andina*. Lima, 1982.
Rostworowski de Diez Canseco, Maria. *Historia Del Tahuantinsuyu*. Lima, 1988.

CHAPTER ONE   INTRODUCTION

Bonavia, D. and R. Ravines. *Arqueologia Peruana: Precursores*. Lima, 1970.
Cieza de León, P. *Part 1 of La Cronica del Peru*. Madrid, 1947.
Cook, N. D. *Demographic Collapse, Indian Peru 1520–1620*. Cambridge, 1981.
Guaman Poma de Ayala, Felipe. *El Primer Nueva Coronica ye Buen Gobierno*. [1614] Trans. J. I. Urioste, Mexico City, 1980.
Menzel, D. *The Archaeology of Ancient Peru and the Work of Max Uhle*. Berkeley, 1977.
Rowe, John H. 'Cultural unity and diversification in Peruvian archaeology', in A. F. C. Wallace, *Men and Culture, Selected Papers, 5th International Congress of Anthropological and Ethnological Sciences*, Philadelphia, 1960: 627–631.
Squier, G. E. *Peru: Incidents of Travel and Exploration in the Land of the Incas*. New York, 1877.
Tello, Julio C. 'Discovery of the Chavin culture in Peru', *American Antiquity* 9:1 (1943): 135–160.
Uhle, Max. *Pachacamac. Report of the William Pepper, M.D., LL.D. Peruvian Expedition of 1896*. Philadelphia, 1903.
Valcarél, L. E. 'Sajsawaman Redescubierto (3 pts)', *Revista del Museo Nacional*, Lima, 2:1–2 (1934–5): 3–26, 211–240; 4:1 (1934–5): 5–24.

CHAPTER TWO   LAND OF THE FOUR QUARTERS

Browman, David L. 'Pastoral nomadism in the Andes', *Current Anthropology*, 15:2 (1974): 188–196.
Browman, D. L., R. L. Burger and M. A. Rivera (eds.). *Social and Economic Organization in the Prehispanic Andes*. British Archaeological Reports, International Series 194, Oxford, 1984.
Brush, S. B. *Mountain, Field and Family: The Economy and Human Ecology of an Andean Valley*. Philadelphia, 1977.
DeBoer, W. 'Buffer zones in the cultural ecology of Aboriginal Amazonia: an ethnohistorical approach', *American Antiquity* 46:2 (1981): 364–377.
Denevan, W., K. Mathewson and G. Knapp (eds.). *Prehistoric Agricultural Fields in the Central Andes*. British Archaeological Reports, International Series 359, Oxford, 1987.
Donkin, R. A. 'Agricultural Terracing in the Aboriginal New World', *Viking Fund Publications in Anthropology 56*, Tucson, 1979.
Flannery, K. V., J. Marcus and R. G. Reynolds. *The Flocks of the Wamani: A Study of Llama Herders on the Punas of Ayacucho, Peru*. New York, 1989.
Frisancho, A. R. 'Growth and Morphology at High Altitude', in P. T. Baker and M. A. Little (eds.), *Man in the Andes: A Multidisciplinary Study of High-Altitude Quechua*, Stroudsburg, Pa., 1976: 180–207.
Kosok, Paul. *Life, Land and Water in Ancient Peru*. New York, 1965.
Masuda, Shozo. *Recursos naturales andinos*. Tokyo, 1988.
Mujica, Elias and Jane Wheeler. 'Produccion y Recursos Ganaderos Prehispanicos en la Cuenca del Titicaca, Peru – Trabajo de Campo 1979–1980', *Informe final al Instituto Nacional de Cultura*, Lima, 1981.
Murra, John V. 'La vista de los chupachu como fuente etnologica', in J. V. Murra (ed.), *Visita de lo Provincia de León de Huánuco en 1562, Iñigo Ortíz de Zúñiga*, vol. 1, Huanuco, Peru, 1967: 381–406.
—, 'El "control vertical" de un maximo de pisos ecologicos en la economia de las sociedades andinas', in *Visita de la Provincia de León de Huánuco [1562], Iñigo Ortíz de Zúñiga* vol. 2, Huanuco, Peru, 1972: 429–476.
—, *Formaciones Económicas y Políticas del Mundo Andino*. Lima, 1975.
Netherly, P. J. 'The management of late Andean irrigation systems on the North Coast of Peru', *American Antiquity* 49 (1984): 227–254.
Orlove, B. S. and D. W. Guillet. 'Convergences and Differences in Mountain Economies and Societies: a Comparison of the Andes and Himalaya', *Mountain Research and Development* 5:1 (1985).
Rostworowski de Diez Canseco, Maria. *Etniá Sociedad: Costa Peruana Prehispánica*. Lima, 1977.
—, *Recursos Naturales Renovables y Pesca, Siglos XVI y XVII*. Lima, 1981.
—, 'Conflicts over coca fields in XVIth-century Peru', *Memoirs of the Museum of Anthropology, University of Michigan 21*, Ann Arbor, 1988.
Salomon, Frank. *Ethnic Lords of Quito in the Age of the Incas: The Political Economy of North Andean Chiefdoms*, PhD dissertation, Cornell University, Ithaca, 1978.
Thompson, L. G., E. Moseley-Thompson, J. F. K. Bolzen, and B. R. Koci. 'A 1500-year Record of Tropical

Precipitation in Ice Cores from the Quelccaya Ice Cap, Peru', *Science* 226 (1985).

Towle, Margaret A. *The ethnobotany of pre-Columbian Peru.* Chicago, 1961.

Troll, C. 'The cordilleras of the tropical Americas', in C. Troll (ed.), *Geo-Ecology of the Mountainous Regions of the Tropical Americas*, Bonn, 1970: 15–56.

Wing, E. S. and J. C. Wheeler (eds.). *Economic Prehistory of the Central Andes.* British Archaeological Reports, International Series 427, Oxford, 1988.

CHAPTER THREE   THE INCA MODEL OF STATECRAFT

Bandelier, A. F. *The Islands of Titicaca and Koati.* New York, 1910.

Bingham, Hiram. *Machu Picchu – A Citadel of the Incas.* New Haven, 1930.

Bueno Mendoza, Alberto. 'El Antiguo Valle de Pachacamac: Espacio, Tiempo y Cultura', *Boletin de Lima* 24, Lima, 1981: 3–52.

Chávez Ballon, Manuel. 'Cuzco, Capital del Imperio', *Wayka* 3, Cuzco, 1970: 1–14.

Cobo, Bernabe. *History of the Inca Empire.* [1653] Trans. Roland Hamilton, Austin, 1983.

Conrad, Geoffrey W. and Arthur A. Demarest. *Religion and Empire: The Dynamics of Aztec and Inca Expansionism.* Cambridge, 1984.

D'Altroy, T. N. (ed.). *Ethnohistory.* Special issue on 'Inka ethnohistory', 34:1, Durham, 1987.

D'Altroy, T. N. and T. Earle. 'Stable Wealth Finance, and Storage in the Inka Political Economy', *Current Anthropology* 25:2 (1985): 187–206.

Demarest, Arthur A. *Viracocha – The Nature and Antiquity of the Andean High God.* Peabody Museum Monographs, No. 6, Cambridge, Mass., 1981.

Dillehay, Tom D. 'Tawantinsuyu Integration of the Chillon Valley Peru: A Case of Inca Geo-Political Mastery', *Journal of Field Archaeology* 4, Boston, 1977: 397–405.

Dillehay, Tom D. and Patricia Netherly (eds.). *La Frontera del Estado Inca.* British Archaeological Reports, International Series 442, Oxford, 1988.

Earle, T. K., T. N. D'Altroy, C. Hastorf, C. Scott, C. Costin, G. Russell and E. Sandefur. *Archaeological Field Research in the Upper Mantaro, Peru, 1982–83: Investigations of Inka Expansion and Exchange.* Monograph 28, Institute of Archaeology, University of California, Los Angeles, 1987.

Garcilaso de la Vega, Inca. *Royal Commentaries of the Incas and General History of Peru.* [1604] Trans. H. V. Livermore, Austin, 1987.

Gasparini, G. and L. Margolies. *Inca Architecture.* Bloomington, Ind., 1980.

Gonzalez, Alberto Rex and Antonio Cravotto. *Estudio arqueologico e inventario de las ruinas Inkallata.* UNESCO, Paris, 1977.

Hemming, John and Edward Ranney. *Monuments of the Incas.* Boston, 1982.

Hyslop, John. *The Inka Road System.* New York, 1984.

—, *Inkawasi, the new Cuzco; Cañete, Launahuana, Peru.* British Archaeological Reports, International Series 234, Oxford, 1985.

—, *Inka Settlement Planning.* Austin, 1990.

Julien, Catherine J. *Hatunqolla: A View of Inca Rule from the Lake Titicaca Region.* University of California Publications in Anthropology, vol. 15, Berkeley, 1983.

Kendall, A. 'Architecture and planning at the Inca sites in the Cusichaca area', *Baessler-Archiv* 22 (1974): 73–137.

—, (ed.). *Current archaeological projects in the Central Andes; some approaches and results.* British Archaeological Reports, International Series 210, Oxford, 1984.

—, *Aspects of Inca Architecture – Description, Function and Chronology.* 2 vols. British Archaeological Reports, International Series 242, Oxford, 1985.

Marcus, Joyce. *Late Intermediate Occupation at Cerro Azul, Peru.* University of Michigan Museum of Anthropology, Technical Report 20, Ann Arbor, 1987.

Morris, C. 'Huanuco Pampa: nuevas evidencias sobre urbanismo inca', *Revista del Museo Nacional* 42, Lima, 1980: 139–152.

Morris, C. and D. E. Thompson. *Huanuco Pampa – An Inca City and Its Hinterland.* London & New York, 1985.

Murra, John V. 'The Economic Organization of the Inca State', Supplement 1 to *Research Economic Anthropology*, Greenwich, CT, 1980.

Niles, Susan A. *Callachaca: Style and Status in an Inca Community.* Iowa City, 1987.

Rowe, John H. 'Inca culture at the time of the Spanish Conquest', in J. H. Steward (ed.), Handbook of South American Indians, Washington, DC, 1946: 183–330.

—, 'The Incas under Spanish Colonial Institutions', *Hispanic American Historical Review* 37:2: 155–199.

—, 'What Kind of a Settlement Was Inca Cuzco?' *Nawpa Pacha* 5, Berkeley, 1967: 59–76.

—, 'An Account of the Shrines of Ancient Cuzco', *Nawpa Pacha* 17, Berkeley, 1979: 2–80.

Spalding, Karen. *Huarochiri: An Andean Society under Inca and Spanish Rule.* Stanford, 1984.

Urton, Gary. *At the Crossroads of the Earth and the Sky.* Austin, 1981.

—, *The History of a Myth: Pacariqtambo and the Origin of the Inkas.* Austin, 1990.

Welch, T. L. and R. L. Gutierrez. 'The Incas: A Bibliography of Books and Periodical Articles', *Hipolito Unanue Bibliographic Series 1*, vol. 8, Washington, DC, 1987.

Zuidema, R. Tom. *The Ceque System of Cuzco.* Leiden, 1964.

—, *La civilisation inca au Cuzco.* Paris, 1986. (Trans. Jean-Jacques Decoster, Austin, 1990).

CHAPTER FOUR   EARLY SETTLEMENT OF THE CORDILLERA

Bird, J. B. 'Excavations in northern Chile', *Anthropological Papers of the American Museum of Natural History* 38:4, New York 1943: 171–318.

—, 'A comparison of South Chilean and Ecuadorian "Fishtail" projectile points', *The Kroeber Anthropological Society Papers* 40, Berkeley, 1969: 52–71.

Cardich, A. 'Lauricocha: fundamentos para una prehistoria de los Andes Centrales', *Studia Praehistorica* 3 (1964).

Chauchat, C. 'The Paijan complex, Pampa de Cupisnique, Peru', *Nawpa Pacha* 13, Berkeley, 1976: 85–96.

—, 'Additional observations on the Paijan complex', *Nawpa Pacha* 16, Berkeley, 1979: 51–64.

Dillehay, T. D. (ed.). *Monte Verde: A Late Pleistocene Settlement in Chile.* Washington, DC, 1989.

Dillehay, T. D. and P. J. Netherly. 'Exploring the upper Zana Valley of Peru; a unique tropical forest setting offers new insights into the Andean past', *Archaeology* 37:4 (1983): 23–30.

Lynch, T. F. *Guitarrero Cave: early man in the Andes.* New York, 1980.

—, 'Glacial-Age Man in South America? A Critical Review', *American Antiquity* 55:1 (1990).

MacNeish, R. S., A. G. Cook, L. G. Lumbreras, R. K. Vierra and A. Nelken-Terner. *Prehistory of the Ayacucho Basin, Peru, II: Excavations and Chronology.* Ann Arbor, Michigan, 1981.

Malpass, M. A. 'The Paijan occupation of the Casma Valley, Peru', *Nawpa Pacha* 24, Berkeley, 1986: 99–110.

Matos Mendieta, R. 'Prehistoria y ecologia humana en las punas de Junin', *Revista del Museo Nacional* 41, Lima, 1975: 37–80.

Ossa, P. P. and M. E. Moseley. 'La Cumbre; a preliminary report on research into the early lithic occupation of the Moche Valley, Peru', *Nawpa Pacha* 9, Berkeley, 1972: 1–16.

Quilter, J. *Life and Death at Paloma: Society and Mortuary*

Practices in a Preceramic Peruvian Village. Iowa City, 1989.
Ravines, R. 'Secuencia y cambios en los artefactos líticos del sur Perú', *Revista del Museo Nacional* 38, Lima, 1972: 133–184.
Richardson, J. B. III. 'The preceramic sequence and the pleistocene and post-pleistocene climate of northwest Peru', in D. W. Lathrap and J. Douglas (eds.), *Variation in Anthropology*, Urbana, Ill., 1973: 199–201.
Rick, J. W. *Prehistoric Hunters of the High Andes.* New York, 1980.

CHAPTER FIVE   THE PRECERAMIC FOUNDATIONS OF CIVILIZATION
Benfer, Robert A. 'The Challenges and Rewards of Sedentism: The Preceramic Village of Paloma, Peru', in M. N. Cohen and G. J. Armelagos (eds.), *Paleopathology in the Origins of Agriculture*, New York, 1984: 531–558.
Bird, Junius B. and John Hyslop. 'The Preceramic Excavations at the Huaca Prieta Chicama Valley, Peru', *Anthropological Papers of the American Museum of Natural History* 62:1, New York, 1985.
Bonavia, D. *Los Gavilanes.* Lima, 1982.
Engel, F. 'Le complexe preceramique d'el Paraiso (Perou)', *Journal de la Societé des Américanistes* 55:1 (1966): 43–96.
—, *Las Lomas de Iguanil y el complejo de Aldas.* Lima, 1970.
Feldman, R. A. *Aspero, Peru: architecture, subsistence economy, and other artifacts of a preceramic maritime chiefdom.* Unpublished PhD dissertation, Harvard University, 1980.
Grieder, T. *Origins of Pre-Columbian Art.* Austin, 1982.
Grieder, T., A. B. Mendoze, C. Earle Smith, Jr. and R. M. Malina. *La Galgada, Peru: A Preceramic Culture in Transition.* Austin, 1988.
Izumi, S. and T. Sono. *Andes 2: Excavations at Kotosh, Peru, 1960.* Tokyo, 1963.
Moseley, M. E. *The Maritime Foundations of Andean Civilization.* Menlo Park, Ca., 1975.
Patterson, T. C. 'The historical development of a coastal Andean social formation in Central Peru, 6000 to 500 BC', in S. Sandweiss, (ed.), *Investigations of the Andean Past*, Ithaca, New York, 1983: 21–37.
Quilter, J. 'Architecture and Chronology at El Paraíso, Peru', *Journal of Field Archaeology* 12 (1985).
Uhle, Max. 'Los aborigines de Arica', *Publicacion del Museo de Etnografia y Anthropologica de Chile* 1:4–5, Santiago, 1917: 151–176.
Weir, G. H., R. A. Benfer and J. G. Jones. 'Preceramic to Early Formative Subsistence on the Central Coast', in E. S. Wing and J. C. Wheeler (eds.), *Economic Prehistory of the Central Andes*, British Archaeological Reports, International Series 427, Oxford, 1988: 56–94.
Wendt, W. E. 'Die Präkeramische Siedlung am Rio Seco, Perú', *Baessler-Archiv* 11, no. 2, 1964: 225–275.

CHAPTER SIX   THE INITIAL PERIOD AND EARLY HORIZON
Alva, Walter. 'Fruhe Keramik aus dem Jequetepeque-Tal, Nordperu', Deutschen Archaeologischen Instituts, *AVA-Materialien*, Brand 32, Bonn, 1986.
Bennett, W. C. 'Excavations in the Callejon de Huaylas and at Chavin de Huantar', *Anthropological Papers of the American Museum of Natural History* 39:1, New York, 1944.
Burger, R. L. 'The Radiocarbon Evidence for the Temporal Priority of Chavin de Huantar', *American Antiquity* 46 (1981): 592–602.
—, *The Prehistoric Occupation of Chavin de Huantar, Peru.* Berkeley, 1984.
Burger, R. L. and L. Salazar-Burger. 'Ritual and religion in Huaricoto', *Archaeology* 33:6 (1980): 26–32.
Conklin, W. J. 'The revolutionary weaving inventions of the early horizon', *Nawpa Pacha* 16, Berkeley, 1978: 1–12.
—, 'The architecture of Huaca Los Reyes', in *Early Ceremonial Architecture of the Andes*, Washington, DC, 1985.

Cordy-Collins, A. 'Chavin art: its shamanic/hallucinogenic origins', in A. Cordy-Collins and J. Stern (eds.), *Pre-Columbian Art History*, Palo Alto, 1977: 352–362.
—, 'An artistic record of the Chavin hallucinatory experience', *The Masterkey* 54, Los Angeles, 1980: 84–93.
Donnan, Christopher B. (ed.). *Early Ceremonial Architecture in the Andes*, A Conference at Dumbarton Oaks, October 8–10 1982. Dumbarton Oaks, Washington, DC, 1985.
Fung Pineda, R. 'Las Aldas: su ubicacion dentro del proceso historico del Peru Antiguo', *Dédalo* 5:9–10, Sao Paolo, 1972.
Fung Pineda, R. and C. Williams. 'Exploraciones y excavaciones en el valle de Sechin, Casma', *Revista del Museo Nacional* 43, Lima, 1979: 111–155.
Grossman, J. 'An ancient gold worker's tool kit; the earliest metal technology in Peru', *Archaeology* 25 (1972): 270–275.
—, 'Demographic changes and economic transformations in the south-central highlands of pre-Huari Peru', *Nawpa Pacha* 21, Berkeley, 1976: 45–126.
Izumi, S., J. J. Cuculiza and C. Kano. 'Excavations at Shillacoto, Huanuco, Peru', *University of Tokyo Museum Bulletin* 3, 1972.
Kroeber, A. L. 'Paracas Cavernas and Chavin', *University of California Publications in American Archaeology and Ethnology* 40, 1953: 313–332.
Larco Hoyle, R. *Los Cupisniques.* Lima, 1941.
Lumbreras, L. G. 'Excavaciones en el Templo Antiguo de Chavin (sector R); Informe de la Sexta Campana', *Nawpa Pacha* 15, Berkeley, 1977: 1–38.
Menzel, D., J. Rowe and L. E. Dawson. *The Paracas Pottery of Ica: A Study in Style and Time.* Berkeley, 1964.
Mohr Chavez, Karen. 'The archaeology of Marcavalle, an Early Horizon site in the Valley of Cuzco, Peru', *Baessler-Archiv* 29, 1981.
Mujica Barreda, E. 'Nueva hipótesis sobre el desarrollo temprano del altiplano, del Titicaca y de sus áreas de interacción', *Arte y Arqueologia* 5–6, (1978): 285–308.
Nuñez L. and T. D. Dillehay *Movilidad Giratoria, Armonia Social y Desarollo en los Andes meridionales: Patrones de Trafico e Interaccion Economica.* Antofagasta, 1979.
Ponce Sangines, C. *Las Culturas Wankarani y Chiripa y su Relacion con Tiwanaku.* La Paz, 1970.
Pozorski, S. and T. Pozorski. *Early Settlement and Subsistence in the Casma Valley, Peru.* Iowa City, Ia, 1988.
Pozorski, T. and S. Pozorski. 'Chavin, the Early Horizon and the Initial Period', in J. Haas, S. Pozorski and T. Pozorski (eds.), *The origins and development of the Andean state*, Cambridge, Mass., 1987: 36–46.
Ravines, R. and W. H. Isbell. 'Garagay: Sitio ceremonial temprano en el Valle de Lima', *Revista del Museo Nacional* 41, Lima, 1975.
Rosas La Noire, H. and R. Shady. *Pacopampa: Un Centro Formativo en la Sierra Nor-peruana.* Lima, 1970.
Rowe, J. H. *Chavin Art: An Inquiry into its Form and Meaning.* New York, 1962.
Tellenbach, Michael. 'Die Ausgrabungen in der formativzeitlichen seidlung Montegrande, Jequetepeque-Tal, Nordperu', Deutschen Archaologischen Instituts, *AVA-Materialien*, Brand 39, Bonn, 1986.
Tello, Julio C. *Chavín Cultura Matriz de la Civilizacion Andina.* Lima, 1930.
—, *Arqueología del Valle de Casma.* Lima, 1956.
Terada, K. and Y. Onuki. *The Formative Period in the Cajamarca Basin, Peru: Excavations at Huacaloma and Layzon, 1982.* Tokyo, 1985.
Watanabe, L. 'Arquitectura de la Huaca Los Reyes', in R. Matos M. (ed.), *Arqueología Peruana*, Lima, 1979: 17–36.
Willey, G. 'The Chavin problem: a review and critique', *Southwestern Journal of Anthropology* 7:2 (1951): 103–144.
Williams, C. 'Arquitectura y urbanismo en el antiguo Perú', *Historia del Peru* 8, Lima, 1979: 389–585.
—, 'Complejos de pirámides con planta en U, patrón arquitectónico de la costa central', *Revista del Museo Nacional* 44, 1980: 95–110.

CHAPTER SEVEN THE EARLY INTERMEDIATE
PERIOD
Aveni, A. (ed.). *The Lines of Nazca*. Philadelphia, 1990.
Bennett, W. C. *The Gallinazo Group, Viru Valley, Peru*. Yale
University Publications in Anthropology 43, New Haven,
1950.
Benson, E. P. *The Moche: A Culture of Peru*. New York,
1942.
Bonavia, Duccio. *Mural Painting in Ancient Peru*. Trans P. J.
Lyon, Bloomington, 1985.
Brennan, Curtis. 'Cerro Arena: Origins of the Urban
Tradition on the Peruvian North Coast', *Current
Anthropology* 23 (1982): 247–254.
Collier, D. 'Cultural chronology and change as reflected in
the ceramics of the Viru Valley, Peru', *Fieldiana:
Anthropology*, Chicago, 1955.
Donnan, Christopher B. *Moche Art and Iconography*. Los
Angeles, 1976.
—, *Moche Art of Peru*. Los Angeles, 1978.
—, 'Moche occupation of the Santa Valley, Peru', *Univ.
California Publications in Anthropology* 8, 1973.
Grieder, T. *The Art and Archaeology of Pashash*. Austin,
1978.
Hocquenghem, Anne Marie. *Iconografia mochica*. Lima, 1987.
Izumi, S. and K. Terada. *Andes 3: Excavations at Pechiche
and Garabanzal, Tumbes Valley, Peru, 1960*. Tokyo, 1966.
Kutscher, G. *Nord peruanische Gefafsmalereien des Moche-
Stills*. Munich, 1983.
Larco Hoyle, R. *Los Mochicas*. Lima, 1938.
Loten, H. S. *Burial Tower 2 and Fort A, Marcahuamachuco*.
Trent University Occasional Papers in Anthropology No. 3,
Peterborough, 1987.
Lumbreras, L. G. *El arte y la vida viscus*. Lima, 1978.
Lumbreras, L. G. and H. Amat. 'Secuencia arqueológica del
altiplano occidental del Titicaca', *Actas y Memorias del 37
Congreso Internacional de Americanistas* 2, 1968: 75–106.
Proulx, D. A. *Archaeological investigations in the Nepeña
valley, Peru*. Amherst, 1973.
—, *An Analysis of the Early Cultural Sequence of the Nepeña
Valley, Peru*. Amherst, 1985.
Quilter, Jeffrey. 'The Moche Revold of the Objects', *Latin
American Antiquity* 1:1: 42–65.
Sachun, Jorge. *Patrones de asentamiento en el proceso cultural
prehispanico del valle de Cajamarca (primera aproximacion)*.
Trujillo, 1986.
Schaedel, R. P. 'Monolithic sculpture of the southern Andes',
Archaeology 1:1 (1948): 66–73.
Shimada, I. 'Horizontal archipelago and coast-highland
interaction in North Peru: archaeological models', in L.
Millones and H. Tomoeda (eds.), *El Hombre y su Ambiente
en los Andes Centrales*, Senri Ethnological Series 10, Lima,
1982.
Silverman, H. and D. Browne. *The Nascas*. London, in press.
Strong, W. D. and C. Evans Jr. 'Cultural stratigraphy in the
Viru Valley, northern Peru', *Columbia University Studies in
Archaeology and Ethnology* 4, 1952.
Topic, T. L. and J. R. Topic. *Huamachuco Archaeological
Project: Preliminary Report on the 1986 Field Season*, Trent
University Occasional Papers in Anthropology 4,
Peterborough, Ontario, 1987: 1–40.
Willey, G. *Prehistoric Settlement Patterns in the Viru Valley,
Peru*. Washington, DC, 1953.
Wilson, D. J. *Prehispanic Settlement Patterns in the Lower
Santa Valley, Peru. A Regional Perspective on the Origins
and Development of Complex North Coast Society*.
Washington, DC, 1988.

CHAPTER EIGHT THE MIDDLE HORIZON
Anders, Martha B. 'Wari Experiments in Statecraft: A View
from Azangaro', in R. Matos M., S. A. Turpin and H. H.
Eling Jr. (eds.), *Andean Archaeology*, Monograph 27,
Institute of Archaeology, University of California, Los
Angeles, 1986.

Bawden, Garth. 'Community Organization Reflected by the
Household: A Study of Pre-Columbian Social Dynamics',
Journal of Field Archaeology 9:2 (1982): 165–181.
Benavides, Mario. *Yacimientos Arqueologicos en Ayacucho*.
Ayacucho, 1976.
Bennett, W. C. 'Excavations at Tiahuanaco', *Anthropological
Papers of the American Museum of Natural History* 34:3
(1934).
—, 'Excavations in Bolivia', *Anthropological Papers of the
American Museum of Natural History* 35:4 (1936): 331–505.
Bermann M. 'Vision de las casas del periodo Tiwanaku en
Lukurmata', in A. Kolata (ed.), *La tecnologia y organizacion
de la produccion agricola en el estado de Tiwanaku*, La Paz,
1989.
Browman, D. L. 'Tiwanaku expansion and altiplano
economic patterns', *Estudios Arqueológícis* 5, 1980: 107–120.
Chavez, S. J. 'The Arapa and Thunderboldt Stelae: A Case
of Stylistic Identity with Implications for Pucara Influences
in the Area of Tiahuanaco', *Nawpa Pacha* 13, Berkeley,
1975: 13–25.
Czwarno, R. M., F. M. Meddens and A. Morgan (eds.). *The
Nature of Wari. A Reappraisal of the Middle Horizon Period
in Peru*. Oxford, 1989.
Foccaci, G. 'Nuevas Fechados para la Epoca del Tiahuanaco
en la Arqueologia del Norte de Chile', *Chungara* 8, Arica,
1982: 63–78.
Goldstein, P. *Omo: a Tiwanaku Provincial Center in
Moquegua, Peru*. PhD dissertation, University of Chicago,
1989.
—, 'The Tiwanaku Occupation of Moquegua', in D. S. Rice,
C. Stanish and P. Scarr (eds.), *Ecology, Settlement, and
History of the Osmorre Drainage*, Oxford, 1989: 219–256.
—, 'La Ocupacion Tiwanaku en Moquegua', *Gaceta
Arqueologica Andina* V(18 & 19), Lima, 1990: 75–104.
Isbell, W. H. 'The Rural Foundations for Urbanism', *Illinois
Studies in Anthropology* 10, Urbana, 1977.
—, 'Environmental Perturbations and the Origins of the
Andean States', in C. L. Redman, M. J. Berman, E. B.
Curtin, W. T. Langhorne Jr., N. M. Versággi and J. C.
Wansers (eds.), *Social Archaeology*. New York, 1978.
Isbell, W. H. and G. F. McEwan (eds.). *Huari Political
Organization: Prehistoric Monumental Architecture and State
Government*. A Round Table Held at Dumbarton Oaks,
May 17–19. Dumbarton Oaks, Washington, DC, 1991.
Isbell, W. H. and K. Schreiber. 'Was Huari a State?',
American Antiquity 43:3 (1978): 372–389.
Kolata, A. 'The Agricultural Foundations of the Tiwanaku
State: A View from the Heartland', *American Antiquity* 51:4
(1986).
—, (ed.). *Arqueologia de Lukurmata* 2, La Paz, 1989.
Larco Hoyle, R. *Cronologia Arqueologica del Norte del Peru*.
Buenos Aires, 1948.
Manzanilla, L. and E. Woodard. 'Restos Humanos Asociados
a La Piramide de Akapana (Tiwanaku, Bolivia)', *Latin
American Archaeology* 1:2 (1990): 133–149.
Menzel, D. 'Style and time in the Middle Horizon', *Nawpa
Pacha* 2, Berkeley, 1964: 1–105.
Mohr Chavez, K. (ed.). *Expedition* 3:3. Special issue on
Andean archaeology. Philadelphia, 1989.
Mujica, E., M. Rivera and T. Lynch. 'Proyecto de Estudio
Sobre la Complementariedad Economica Tiwanaku en los
Valles Occidentales del Centro-Sur Andino', *Chungara* 11,
Arica, 1983: 85–109.
Ponce Sangines, C. *Nuevo Perspectiva Para el Estudio de la
Expansion de la Cultura Tiwanaku*. La Paz, 1979.
—, *Tiwanaku: Espacio, tiempo y cultura*. La Paz, 1981.
Posnansky, Arturo. *Tihuanacu. The Cradle of American Man*.
La Paz, 1957.
Ravines, R. 'Un deposito de ofrendas del Horizonte Medio
en la Sierra Central del Peru', *Nawpa Pacha* 6 (1968):
19–46.
Schaedel, R. P. 'Incipient urbanization and secularization in
Tiahuanacoid Peru', *American Antiquity* 31 (1966): 338–44.

Shady, R. 'La Epoca Huari como interaccion de las sociedades regionales', *Revista Andina* 6:1, Cuzco, 1988: 67–99.

Shimada, I. 'Economy of a prehistoric urban context: commodity and labor flow at Moche V Pampa Grande, Peru', *American Antiquity* 43:4 (1978): 569–592.

Tello, Julio C. 'Las ruinas de Huari', in R. Ravines (ed.), *100 Años de Arqueología en el Perú*. Lima, 1970: 519–525.

Wallace, D. T. *The Tiahuanaco Horizon styles in Peruvian and Bolivian highlands*. PhD dissertation, University of California, Berkeley, 1957.

CHAPTER NINE   THE LATE INTERMEDIATE PERIOD

Bawden, Garth. 'The Tumilaca Site and Post-Tiahuanaco occupational stratigraphy in the Moquegua Drainage', in D. S. Rice, C. Stanish and P. Scarr (eds.), *Ecology, Settlement and History in the Osmorre Drainage*, British Archaeological Reports, International Series 545, Oxford, 1989.

Bonavia D. *Las Ruinas del Abiseo*. Lima, 1968.

Browman, D. *Early Peruvian Peasants: The Culture History of a Central Highlands Valley*. PhD dissertation, Harvard University, Cambridge, Mass., 1970.

Conrad, G. W. 'Chiquitoy Viejo: an Inca administrative center in the Chicama Valley, Peru', *Journal of Field Archaeology* 14 (1977): 1–18.

Donnan, C. B. and C. J. Mackey. *Ancient Burial Patterns of the Moche Valley*. Austin, 1978.

Donnan, C. B. and G. A. Cock, (eds.). *The Pacatnamu Papers*, vol.1. Museum of Culture History, Los Angeles, 1986.

Earle, T. K., T. N. D'Altroy, C. A. Hastorf, C. Scott, C. L. Costin, G. S. Russell and E. Sandefur. *Archaeological Field Research in the Upper Mantaro, Peru, 1982–1983: Investigations of Inka Expansion and Exchange*. Los Angeles, 1987.

Ghersi Barerra, H. 'Informe sobre las excavaciones en Chiribaya', *Revista del Museo Nacional* 25, Lima, 1956: 89–119.

Keatinge, R. and G. W. Conrad. 'Imperialist expansion in Peruvian prehistory: Chimu administration of a conquered territory', *Journal of Field Archaeology* 10 (1983): 255–283.

Lumbreras, L. G. 'Los Reinos Post-Tiwanaku en el Area Altiplanica', *Revista del Museo Nacional* 40, Lima, 1974: 55–85.

Matos M. R. and J. R. Parsons. 'Poblamiento Prehispanico en la Cuenca del Mantaro', in R. Matos (ed.), *Arqueologia Peruana*. Lima, 1979: 157–171.

Menzel, D. *Pottery Style and Society in Ancient Peru: Art as a Mirror of History in the Inca Valley, 1350–1570*. Berkeley, 1976.

Moore, J. D. 'Chimu Socio-economic Organization: Preliminary Data from Manchan, Casma Valley Peru', *Nawpa Pacha* 19, Berkeley, 1981: 115–128.

Moseley, M. E. and A. Cordy-Collins (eds.). *The Northern Dynasties: Kingship and Statecraft in Chimor*. Dumbarton Oaks, Washington, DC, 1991.

Moseley, M. E. and K. C. Day (eds.). *Chan Chan: Andean Desert City*. Albuquerque, 1982.

Mujica, M. (ed.). *Gaceta Arqueologica Andina*. Special issue, Arqueologia de los Valles Occidentales del Area Centro Sur Andina. Lima, 1990.

Muñoz O., I. 'La Aldea de Cerro Sombrero en el Periodo del Desarrollo Regional de Arica', *Chungara* 7, Arica, 1981: 105–142.

Rice, D. S., C. Stanish and P. Scarr (eds.). *Ecology, Settlement and History in the Osmorre Drainage*, British Archaeological Reports, International Series 545, Oxford, 1989.

Rivera, Mario. 'Una hipotesis sobre movimientos poblacionales altiplanicos y trasaltiplanicos a la costa del norte de Chile', *Chungara* 5, Arica, 1975: 7–31.

—, *Prehistoric Chronology of Northern Chile*. PhD dissertation, University of Wisconsin, Madison, 1977.

Rostworowski de Diez Canseco, Maria. 'Mercaderes del valle de Chincha en la epoca prehispanica: un documento y unos comentarios'. *Revista Española de Antropologia Americana* 5, Madrid, 1970: 135–177.

Sandweiss, D. H. 'The Fishermen of Chincha: Occupational Specialization on the Late Prehispanic Andean Coast', in E. S. Wing and J. C. Wheeler (eds.), *Economic Prehistory of the Central Andes*, British Archaeological Reports, International Series 427, Oxford, 1988.

Stanish, C. 'A Late Pre-Hispanic Ceramic Chronology for the Upper Moquegua Valley, Peru', *Fieldiana Anthropology*, New Series 16, Chicago, 1991.

—, 'Household Archaeology: Testing models of zonal complementarity in the south central Andes', *American Anthropologist* 91:1 (1989): 7–24.

Watanabe, L. K., M. E. Moseley and F. Cabieses (eds.). *Trabajos Arqueologicos en Moquegua, Peru*. 3 vols. Lima, 1990.

Sources of illustrations

Numerals in *italics* refer to line illustrations; numerals in **bold** refer to plates

M. Allison et al. 'Chinchorro, momias de preparacion complicada. . .', *Chungara* 13 (1984): *40* · American Museum of Natural History **86** · Jose Canziani Amico, *Asentamientos humanos y formaciones sociales en la costa norte del antiguo Perú (del Paleolítico a Moche V)*, 1989: *48, 57* · Ferdinand Anton, *The Art of Ancient Peru*, Thames and Hudson, London 1972: *39, 41, 72, 86, 91, 95* · Ferdinand Anton, *Ancient Peruvian Textiles*, Thames and Hudson, London 1987: *3, 18, 19, 43, 47, 60, 63, 69, 85, 94, 104, 105, 112*; **89** · George Bankes, *Peru before Pizarro*, Phaidon, Oxford 1977: *62* (drawing Michael Jones) · R. Braunmüller, Museum für Volkerkunde, Munich **69, 70, 90** · British Museum **61** · Geoffrey H. S. Bushnell, *Peru*, Thames and Hudson, London 1965: *6, 29* (drawn by Mrs G. E. Daniel), *82* (redrawn from Larco) · Cambridge University Museum of Anthropology and Ethnography **10, 19, 22, 23, 68, 92** · Chan Chan-Moche Valley Project *73–80, 99, 101, 102, 113, 116, 117, 118, 119, 120, 121*; **35, 36, 60, 100, 102** · C. Chauchat *37* · Cleveland Museum of Art **21** (The Norweb Collection, CMA 40.530) · William Conklin *59*; **87** · Christopher B. Donnan *13, 15, 16, 81, 83, 84*; **66** · Simon S. S. Driver *35* · José Emperaire, Annette Laming-Emperaire, and Henry Riichlen, 'La Grotte Fell et autres sites de la région volcanique de la Patagonie Chilienne', *Journal de la Societé des Américanistes*, 1963: *36* · Patricia A. Essenpreis **12, 42** · Robert Feldman *50, 51, 106*; **25, 26, 41, 78, 91, 93, 96** · Field Museum of Natural History, Chicago **26, 88** · Paul Goldstein *30, 96, 97, 107, 108, 109, 110* · Terence Grieder, *Galgada Peru: A Preceramic Culture in Transit*, 1988: *49* · Abraham Guillen M. **97** · Ann Kendall, *Everyday Life of the Incas*, Batsford, London 1973: *11, 33* (after Zuidema) ·

Alan Kolata *92*; **74, 83–85** · George Kubler, *The Art and Architecture of Ancient America*, Penguin Books, Harmondsworth and Baltimore 1962: *44, 55, 56, 70, 93* (drawings by K. F. Rowland) · Rafael Larco Hoyle **37, 38, 44, 46, 51, 52, 53** · Thomas F. Lynch *38*; **27, 28** · Hans Mann **1, 3, 4, 8, 9, 11, 18, 31, 67, 101** · Craig Morris and Donald E. Thompson *Huánuco Pampa: an Inca City and its hinterland*, Thames and Hudson, London and New York 1985: *23, 24, 28, 31* · Michael E. Moseley *9, 26, 45, 46, 52, 61, 66* (after Lumbreras), *87, 88, 90*; **30, 32, 33, 34, 43, 47, 48, 49, 55, 72, 73, 76, 77, 79, 80, 98, 99** · Musée de l'Homme **71, 75** · Museo Arqueologico, Cuzco **24** · NASA **7** · National Museum of Archaeology, Lima **95** · The Newark Museum **20** · Peabody Museum, Harvard University **57, 58, 62, 65, 103** · Annick Peterson *1, 2, 10, 34, 42, 53, 67, 71, 98, 111* · Philadelphia University Museum **45** · Guaman Poma *4, 14, 17, 21, 22, 25, 27, 28* (above left) · R. Ravines *58* · James Richardson III **63, 64** · John H. Rowe *32, 68* · Dennis Satterlee *9* · Alan R. Sawyer, *Tiahuanaco Tapestry Design*, 1963: *103* (drawing Milton Franklin Sonday, Jr; courtesy the Museum of Primitive Art, New York) · Servicio Aerofotografico Nacional, Peru **5** (photo Hans Mann), **6, 29, 50** · Izumi Shimada **100, 114, 115** · Shippee-Johnson Expedition, American Museum of Natural History **2, 39, 54, 55, 56, 86** · Bunny Stafford **13, 81, 82** · Nicholas J. Saunders, *People of the Jaguar: the living spirit of ancient America*, Souvenir Press, London 1989: *20* (after Roe *1974*, Fig. *29a*), *64* (after Rowe *1967*, Fig. *11*), *65* (after Roe *1978*, Fig. *1*) (all drawings by Pauline Stringfellow); **17** · H. Ubbelohde-Doering, *On the Royal Highways of the Inca*, Thames and Hudson, London, 1967: **16** · Carlos Williams, 'A Scheme for the Early Monumental Architecture of the Central Coast of Peru', in Christopher B. Donnan (ed.), *Early Ceremonial Architecture in the Andes*: *54* · Nicholas Young **14**

Index

Taycanamu 248, 250, 254–5
Taymi Canal 252
technology 121, 157, 159, 219; western 262, 27; see also lithic remains, tools
Telarmachay Cave 142
Tello enclosure 260
Tello, Julio C. 19–20, 141, 156
Tello Obelisk 156
terracing 68, 74–5, 100, 116, 137, 143, 165, 201–2, 218–19, 223, 227, 229, 232, 241, 243, 2
textiles 17, 44, 48, 50, 68, 70, 72, 96–7, 107–8, 116, 144–5, 149, 157–8, 186–7, 241, 243, 246, 248, 259, 69, 76–8, 18–21; back-strap loom 17, 18; batik 157; Chancay 112; cordage 68, 96; embroidery 152; heddle loom weaving 114, 125, 157; horizontal loom 68; motifs in 68, 186, 19, 43, 45–7, 63, 69, 103, 112, 20–1; Paracas 186, 47, 63, 20–1; Pukara 149–50; tapestry 157, 226, 70; taxation 65, 68–9; vertical frame loom 68; weaving 68, 70, 147, 256, 26, 19; see also cotton, fabric, wool
Thunderbolt Stelae 204, 79
Tierra del Fuego 25, 84
Tiliviche 92
time, conception of 12–13, 55–7
Titicaca 29, 32, 42, 46, 77, 91, 112, 142, 146, 158, 164, 203, 208, 220, 222, 224, 228–30, 8
Titicaca Basin 14, 18, 45–6, 72, 76, 96, 99, 102, 145–50, 203, 209, 226, 229, 231; Lake 13–15, 26, 29, 31, 112, 137, 145, 149, 185, 202, 204, 216, 228
Tiwanaku 13, 15–16, 18–21, 32, 42, 46, 72, 110, 112, 146, 149–50, 202–3, 205–9, 211, 216, 219–22, 224–31, 241, 243, 92, 74–88; art of 18, 203–4, 207, 219, 241, 74–5, 77–9, 85; ceramics 232, 81, 84; Classic Tiwanaku Phase 203–4; demise of 230; iconography 205, 208, 220, 74–5
tombs 16–17, 114, 128, 180, 182, 192, 201, 217, 224, 246, 253, 64

Tomoval Castillo 166
tools 83–7, 92, 38, 28; tumi knives 253, 97
Topa Inca 13, 15, 76, 246
Topic, John and Theresa 163, 191
Toquepala 91
trade 42, 47, 190–1, 247, 253–4
transport 10, 17, 28, 45, 74, 76, 148, 191, 214, 216, 223, 228, 232, 1–2
Tres Ventanas Cave 97
Tropical Forest lifeway 25, 27, 48, 8–11
Tschudi, J. J. Diego de 18
Tucume 251–2
Tullamayo, Río 14, 77
Tumbes Valley 143, 254
Tumi Bamba 10–11, 74
Tumilaca Phase 227–8
Tutishcainyo 143

Ucayali, Río 143
Uhle enclosure 260, 101
Uhle, Max 18–21, 115, 209
Urton, Gary 55–6
Urubamba Valley 32, 68, 202, 243–4, 2
Uruguay 85
U-shaped centers 119, 121, 124, 128, 137–42, 144, 152–3, 157, 162, 165, 184, 256, 258, 39, 100
Ushumachay 84

Valcarcel, Luis E. 20
Valdivia, people 118, 143; pottery 109
Vega, Garcilaso de la 78
Ventanilla Bay 106
verticality 28, 42–6, 48, 100–1, 125, 142, 148–9, 190–1, 201, 202, 208, 224, 232, 246, 262
vicuña 89
vicus 181–3, 213
Viracocha 13–16, 78, 230
Viracochapampa 223

Viru 162–6, 183, 212, 260
Viru, Río 41, 142, 162, 7
Vitor Valley 241
volcanic activity 21, 27
von Humboldt, Alexander 17, 95

Waira-jirca 144
Wanka 245
Wankarani 147
warfare 7, 10–12, 15–16, 20–1, 32, 157, 162–4, 202, 209, 212, 216, 221–3, 244, 255, 260, 25, 82, 84, 33–4; military 68–9, 246; revolts 182, 227, 255; weaponry 85, 181
Wari Willka 245
warrior priest 180–1, 64–5
wasi 75, 78, 146
water 55, 79, 260; ritual manipulation of 78, 143, 155, 192, 205
watercraft 28, 47, 94, 104–5, 8
Wayna Capac 10–11, 15, 74
Waywaka 144
weaving see textiles
West, Michael 164
Wichquana 144
Williams, Carlos 121, 137, 139
Willkawain 192
Wina-Wayna 32
wood 17, 82–3, 85, 96, 108, 256; artifacts 83, 207; firewood 104; woodwork 72
wool 43, 67–8, 125, 201, 63; alpaca 152, 186; camelid 157; vicuña 69

Yanamarca Valley 245
Yaya-Mama Religious Tradition 146, 149–50, 202
Yupanqui 14

Zaña, Río 41, 86, 88, 100, 125, 143, 251–2
Zolzdoni 250
Zuidema, Tom 79, 33